Education and Emergency in Italy

Education, Culture, and Society

Founding Editor

Bernardo Gallegos†

Editorial Board

Ming Fang He (*Georgia Southern University, USA*)
Paula Groves-Price (*Washington State University, USA*)
Isabel Nuñez (*Indiana University/Purdue University, Fort Wayne, USA*)
Rodolfo Palma-Rojo (*Universidad Nacional Autónoma de Mexico, Mexico*)
William Schubert (*Emeritus, University of Illinois at Chicago, USA*)
Mette Marie Wacher Rodarte (*Instituto Nacional de Antropología e Historia, Mexico*)

VOLUME 5

The titles published in this series are listed at *brill.com/ecas*

Education and Emergency in Italy

How the Education System Reacted to the First Wave of Covid-19

Edited by

Maddalena Colombo, Marco Romito,
Massimiliano Vaira and Martina Visentin

BRILL

LEIDEN | BOSTON

All chapters in this book have undergone peer review.

The Library of Congress Cataloging-in-Publication Data is available online at https://catalog.loc.gov

Typeface for the Latin, Greek, and Cyrillic scripts: "Brill". See and download: brill.com/brill-typeface.

ISSN 2590-0005
ISBN 978-90-04-52321-0 (paperback)
ISBN 978-90-04-52322-7 (hardback)
ISBN 978-90-04-52323-4 (e-book)

Copyright 2022 by Maddalena Colombo, Marco Romito, Massimiliano Vaira and Martina Visentin.
Published by Koninklijke Brill NV, Leiden, The Netherlands.
Koninklijke Brill NV incorporates the imprints Brill, Brill Nijhoff, Brill Hotei, Brill Schöningh, Brill Fink, Brill mentis, Vandenhoeck & Ruprecht, Böhlau and V&R unipress.
Koninklijke Brill NV reserves the right to protect this publication against unauthorized use. Requests for re-use and/or translations must be addressed to Koninklijke Brill NV via brill.com or copyright.com.

This book is printed on acid-free paper and produced in a sustainable manner.

Contents

List of Figures and Tables   VII
Notes on Contributors   X

Introduction: Social Needs, Emergency Policies and Solidaristic Attitudes throughout the Italian Education System: Sociological Research during the Covid-19 Pandemic Outbreak   1
    Maddalena Colombo, Marco Romito, Massimiliano Vaira and Martina Visentin

1   Challenges for Early Childhood Professionals: An Empirical Research Project on the Strategies, Practices and Effects of LEADs   32
    Rita Bertozzi and Tatiana Saruis

2   Rethinking the Role of No Schooling during the Pandemic   56
    Maurizio Merico and Fausta Scardigno

3   Rhetoric, Problem or Necessity? A Study of Parental Involvement during Covid-19   77
    Mariagrazia Santagati and Paolo Barabanti

4   From Classroom to Screen: An Exploratory Study of University Students in Sicily during the Covid-19 Lockdown   104
    Umberto Di Maggio

5   A New World Is Open? Distance Teaching in Italian Universities during the Covid-19 Emergency   122
    Francesco Ramella and Michele Rostan

6   Young Europeans, Distance Learning and Trust in Educational Institutions: A Comparative Analysis after Covid-19   151
    Diego Mesa

7   Inside the Emergency: Digital Teaching from the Point of View of Teachers   175
    Eduardo Barberis, Nico Bazzoli, Domenico Carbone and Joselle Dagnes

8   Distance Learning/Teaching during the Covid-19 Emergency: The
     Perspective of School Principals   192
         Stefania Capogna, Maria Chiara De Angelis and Flaminia Musella

9   The Platformization and Commodification of Italian Schools during the
     Covid-19 Crisis: Implications for Policy and Future Research   219
         Gianna Cappello

     A Post-Commentary from the UK: Educational Challenges after the
     Covid-19 Pandemic   238
         Spyros Themelis

     Index   251

Figures and Tables

Figures

1.1 Activities offered to the children during the lockdown period: Percentage of respondents who answered 'Frequently' (Source: Fieldwork data).   42
1.2 How the interviewees' relationship with IT tools changed during the lockdown (Source: Fieldwork data).   49
4.1 Question: 'Do you prefer DL, LP or both solutions?' (% value) (Source: 'Stay Home & Keep in Touch' data, LUMSA University (Palermo) students, March 2020).   114
4.2 Pleasant or unpleasant sensation perceived during DL in pandemic (% value) (Source: 'Stay Home & Keep in Touch' data, LUMSA University (Palermo) students, March 2020).   114
4.3 Question: 'What do you miss from your college life routine before Covid?' Textual analysis with IRaMuTeq software (Source: 'Stay Home & Keep in Touch' data, LUMSA University (Palermo) students, March 2020).   115
4.4 Question: 'What do you miss from your college life routine before Covid?' Occurrences over 10. Textual analysis of similarities with IRaMuTeq software (Source: 'Stay Home & Keep in Touch' data, LUMSA University (Palermo) students, March 2020).   116
5.1 Respondents' ratings of how the emergency was managed.   130
5.2 The teaching strategies employed for online classes, by level of support and variety of channels used by respondents in the transition to distance teaching (1–10 scale for support; 1–7 scale for channels).   138
8.1 Difficulties experienced by teachers and students in terms of access to digital tools.   198
8.2 Difficulties encountered by families during the emergency.   199
8.3 The frequency of updating activities.   199
8.4 The tools used to provide teaching activities.   201
8.5 Scree plot for the selection of the factors.   204
8.6 Scree plot of the selection of the factors.   207
8.7 Scree plot of points of satisfaction.   208
9.1 GAFAM growth (2010–2020) (from statista.com/chart/20285/market-capitalization-of-google-apple-facebook-amazon-and-microsoft/, CC BY-ND).   223

Tables

1.1 Type of services/schools and geographical areas in which the respondents work (% of columns). 38
1.2 Index of the school-family connection. 45
1.3 Index of school-family connection by geographical areas. 45
1.4 Index of school-family connection by type of services. 46
1.5 Difficulties experienced by teachers/educators in carrying out online activities. 47
3.1 Participating sample in Vo.Ca.Le. project (absolute values). 85
3.2 Ways used by schools to inform parents about school activities organization in March-May 2020 (answers 'Often' + 'Always or Nearly Always' by parents and teachers, in percentages). 86
3.3 School collective bodies involved in decision-making about distance learning in March-May 2020 (teachers' answers, in percentages). 87
5.1 When did you start distance teaching? (%). 124
5.2 What form did your distance teaching take? (%). 125
5.3 Were the internet connection and IT tools available to you during the emergency good enough to enable you to choose the teaching approaches you felt were most appropriate? (%; stage II). 126
5.4 What kind of training and support did you receive, and from whom? (%). 127
5.5 Were you able to choose what kind of distance teaching you used? (%). 128
5.6 Levels of support by institutional response style (support received by faculty members through institutional networks: average scores on a 1–10 scale). 129
5.7 Perception of the distance learning experience as an opportunity for increasing professional skills, by support from networks (average values; scores from 1 to 10). 130
5.8 Institutional support and respondents' ratings of emergency governance (average values; scores from 1 to 10). 131
5.9 Ratings of the experience during the emergency (% Very + Fairly). 133
5.10 What would you like to keep from this distance teaching experience once the Covid-19 emergency is over? (%). 134
5.11 In your experience with distance teaching, how problematic were the following aspects? (Very + Fairly; %). 135
5.12 Please indicate your teaching activities prior to the Covid-19 emergency and your distance teaching activities (for your main courses) (%; multiple responses possible). 136
5.13 How much do you think hybrid teaching, which combines in-person classes with online activities, can contribute positively to the following goals? (A lot + Some; %). 140

FIGURES AND TABLES   IX

5.14   How much do you think distance teaching can help enlarge the pool of potential students in the following categories? (A lot + Some; %).   140
5.15   How much do you agree with the following statements? (A lot + Some; %).   141
5.16   Preferences regarding post-emergency teaching according to the type of in-person teaching strategy (% per line).   142
5.17   Preferences regarding post-emergency teaching according to experience during the emergency (% per line).   143
6.1   The use of distance learning by country (percentage values).   157
6.2   The use of distance learning by gender, age, educational attainment and main activity by country (use today or in the past; percentage values).   159
6.3   Satisfaction of distance learning (DL) by country (mean and st. dev.).   160
6.4   Satisfaction of distance learning (DL) by gender, age and educational attainment by country (mean and st. dev.).   161
6.5   Frequency of consulting apps/websites/social networks/forums and blogs by use of distance learning and country (very or fairly frequent use; percentage values).   163
6.6   Trust in school and university by use of distance learning and country (percentage values).   164
6.7   Independent variables included in logistic regression.   165
6.8   Results of logistic regression models of use of distance learning in the past, use in the current phase and satisfaction with distance learning.   167
7.1   Teachers' motivation to start their job; matrix of rotated components.   181
7.2   According to your direct experience, on average what share of students... (Mean values, % for selected groupings in the sample).   182
7.3   In your view, how relevant were the following reasons why students struggled to participate? (Selected items, mean value, range 1–4).   183
7.4   During the pandemic, how often did you feel... (mean value, range 1–4).   185
7.5   How often did you use the following teaching methods before and during the Covid-19 emergency? (Only comparable items; columns A and B: sum of answers 'Often + Always'; column C and D: difference in the frequency of use).   187
7.6   Share of respondents who often used a few methods among the above.   188
8.1   Organizational response factors.   205
8.2   Evaluation of strategic organizational-process factors.   207
8.3   Overall factors of satisfaction.   209
8.4   Factorial weights and communality of extracted and rotated factors (sorted rotated factor loadings and communalities).   210
8.5   Factorial weights and communality of extracted and rotated factors (sorted rotated factor loadings and communalities).   211
8.6   Factorial weights and communality of extracted and rotated factors (sorted rotated factor loadings and communalities).   212

Notes on Contributors

Paolo Barabanti
holds a PhD in Education & Assessment and teaches Sociology of Education at the Università Cattolica del Sacro Cuore in Brescia (Italy), where he carries out research for CIRMiB (Centre of Initiatives and Research on Migration-Brescia) and LaRIS (Laboratory of Research and Intervention on Society). He works as a primary school teacher in Brescia. His publications deal with educational inequalities, school assessments with standardized tests (such as INVALSI and OECD-PISA), top-performing students, multicultural schools, and the school-family relationship.

Eduardo Barberis
is Associate Professor in Sociology at the University of Urbino Carlo Bo (Italy), where he teaches Comparative Welfare Systems, Immigration Policy and Methodology of Social Research. His main research interests include the territorial dimension of welfare policies and of migration processes, with a special focus on non-metropolitan contexts.

Nico Bazzoli
is a postdoc in Urban and Environmental Sociology at the University of Urbino Carlo Bo (Italy), where he also lectures on Economic and Political Geography. His research interests include spatial transformations and the study of the built environment, youth conditions, urban and environmental conflicts, and strategic and urban planning.

Rita Bertozzi
is Associate Professor of Sociology of Cultural and Communicative Processes at the University of Modena and Reggio Emilia (Italy), where she teaches Sociology of Education and Sociology of Socio-Educational Policies. She is a member of the National Observatory for the Integration of Foreign Students and Interculturalism (of the Italian Ministry of Education). Her academic research focuses on educational inequalities, youth participation, education and migration, unaccompanied minors, poverty and social exclusion, and child-centred research approaches. She was a member of the Scientific Committee of the Italian Sociological Association's Sociology of Education section (AIS-EDU) from 2009 to 2015.

NOTES ON CONTRIBUTORS   XI

Stefania Capogna

is Associate Professor at Link Campus University (Rome, Italy), Director of DiTES (Digital Technologies, Education and Society), and a member of the CRES-IELPO Research Center. In particular, she deals with research applied to public policies, especially on education and innovation, and also in relation to digital technologies.

Gianna Cappello

is Associate Professor at the Department of Cultures and Societies at the University of Palermo (Italy), where she teaches Social Media Studies and Sociology of Education and Digital Media. She is a member of the Scientific Committee of the Italian Sociological Association's Sociology of Education section (AIS-EDU) (2021–2024); President of MED, the Italian Association for Media Education; Co-editor of the journal *Media Education* (Firenze University Press); a member of the advisory board of the McLuhan Foundation; and Associate Editor of *The International Encyclopedia of Media Literacy* (Wiley). Her fields of research include media studies, the digitalization of education and media education.

Domenico Carbone

is Associate Professor in General Sociology at the University of Eastern Piedmont in Novara-Alessandria (Italy), where he teaches Sociology and Methods and Techniques of Social Research. His main research interests include gender-based and intergenerational inequalities, and the comparative study of welfare systems.

Maddalena Colombo

is Full Professor in Sociology of Cultural and Communicative Processes. She teaches Sociology of Education, Sociology of Educational Policy and Sociology of Inequalities and Differences at the Università Cattolica del Sacro Cuore in Milan and Brescia (Italy). She is Director of the CIRMiB (Centre of Initiatives and Research on Migration-Brescia) and LaRIS (Laboratory of Research and Intervention on Society). She co-ordinated the Italian Sociological Association's Sociology of Education section (AIS-EDU) from 2018 to 2021. Her main areas of study are educational inequalities, training and socialization processes and supply, education systems, impacts of migration in schools and the curriculum, social changes in teachers' role, and intercultural competences.

Joselle Dagnes

is tenure-track Assistant Professor of Economic Sociology at the University of Turin (Italy), where she teaches Sociology of Markets. Her main research interests include financialization processes and financial markets, formal and informal regulation, the Mafia's processes of territorial expansion at both national and international level, and the foundational economy.

Maria Chiara De Angelis

is Research Fellow at the Education Science Department of the University of Roma Tre (Italy), member of the Steering Committee of the DiTES (Digital Technologies, Education and Society) research centre of the Link Campus University, and a member of the editorial board of the journal *Quaderni di Comunità*. She carries out research on the impact of digital innovation on people, education systems and organizations; training and socialization processes; and ethical dimension of digital culture.

Umberto Di Maggio

has a PhD in Social Policies and Local Development and teaches Sociology at LUMSA University (Palermo, Italy, campus). He was a visiting scholar at Deusto University of Bilbao (Spain), where he taught and carried out research on Social Impact Assessment. He collaborated with the Research Center on Transnational Organized Crime, University of Catania, within the European program Erasmus+ 'Jean Monnet'. He is a member of the Migration Observatory at the Pedro Arrupe Institute (Palermo).

Maurizio Merico

is Associate Professor in the Department of Social and Political Studies, University of Salerno (Italy), where he currently teaches Sociology of Education and Sociology of Youth Cultures. His research interests are mainly focused on youth cultures, youth policies, non-formal education and youth work. He is Editor-in-chief of the *International Bulletin on Youth Research* (ISA-RC34 Sociology of Youth) and Deputy Chairman of GENESIS (Generation and Educational Science Institute) (Austria). He is also the national scientific coordinator of *Youth Wiki*, the European online encyclopaedia on youth policies.

Diego Mesa

(PhD in Sociology and Methodology of Social Research) is Project Manager at Caritas Italia. He teaches Sociology of the Family at Università Cattolica del Sacro Cuore in Brescia (Italy), where he collaborates with CIRMiB (Centre of Initiatives and Research on Migration-Brescia), LaRIS (Laboratory of

Research and Intervention on Society) and CESVOPAS (Centre for Studies on Volunteering and Social Participation). His academic research focuses on youth studies, education, volunteering, religiosity, gender policies and services for youth and family.

Flaminia Musella
is Associate Professor of Statistics at the Link Campus University (Rome, Italy). She is interested in analysing socio-economic and managerial phenomena by statistically modelling complexity. Her main research interests are Bayesian networks both from a computational point of view and in an applicative way with a particular focus on the what-if analysis.

Francesco Ramella
is Full Professor of Economic Sociology at the University of Torino (Italy), where he is Chair of the Department of Cultures, Politics and Society and Co-director of the Luigi Bobbio Centre for Public and Applied Social Research. He co-founded and was the first president of the Italian Society of Economic Sociology (SIPED). He is a member of the editorial and scientific boards of the journals *Il Mulino, Stato e Mercato, South European Society and Politics*, and *Sociologias*. His studies deal with issues related to innovation, the economy of collaboration, local and regional development, and urban and territorial governance.

Marco Romito
is Assistant Professor at the Department of Sociology and Social Research at the University of Milano-Bicocca (Italy), he is member of the Scientific Committee of the Italian Sociological Association's Sociology of Education section (AIS-EDU) and member of the editorial board of the journal *Scuola democratica*. He carries out research on educational inequalities in schools and higher education, on educational transitions and on the digitalization of education.

Michele Rostan
is Full Professor of Economic Sociology and Labour Studies at the University of Pavia (Italy), where he directs the Interdepartmental Center for Studies and Research on Higher Education Systems. He is a member of the Consortium of Higher Education Researchers, and of the editorial boards of the following journals: *Higher Education, International Journal of Higher Education Research*, and *Studies in Higher Education*. His main fields of research include graduate employment and work, the academic profession, universities' third mission, and the life and career of university students.

Mariagrazia Santagati
is Assistant Professor in Sociology of Education at the Università Cattolica del Sacro Cuore of Milan (Italy). She is the Scientific Secretary of the CIRMiB (Centre of Initiatives and Research on Migration) and manages the Department for Education of the ISMU Foundation (Initiatives and Studies on Multiethnicity). Her main scientific interests deal with educational inequalities, students with a migrant background, interculturalism and biographical approach to research. She was a member of the Scientific Committee of the Italian Sociological Association's Sociology of Education section (AIS-EDU) from 2015 to 2018, and she contributed to the creation of a Southern European network of Sociologists of Education.

Tatiana Saruis
(PhD in Sociology) has worked at the University of Modena and Reggio Emilia (Italy) since 2017, where she teaches Sociology of Education and Childhood. Her research focuses on education and welfare policies and services, professionals and organizations, social innovation and participation. She has also worked as a researcher with the University of Bologna and the Agency on Health and Social Care of the Emilia-Romagna region.

Fausta Scardigno
is Associate Professor of Sociology of Education and Cultural Processes at the Department of Humanistic Research and Innovation at the University of Bari Aldo Moro, where she teaches Sociology of Education and Sociology of Institutional Communication. She is a member of the Scientific Council of the Italian Universities Network for Lifelong Learning (RUIAP), member of the National Agency (ANVUR) for the academic evaluation of the Third Mission (VQR in progress). She is also, since 2016, Director of CAP (Centre for Lifelong Learning), which promotes migrant and refugee students. Her topics of research are integration and enhancement of the human capital of migrant people as well as assessment and analysis of public policies (mainly in the area of education).

Spyros Themelis
is Associate Professor in Education at the School of Education & Lifelong Learning, University of East Anglia (UK). He is Editor (formerly Deputy Chief Editor) of the *Journal for Critical Education Policy Studies* (*JCEPS*) and a member of the editorial board of *The SoJo Journal: Educational Foundations and Social Justice Education*. His current research interests span different fields and his research focuses on educational and social issues in the UK, Greece, Brazil and Chile.

Massimiliano Vaira
is Associate Professor of Sociology of Economy at the University of Pavia (Italy). He is member of the Consortium of Higher Education Researchers (CHER) and of the Scientific Committee of the journal *Scuola democratica*. His main research interests are comparative analysis of higher education systems, the academic profession and work conditions, university and industry relationships, the Third Mission of universities and public engagement. He was a member of the Scientific Committee of the Italian Sociological Association's Sociology of Education section (AIS-EDU) from 2018 to 2021.

Martina Visentin
is Assistant Professor at the University of Padua (Italy), where she teaches Sociology and Social Policies. Her academic research focuses on social innovation, youth studies and cultural transformation. She has collaborated as a researcher and as a consultant with a large number of services and universities. She was a member of the Scientific Committee of the Italian Sociological Association's Sociology of Education section (AIS-EDU) from 2018 to 2021.

INTRODUCTION

Social Needs, Emergency Policies and Solidaristic Attitudes throughout the Italian Education System

Sociological Research during the Covid-19 Pandemic Outbreak

Maddalena Colombo, Marco Romito, Massimiliano Vaira and Martina Visentin

1   History, Objectives and Targets of the Book

During the first wave of the Covid-19 pandemic (March 2020), Italy was the only European country where all the schools, universities, as well as other formal and informal educational institutions, were completely closed down (until June 2020), with distance teaching being introduced for the first time. As in other countries, many Italian scholars and practitioners began to question the capacity of the system to maintain its performance despite the complete disappearance of the socio-material embeddedness of the education provided. Another highly pressing matter was to guarantee the persistence of the 'education for all' principle with concrete measures for the more disadvantaged students, asking whether the system was fully prepared to monitor the 'old-and-new' forms of inequality in a frame of suspended social institutions (Lupton & Willis, 2021, p. 11) as well as, if required, to introduce equalization solutions.

In June 2020, the Italian Sociological Association's Sociology of Education section (AIS-EDU)[1] invited the community of Italian sociologists of education to present papers on the topic, based on ad hoc field research and/or theoretical reflections. The focus was on how the Italian education system at any level of education reacted to the changes brought about by this pandemic and what changes and innovations were implemented, in order to work out if they were directed at resisting, adapting or reconfiguring the learning-teaching routine. Lastly, we were interested in understanding what lessons the different levels of schooling and university could have drawn from the emergency.

The AIS-EDU team received eighteen proposals of which nine were selected on the basis of quality and innovation, in terms of both content and methods used for the field research. The result is a composite and unprecedented collection of essays, produced by a set of senior and junior academic researchers and professors in the field of the sociology of education working in thirteen universities located in the north, centre and south of Italy. The chapters cover different topics on students, teachers, parents, school principals and academic staff, along with in-field studies carried out in pre-primary, primary, secondary education, higher education, as well as out-of-school education services.

The idea underpinning the book is that every unit in the education system has been seriously affected by the shock of the school closure and that the sudden disruption of the learning routine could have brought about either negative or positive effects, depending on how the institutional settings and educational network had been hit by the crisis and how they responded to it. This particular 'dissociative' experience (i.e. offering lessons without schools, managing schools without lessons, teaching instructional content, receiving emotional feedback, etc.) was a *unicum* in time and space, at least so far, and deserved an extra effort to be understood by researchers in many of its dimensions and processes, from the first adjustments and survival solutions up to the long-term consequences of distance teaching.

From a sociological standpoint, the book considers the interplay between: 1) the structural level (the system governance, including the normative frame); 2) the organizational level (the management of the school/university in a context of radical uncertainty and fear, the ICT equipment and platformization of teaching, etc.); and 3) the life-world level (the micro-sociological connection among the participants). All the levels are implied in the profound systemic change, but the different essays touch them in several ways, giving information about both the systemic and punctual responses to the crisis.

Regarding the methodology adopted and the territorial scale, the essays present several differences. Some analyses are based on convenience samples, taken during the emergency period, that reached the available self-selected respondents and are structured as local case studies, while others are based on more or less wide samples at a national level. The differences are due both to the research interests of the authors as well as to the physical restrictions imposed at the time that affected the research designs and methods. It is worth remembering that in some cases these limitations encouraged the search for new sampling and testing methods.

This introductory chapter aims to contextualize the essays by showing, firstly, what occurred in Italy during the initial Covid-19 outbreak and how the government and the Ministry of Education managed the sanitary crisis. Secondly, the state of the Italian education system before the health emergency is discussed in order to highlight how the pandemic emphasized the ordinary systemic criticalities. Thirdly, we offer several key concepts to interpret some empirical data, taken from cultural studies and the sociology of change, from the well-known notions of risk (Beck, 1992), ontological insecurity (Giddens, 1984), fear (Furedi, 1997, 2018) and trauma (Alexander, 2012), to the less used concept of suffering as a social construction (Bourdieu et al., 1999; Das et al., 2001; Wilkinson, 2005; Giarelli, 2018, 2021), applied to education. In this way, we try to delineate the leitmotif that brings the studies together, in terms of the common issues emerging from the theoretical and empirical contributions.

The sociologist Nicholas Christakis distinguishes between the intermediate pandemic and the post-pandemic. In the former, people are recovering from the clinical, psychological, social and economic shock of the pandemic and the adjustments it required. In the latter, they hope things will return to 'normal', albeit in a world with some persistent changes. It is possible to assume that we cannot expect schools and universities to snap back to a pre-pandemic normality, but we hope this book will be a useful window on the past through which to learn how to manage new traumatic changes like this.

The book addresses every social actor committed to organizing and realizing education in both the public and private spheres, especially those who were called upon to cope with a social emergency like the Covid-19 infection during 2020 (teachers and professors, school managers, school administrators, students, parents, and early childhood professionals). We hope the 'Italy case', with its specific response to the sanitary crisis and the prolonged school closure, will also be useful for other countries within and outside of Europe. One of the purposes of this book is to give international readers suggestions for future advancement in understanding personal and collective agency during the turbulence, in light of the main mandate of education: to reduce structural inequalities, while fostering human care and promotion through education.

2   The Covid-19 Pandemic Outbreak in Italy and the Responses of the Government and the Ministry of Education

2.1   *A Brief Chronology*

As many readers already know, the story of the Covid-19 pandemic began over a few days in the winter of 2019. On December 31st 2019, the Chinese authorities reported to the World Health Organization (WHO) that a new acute pulmonary disease, similar to SARS, had been observed in Wuhan. In the beginning, and up to January 19th 2020, the Chinese health authorities stated that the transmission of the virus was from living animal to human and that there were no indications that transmission could be from human to human. The WHO believed this information to be reliable, but on January 20th, the Chinese authorities confirmed that the virus could be transmitted from human to human. Three days later, the Chinese government announced a strict lockdown in Wuhan and other districts. On February 11th 2020, the WHO labelled the new virus SARS-CoV-2 and the resulting illness Covid-19. A month later, the

WHO declared Covid-19 a pandemic, with the virus having spread to 114 countries, infecting 118,000 people and killing 4,291.

Italy was the first European country that detected and dealt with the new virus. On January 31st 2020, the first two cases of Covid-19 were identified in a couple of Chinese tourists and the Prime Minister Giuseppe Conte declared a public health emergency, without taking any restrictive or special measures, except the provision that the Department of Civil Protection was assigned to define and implement any appropriate actions in the event of further diffusion of the virus.

On February 21st, the first Italian case of Covid-19 was detected in Codogno, a small town near Milan; on the same day, the first victim of the virus was recorded in Vò, a village in the Veneto region. It is worth mentioning that the health authorities and virologists identified the Champions League football match between Atalanta (a football team from Bergamo, Lombardy) and Valencia, played on February 19th 2020, as the diffusion epicentre of the virus. The area of Bergamo had the highest mortality rate during the first wave of the pandemic: between February and March 2020, about 7,000 people died and the province recorded a growth in the death rate equal to 568% with respect to the period 2015–2019.

On February 23rd 2020, the government declared the first local red zones and a strict lockdown was ordered in eleven Veneto and Lombardy municipalities. On March 4th, relevant limitations were extended to the whole national territory. The decree banned any form of gathering in public places as well as both amateur and professional sports activities. Professional sport competitions had to be held behind closed doors. On March 23rd, a new decree instituted a complete and strict lockdown: the country stopped every activity (with the exceptions of those considered necessary) and the mobility of people was largely restricted. Italy was the first Western country to implement a lockdown measure to contain the spread of the virus.

The strict lockdown lasted until May 2020. It was significantly loosened during the summer, but starting in October 2020 it was re-instituted to cope with the second wave of the pandemic, which lasted until March 2021. Since summer 2021, the epidemic has been evaluated as 'under control' by the national health authorities, thanks to an intense vaccination campaign, which included more than 80% of the population over twelve years old with a complete cycle of two doses and almost 90% of the population with a first dose of the vaccine.

2.2   *Coping with the Covid-19 Outbreak in the Educational System*

Focusing on the role and actions taken by the Italian government for the educational sector during the first pandemic wave (February–May 2020), the first provision was a decree issued on February 23rd 2020, when the first Covid-19 cases were detected and recorded. It was quite narrow in scope since it stated that in-presence teaching had to be stopped in all schools and higher education institutions (in Lombardy and Veneto only) and replaced by distance teaching. On the same day, for precautionary purposes, this provision was extended to another northern region, Emilia-Romagna, which borders both Lombardy and Veneto.

Both the seriousness of the virus and its pandemic nature were still unclear. It seemed that it could be managed given its spread was still territorially circumscribed, albeit it affected three of the most populated regions in Italy. On March 2nd, the Ministry of Education, University and Research (MIUR) announced its support, in collaboration with the schools of other regions and the National Institute of Educational Documentation, Innovation and Research (INDIRE), to close schools in Lombardy and Veneto so as to help them with online remote teaching. They offered teachers: webinars for remote teaching training, free access and use of teaching platforms, multimedia contents, collaboration and exchanges with schools with advanced infrastructures and experience in distance teaching.

The situation worsened dramatically in only a few days: the disease broke out in Lombardy and Veneto with thousands of contagions, hospitalizations – both in ordinary and intensive care units – and deaths, while it continued to spread across the country. On March 4th, the government issued the first lockdown decree[2] through which schools of every level (from kindergartens to upper secondary schools), higher education institutions and extra-school recreational and sport centres had to suspend every in-presence activity up to March 15th 2020. This decision, based on a very optimistic prevision, was due to several interacting factors: the WHO had yet to define Covid-19 as a pandemic (with there being no homogeneous agreement among scientists and physicians on the seriousness of the disease); secondly, since the epidemic was located primarily in the northern regions of Italy, the government thought that it could be contained with a strict, limited-time lockdown. They avoided alarming the population and creating panic. However, the logic of this action was incremental and based on the constant monitoring of the evolution of the disease. In order to imagine the impact of the educational lockdown in Italy, it is worth mentioning that the number of people affected can be approximately estimated to be more than one-sixth of the entire population (Giancola & Piromalli, 2020).

Regarding the actions carried out by the national education system, in March 2020, MIUR extended the Scuola-web platform, useful for delivering distance learning (*didattica a distanza*, DAD) to all lower and upper secondary schools, nationwide in order to support distance teaching until the end of the 2019/2020 academic year. Furthermore, the ministry launched the webpage Inclusion via Web, a dedicated web channel offering targeted tools for students with learning disabilities.

The government and MIUR gave significant autonomy to all schools and higher education institutions to organize their distance teaching. At the same time, in a Ministry Note (no. 338, March 17th 2020), the government recommended the use of distance teaching only in emergency situations and urged teachers 'not to use distance teaching as a formal or bureaucratic task' and to embrace the goal of returning 'to the essential coordinates of the school system action' as soon as possible. The ministry specified 'the uselessness of just sending materials or homework', which were not preceded by any explanation or which did not provide for subsequent clarification or comments by the teacher. It also recommended finding 'a balance between learning activities and moments of rest, to guarantee that children did not spend too much time in front of screens' (Banchio et al., 2021, p. 276).

Despite a long-standing frame of school autonomy in Italy (Landri, 2009; Colombo & Desideri, 2019), during the Covid-19 emergency, the Ministry of Education assumed the role of the leading institution, with its pyramidal decision-making, and it may have caused a sort of retrocession in the capacity of school managers (and even of the middle management) to take autonomous decisions (Colombo et al., 2020).

We think this aspect highlights a double effect. Although the whole Italian education system had been reformed (since 1997) towards a quasi-market regime, endowing schools and universities with (formally) greater autonomy, the governance structure and logic remains largely centralized and bureaucratic. Only during the pandemic, could the majority of educational professionals have gained a larger leeway in terms of organizational and teaching flexibility to organize and manage an unprecedented situation. This was not only due to the situation itself and the conditions of emergency it generated, but also – to some extent – to the inability of the centralized administration to monitor and follow what teachers were doing. Although errors did occur, and the limits of this experience were present somewhere, the educational institutions were able to cope with the situation they faced and, above all, to warrant the offer of education and the teaching activities in spite of a dramatic and disorienting scenario. This happened because, we argue, they had assumed the necessary orientation to act and react autonomously to develop their mandate in any given situation.

After the four months of lockdown (March to June 2020), schools opened for the final examinations and – given the decline in the infection level in the entire population during summer 2020 – the ministry stated that for the 2020/2021 school year, pre-primary and primary schooling could regularly take place, while secondary education should be re-organized with 50% of its time dedicated to distance learning. In guidelines dated June 26th 2020, the Ministry of Education recommended 'not to neglect or dissipate what schools were able to carry out during the school lockdown' (MIUR, 2020). Thus, the ministry stipulated that each school was required to prepare a specific DAD plan (now called DID, digital integrated didactic), capitalizing on the experience gained during the months of closure. Each school was also asked to undertake a survey to verify that any specific needs for tablets, PCs and internet connections and other infrastructural equipment for students and teachers were catered for; 80m euros were allocated for this. Planning the re-opening of the schools in September 2020, and according to the need to prevent infection and to track the possible increase of contagion, a further 95m euros were allocated for the renewal of classroom furniture (i.e. the ministry purchased 1.5m single 'wheeled school desks', whose utility was immediately questioned by the public). The idea was to take the sanitary precautions as an opportunity to change the learning spaces and infrastructures, notoriously old and organized in a hyper-traditionalist manner, and contribute to improving safety and flexibility in the school environment. This should have been the first step for a more profound teaching reform, where pedagogical method, technology and architecture would be integrated (Neill & Etheridge, 2008) and students re-engaged after the long school closure.[3]

For the second pandemic wave (from autumn 2020 to spring 2021), a more selective closure of educational institutions was decided, based on the distinction between 'red', 'orange', 'yellow' and, from January 2021, 'white' zones, according to the severity of contagion at a regional level. With the arrival of the third wave, stricter rules were introduced for the closure of all the schools in 'red' zones, covering more than a half of the national territory between March and mid-April 2021. The general re-opening of schools occurred in April 2021, once the vaccination campaign of the adult population began.

Regarding students with disabilities, whereas during the first lockdown they were subjected to restrictions imposed on all the students (which placed a heavy burden on their families), from September 2020 onwards, they received special provisions: in the case of blended learning (remote and in-presence), they would be given priority in receiving face-to-face learning with their teachers. In cases where school closure became necessary, online lessons would be synchronous for the whole class and a minimum timetable would have to be guaranteed for all the students. This measure was strongly requested by both the parents as well as other stakeholders, who wanted public attention for their special needs after they had been neglected during the school closure (Human Rights Watch, 2021).

3   The Italian Education System: Features and Criticalities beyond the Covid-19 Pandemic

It is worth helping the reader to contextualize the practices and issues analysed throughout the book. To make sense of the ways through which educational actors reacted to the necessities and urgencies of making education possible during the lockdown, we highlight some of the key features characterizing the Italian education system before it was hit by the pandemic emergency.

Considering the structure, Italy had belonged for a long time to the 'centralized type', as Margaret Archer (1979) depicted: strong central control over educational institutions, central regulation on the main structural, organizational and activity issues, structural inertia, political difficulties to reform, change and innovate the system, structural and organizational rigidity, and a high degree of bureaucratization throughout the whole system.

This does not mean that nothing has changed over time. Since the mid-1960s, some structural innovations have been introduced to the system, such as the institution of the compulsory lower secondary school track (1962), the reform of a secondary school graduation examination (1969) and others. However, these innovations have had rather an episodic, circumscribed and sectorial nature without generating an overall reforming and restructuring of the system (Dei, 1993).

Since the national unification process (1861), a high degree of centralization had characterized the system and lasted for a little less than 150 years. It was not until the beginning of the 1990s that the first change occurred, when universities were reformed to grant them a greater degree of institutional autonomy. In the second half of the 1990s, the entire educational system was reformed under the buzzwords of autonomy, marketization and competition. The political idea behind this reform was to construct an educational quasi-market, where schools compete to attract 'consumers' on the basis of a single institution's educational supply. The central governance of education, therefore, was (formally) reduced to a guide-at-a-distance role, allowing the educational institutions to organize themselves within a general normative and regulative framework.

Even if the school and university reforms were overarching, intended to innovate the Italian educational system significantly, the central control over educational institutions has not disappeared. Quite paradoxically, market-driven reforms have generated a different form of centralization. Bureaucratization has grown significantly: the traditional bureaucratic form based on norms, compliance and conformity has been substituted for rules of assessment and accountability schemes that generate a huge amount of administrative work, linked to an increasing number of projects carried out with extra budget funds (like European Union or private funding), which did not change the functioning of schools radically. This brief account of centralization and bureaucratization is relevant, as mentioned above, in relation to the Covid-19 pandemic crisis: in such a circumstance, the ministry has awarded educational institutions a greater operational autonomy but within the framework given by ministerial decrees, in order to cope with the challenges conditioned by the crisis.

Another feature of the Italian education system is the slow improvement of its systemic performance. Italy has long been characterized by:
– low participation rates at the higher levels of education,
– high rates of intergeneration transmission of educational credentials,
– high dropout rates (in both secondary and tertiary education),
– inequalities based on social origins, and
– sharp territorial divides, with the southern regions and islands significantly below the European average in educational attainment and achievement.

A recent report from the Institute of National Statistics (Istat, 2021) points out that in Italy only 20.1% of the population (aged 25–64) have a university degree against the EU average of 32.8%. The same report shows stark differences between the northern and southern regions, with Italy also being below the EU average when considering the proportion of adult population having at least an upper secondary education diploma (62.9% against 79% in the EU). Even more significantly, the report highlights that, although there has been an increase in the participation rate in higher levels of education in recent years, this has been much slower than in other European countries. University graduates have increased by 0.5% from 2019 to 2020, against 1.2% in the EU27 (+1.7 in France, +1.1 in Spain, +1.4 in Germany).

These features are legacies of the historical process of industrialization and urbanization that has taken place in Italy during the last century, which has been accompanied by a movement out of illiteracy much slower than in other European countries, especially in the south (De Mauro, 2017). According to 2018 PISA survey data, Italy ranks between the 23rd and 29th places for literacy among the OECD countries (Puccetti & Luperini, 2020). In this context, Italy has been, and still is, characterized by a lower public expenditure on education when compared to other European and OECD countries (World Bank, 2021).[4] This has a serious impact on the capacity of the system to address the country's historical delays.

A country, where the adult population scores relatively low in regard to educational levels and where a significant proportion of it lacks basic skills in reading and math (OECD, 2013), found it difficult to face the school lockdown and to shift suddenly to distance teaching in place of traditional learning environments.

As the chapters of this book will show, and as it has been outlined by research carried out in other countries (Lupton & Willis, 2021), digital technology constituted a key asset to make formal education possible during the pandemic emergency. On the one hand, ICT allowed some basic forms of interaction and communication among teachers, students and families during the school lockdown. On the other, ICT opened up spaces to reshape these interactions and to produce teaching innovations. This has also happened in Italy, thanks to recent investments made by the Italian government to introduce digital technologies and to promote digitally mediated teaching at every school level (Avvisati et al., 2013). Since the 2000s, a number of initiatives have been launched aimed not only at providing school with ICT, but also to increase their use in teaching. The percentage of schools having an internet connection in each classroom has increased significantly, reaching about 74% in 2017, and the percentage of teachers using ICT in their work has increased from 20% in 2014 to 53% in 2017 (Gui, 2019). The introduction of specifically trained teachers as 'digital animators' (see the National Plan for Digital Schools in 2015), aimed at incentivizing the use of digital technologies in classrooms, might have had a role in the spread of digitally mediated teaching practices.

However, broadband connectivity is still lacking in Italy, especially outside urban contexts, a fact that heavily limits the potential of digital education tools (AGCOM, 2019). Although the majority of teachers use IT, they do it mainly in the backstage of teaching activities as tools to prepare lessons. Before the pandemic, teachers using digital devices, software for teaching and the internet in classrooms were still a minority and they mostly used these tools to support a traditional model of teaching (Pitzalis et al., 2016). Teaching innovations as a means to share contents, boost interactions and enable cooperation were limited, and some authors have highlighted a lack of direction and systematization of 'good practices' at a national policy level (Gui, 2019; Salmieri, 2019).

Studies have also pointed out that teachers often fail to embrace the teaching potential of ICT due to their lack of digital skills and to the bad quality of both the digital infrastructures as well as the training received (Pandolfini, 2016). Moreover, research has also shown that digital tools are widespread among students and families, but digital competences are lacking, even among the so-called 'digital natives' (Gui & Argentin, 2011; Vaira & Romito, 2020). This is closely correlated to students' social and geographical origin, so that the impact of the school lockdown has been greater for students coming from families with lower economic, educational and technological resources and housing conditions (Cordini & De Angelis, 2021; Pitzalis & Spanò, 2021).

In summary, as this book shows, Italian schools and families did have access to digital tools and infrastructures when the Covid-19 emergency occurred. However, the quality of these tools was unequally distributed and the policies enacted in recent years seemed ineffective in both reducing any technological gaps and working to favour the acquisition of digital skills and knowledge, among teachers and students, to make quality education possible during the pandemic emergency.

4   Some Key Concepts to Interpret Empirical Data

Italy is the European country that, together with the United Kingdom (see Themelis, this volume), kept its school system closed for the most days and where the choice to keep schools closed was made much more strictly than economic activities (Pavolini et al., 2021, p. 261 et seq.). The 'stay at home' mandate hit many social categories, with the greatest impact being on families with children and teenagers, whose lives were completely overturned. Distance learning was particularly difficult for children in poor, and even modest-income, households who lost not only socialization and equity opportunities, but also the only free nutritious meal they were given in school in 'normal' times (Saraceno, 2020, p. 148).

Given the severity of the health risks (with many lives lost in a few weeks and thousands of people being hospitalized, half of them concentrated in the most industrialized region of Italy, Lombardy) and the initial underestimation of risk by the public, the national authorities carried out a communication campaign focused predominantly on the state of the emergency, the extent of the danger and the battle against the virus. The war metaphor was rampant: several TV channels informed Italians that authorities 'hunt down the infected', that doctors valiantly 'fight' the virus 'like heroes', that victims 'courageously succumb', that a desperate search is on for a 'weapon' against Covid-19' (Moretti & Maturo, 2021, p. 90).

This situation can be interpreted using the sociological concept of *risk*. As Mary Douglas (1992) argued, the ubiquity of risks today makes the distinction between danger and risk irrelevant. In scientific terms, while danger is real, risk is a socially constructed representation and projection, i.e. the probability of an event combined with the magnitude of the losses and gains that it will entail. The ongoing increase of dangers linked to the ever-new technological assets, environmental exploitation and bio-chemical manipulation of organic matter, together with the globalization of the risk itself (Beck, 1992), have produced a suspension of their awareness of risks and, by consequence, more vulnerability:

> A sense of *'fate'*, whether positively or negatively tinged – a vague and generalised sense of trust in distant events over which one has no control – relieves the individual of the burden of engagement with an existential situation which might otherwise be chronically disturbing. (Giddens, 1990, p. 133)

When the threat of SARS-CoV-2 stormed the Western societies, and Italy first, it easy to imagine the psychological and social impact on everyday life as an evaporation of the 'ontological security' postulated by Giddens (1984). At an interactional level, the fear of contagion, the use of face masks and social distancing changed the rituals and habits of everyday life, pushing people towards satisfying the need of sociality in the virtual (and domestic) environment. At an institutional level, the difficulties in managing the spread of the virus (along with the overcrowded hospitals and the *uncertainty* coming from virology, immunology and medical science, in general), lead the government to impose general restrictions on the entire population, taking full sovereignty over their lives. This new 'welfarist' regime, which included since the beginning the interruption of in-person education and the control over any individual movement out of the home, contributed to delineating a condition of constant trauma (Alexander et al., 2004; Alexander, 2012) in dealing with the pandemic.

The concept of *cultural trauma* is also useful in understanding how and how much the foundations of individual and collective identity are shattered, generating a discursive process to make sense of what happened, assign blame and find pathways to repair an interpreted situation. Cultural trauma is 'a specific form of collective trauma, affecting collective identity, where groups of individuals feel similarly affected by a fracturing of the existential security that a firm sense of identity afford' (Demertzis & Eyerman, 2020).

As the anthropologist Thomas Hyll and Eriksen reports (2021), during the first wave, in the home confinement regime the 'metaphysics of absence' made itself known in a very acute way since all the things we took for granted were not there anymore. In such a moment of true disruption, we were able to see how much the routines of our daily lives are so pervasively embedded into our lives. And, as Randal Collins reminded in a piece written just as the first wave of infections was about to decline,[5] we lived a strong partial restriction of the ingredients of interaction rituals: even when people were bodily co-present, the face-to-face element was hugely reduced. Masks covered our mouths and lower faces, making it harder to recognize other people's emotions and sometimes even to understand what they were saying when interacting with each other. Undoubtedly, in the near future we will see the proliferation of narratives, images and metaphors with men, women and children wearing white protection suits and face masks that will foster a 'culture of fear' (Furedi, 2018) in every social activity, attaching the fundamentals of social solidarity.

Applied to students, teachers and school staff, the trauma was prolonged as a sort of *shared suffering* (Giarelli, 2018), which, to a certain degree, was 'discovered' for the first time, when school life normally relegates pain and illness 'into darkness', eluding any form of description, explanation or reference to them within the educational discourse and practice.

The shock has been multifaceted, including the economic trauma for the loss of income among families (and in some cases, as previously mentioned, food insecurity), along with the psychological stress and anxiety that impacted on mental health (Capurso et al., 2020; Egan et al., 2021). Learning and teaching were also undermined by the pain experienced among those who had a family member infected, worsening the sense of inadequacy to the new situation on both sides, who were asked to learn and who were asked to teach without the school infrastructure around them. Within the walls of the home, both stress levels and the disease increased, especially when learning/teaching had to be negotiated with other family needs, often sharing a limited space and, for those lucky enough to have it, access to connectivity and digital devices. In addition, the prolonged stress caused by *uncertainty* about the evolution of the pandemic and arising from the knowledge that everybody could be infected and potentially die, exacerbated the traumatic context for many that undermined the necessary focus and dedication to school work (Reimers, 2022, p. 2).

5 Determinants of the Emergency in Education: Open Issues from the Covid-19 Pandemic

In this context, the main axis of the school life (spaces, times, patterns of behaviour, public values, etc.) started to exert a new power over the actors as determinants (or co-determinants) of the emergency itself. Deeply hit by the prolonged school closure, all the educational actors found themselves in the position of imagining new ways of interacting with each other and making education possible. As previously mentioned, the pre-pandemic structures and pre-existing inequalities among students based on family resources played a role in the capacity to respond to the pandemic challenges. Research is highlighting how the student's engagement, learning and participation declined progressively, particularly among those from a disadvantaged social background (Reimers, 2022), giving life to a new emergency within the Covid-19 emergency.

If co-presence constituted the unnoticed 'normality' of teaching and learning processes, the replacement of physical social interactions by those enabled by digital platforms have had an enormous effect on educational practices. Research is fundamental in trying to understand how education has been reconfigured in its remote or blended forms and several chapters of this book provide an attempt in this direction. In our view, two main issues have been opened up by the pandemic disruption: the acceleration of digitalization and the change of the school/university form.

Firstly, the pandemic emergency brought about an acceleration of digital education all over the world. Teaching and learning have been transformed into processes that could unfold remotely through the mediation of an online platform and, as far as digital infrastructures were already in place, educational platforms allowed schools and universities to operate even in the midst of the spreading of the virus, when in many countries thousands of deaths and severe illness occurred (Grek & Landri, 2021). Paying the price of collapsing the spatial and temporal dimension of ordinary processes, digital technologies allowed public educational systems to continue pursuing their key functions: transmission of knowledge, acquisition of skills, production of human capital and – to some extent – the maintenance of social capital and the safeguarding of civic rights.

However, the acceleration of digitalization also meant increasing the role of the private sector in education, raising questions about if, and how, the pandemic emergency represented a window of opportunity not only for the advancement of the digital agenda but also for the penetration of private interests in the ecology of education practices (Williamson, 2021). As far as solutions had to be enacted in a state of emergency, governments and educational institutions – which had scarcely invested in the creation of public digital ecosystems in previous years – resulted in promoting only the already existing educational technologies, platforms, applications and software (cf. Chapter 9). This has led many countries, such as Italy, to rely on private companies like Microsoft, Google, Facebook, Amazon and other ed-tech enterprises to provide technical solutions to the education emergency. Everyday school and university activities soon become mediated by privately owned platforms. National governments and supra-national institutions launched public-private partnerships, institutionalizing the increasing role of ed-tech companies in education, raising the issue of who/what controls users and providers, and which kind of new organizational form is growing (Pais & Stark, 2020), while students and teachers still trust the cultural delivery as an independent action. There still remains the question about whether the pandemic 'exception' will constitute a new normality where education will provide an expanding and increasingly profitable space for private investors, along with if and how privately owned digital instruments will shape new forms of teaching, pedagogy and the meaning of education (Taglietti et al., 2021).

Secondly, an issue raised by the pandemic emergency regards the changing features of the school and university form itself. For many decades, modern education systems have been characterized by clear borders between formal and non-formal education as well as between the times and spaces where education takes place, through mechanisms of control and discipline that were focused on students' bodies, as systems of evaluation that assumed the co-presence of teachers and students in the same space-time (Maulini & Perrenoud, 2005). The 'de-materialization' and physical closure of educational institutions made these arrangements impossible and forcefully re-configured the teaching/learning processes which are now embedded in digitally mediated environments. As many authors describe, educational arrangement suddenly became more fluid, blurred and virtualized, with the time of education becoming de-standardized for both teachers and students. Learning processes became more dependent on individual activation and motivation, being impossible to activate the old mechanisms of incentives and control based on the co-presence of teacher and student bodies (López et al., 2021). Non-cognitive skills such as self-control, self-efficacy, resilience and tenacity became crucial to overcome the state of fear and distress (Tannert & Gröschner, 2021).

In both schools and universities, teachers have been forced to craft new meanings to their everyday working situation and new ways of engaging students. On the one hand, they have acquired skills that were relatively rare before the pandemic (at least in Italy) and contributed to expanding the digital agenda in education. On the other, old and new forms of inequalities still intersect the academic performance, calling into question:
- the stock of student resources (based on their family cultural, economic and housing capital),
- the stock of teacher resources (based on their technological skills, but also on the individual work-family balance, family capital and housing), and –
last but not least –
- the resources they can count on through the educational institution they belong to, which interrogate the so-called 'educating community': what is this like in a turbulent and challenging situation?

The 'revolution' of the de-materialized school, experienced during the pandemic, leaves us to imagine an emerging new paradigm for education (Messeri, 2019), within and outside the school itself, which possesses features that are both unfamiliar and blatant. For this reason, the in-field research presented here promises to fill the gap.

6   What the Essays Teach: Impact of the Lockdown on Educational Provision in Italy

Going through the content of this book, the nine studies collected here report the different impacts of the lockdown on educational provision in Italy, and analyse the immediate reactions of the different school/educational levels. It is worth briefly mentioning the main results.

The first essay, 'Challenges for Early Childhood Professionals: An Empirical Research Project on the Strategies, Practices and Effects of LEADs' by Rita Bertozzi and Tatiana Saruis, shows how education professionals built and managed 'distance education relationships', or LEADs (*legami educativi a distanza*), even before these were formalized, by comparing professionals' reports (via an online survey of 1,086 educators and teachers of children 0–6 years across Italy) and subsequent ministerial guidelines that noted the need to build LEADs in pre-primary education. It discusses in detail how the professionals performed their roles and whether (and how) they redefined tasks and objectives. The data collected at the outset show some inconsistencies, since the decision-making processes were more frequently individual rather than collegial. Professionals perceived weak support from coordinators, principals and institutions. However, the practical effort to manage the activities and contact the families were often left to them, boosting their creativity. Despite LEADs necessarily requiring the parents' mediation and engagement, parents were only marginally consulted in the decision-making processes. The data also show that digital technologies usage is still a challenge for Italian teachers/educators of children aged from 0 to 6 (remarking the minimal public investment in 'digitalization at school' in recent decades). Finally, the survey confirms the expected heterogeneity among the sample: continuity of contact was influenced by the stability of services and employment contracts (greater in the public sector) compared to flexibility and intermittence (in the private and Third sectors). Marked territorial differences also emerged between crèches and kindergartens in the northern and southern/central regions.

The second contribution is of a theoretical nature: 'Rethinking the Role of No Schooling during the Pandemic' by Maurizio Merico and Fausta Scardigno.

It focuses on the lack of this topic emerging in the current discourse on educational processes. The authors argue that during the first wave of the Covid-19 pandemic, children, adolescents and youngsters have been silently expropriated of the wide variety of educational opportunities – both non-formal and informal. Despite there being clear evidence of how (and how much) non-formal and informal activities produce lasting positive effects on the learning process, the Covid-19 emergency caused the (re)emergence of the (apparently old-fashioned) critical issue of the relationship between schooling and no schooling, and more generally, the need of conceiving a more integrated educational system. From the reconstruction of some international experiences, they highlight the prevailing imbalance, especially related to the management of spaces (indoor/outdoor) and times (synchronous/asynchronous) of the initiatives. Without doubt, during the lockdown, especially in Italy, no schooling played a residual role in the public debate. Due to the need for social distancing, informal education has been forced into a sort of (indefinite) deferral, situated in a non-place and a non-time. In the next stage of recovery from the pandemic and post-pandemic reconstruction, that 'spirit of community' brought by no schooling will probably become even more vital and indispensable.

In the third chapter, 'Rhetoric, Problem or Necessity? A Study of Parental Involvement during Covid-19' by Mariagrazia Santagati and Paolo Barabanti, the reader can find an in-depth analysis of the family-school relationship during the lockdown. The literature on parental involvement highlights problems and tensions from the asymmetrical teacher-parent relation; during the pandemic emergency, the pre-existing inequalities among parents affected the cooperation strategies. Through the use of a mobile instant messaging interview (MIMI) methodology, the author collected WhatsApp voice messages from February to August 2020 that were sent by students, parents and teachers living in some of the Italian cities most affected by the initial spread of the virus (Bergamo, Brescia, Milan and Turin). The results show that, although parental involvement has long been recognized as crucial by the Italian legislation and teachers and parents brought out positive narratives, the Covid-19 pandemic led to the emergence of tensions that were once hidden. A feeling of distress, overload and inability to cope with teachers' requests have profoundly impacted on student achievement and well-being during the pandemic, especially for disadvantaged families. Conversely, in some instances teachers and schools have developed formal and informal strategies that involved constant dialogue and communication with families (i.e. taking care not to place an excessive burden on vulnerable families with many children or on children with special needs, learning or relational difficulties, etc.). This involved negotiating the timetable, workload, learning objectives, etc. The authors highlight the meaningful capacity of some teachers and/or schools to respond to the emergency properly. However, these individuals inhabit a context lacking any form of systematization and clear indications about the pedagogical objectives and strategies to make parental involvement useful so as to improve the quality and equity of the students' learning process.

The fourth chapter, 'From Classroom to Screen: An Exploratory Study of University Students in Sicily during the Covid-19 Lockdown' by Umberto Di Maggio, presents the results of an exploratory quali-quantitative analysis on how students enrolled in social sciences degree courses (attending a small private university) had lived, perceived and evaluated the learning-at-a-distance experience. It sheds light on the investigated phenomena on the students' side, looking at how students lived the disruption of everyday life routines and interaction rituals at university. They consider remote teaching and learning a substitute or surrogate of traditional in-presence activities; a significant quota of them think that distance teaching could never substitute the traditional in-presence system. Moreover, students mostly perceived remote teaching to be an unpleasant experience (e.g. stressful, tiring, lonely); only a minority found it pleasant to learn at home. These students largely missed the interactional dimension with peers and teachers, the face-to-face exchanges and discussions, that they consider not only the 'social side' of the university experience but the core of teaching-learning itself.

Chapter 5, 'A New World Is Open? Distance Teaching in Italian Universities during the Covid-19 Emergency' by Francesco Ramella and Michele Rostan, is based on a survey of 3,398 academics working in Italian public universities. Organizational arrangements enacted by institutions, the new distance teaching experience and the possible consequences of distance learning on student engagement are the points under scrutiny. As a result, firstly, half of the academics were able to implement distance teaching immediately, even if only 8% of them had had some experience with e-teaching before. Secondly, the vast majority of academics enjoyed structuring, organizing and delivering distance teaching activities: they were free to organize themselves for the purpose (due to the lack of mandatory guidelines issued by the ministry); more specifically, about 70% of the interviewees answered they were free to choose the organization by themselves or within a range of options provided by their institutions, while the remaining 30% had to follow what their institutions had established (platforms, calendars, rules for students engagement). Their general satisfaction is due not only to the accomplishment of their teaching duties (and the fact that they were able to deliver the courses despite the emergency), but also to the acknowledgment that they had learnt something new that enriched their professional skills. There were several critical aspects of the academics' experience that emerged from the survey: during the lockdown, the workload grew dramatically (i.e. in lectures and material preparation); the more innovative and cooperative strategies were curtailed, while the most traditional teaching methods and practices doubled. The scarcity of confidence with e-teaching platforms, as well as the lack of training in IT-mediated teaching methods, are fundamental to understand the working conditions of academics and their future orientations to cope with an emergency like this.

Chapter 6, 'Young Europeans, Distance Learning and Trust in Educational Institutions: A Comparative Analysis after Covid-19' by Diego Mesa, showcases an international perspective, with a data analysis on five national samples (Italy, Spain, UK, France and Germany) of young respondents (aged 19–33). The data confirm that the use of distance learning has increased greatly in all the countries with an overall effect of reducing the gap between the various systems. The greatest effort in terms of activation has been made by the Italian education system, in which prior to Covid-19 young people had fewer opportunities to experience formal education of this kind than their counterparts abroad. The process of technological development and the forced 'reconversion' of teaching staff to a teaching method based on ICT resulted in a sort of 'de facto reform' of educational methods and practices (and Italy seems to have profited from it more than any other EU country). Italy seems to be the country with the most positive evaluation of distance learning, followed by Great Britain and Spain. Young Italians also declare the highest level of increase in trust in educational institutions, followed once again by Spain and Great Britain. Young Germans and French expressed considerably more critical assessments of distance learning. The youngsters' positive orientation towards e-learning highlights their desire for more dynamic education systems that are open to innovation, especially in relation to work. The average high level of trust in schools and universities expressed by the respondents was probably a sign that these systems showed their reactivity and 'care' about the educational demand at the very moment when access to the classrooms was banned. However, among the respondents, there is a greater polarization – especially in Italy – between confidence and distrust of institutions; between those who have experienced at first hand the 'fibrillations' of the system, feeling intensely its limits and iniquities, and those who, on the other, have recognized its practical and symbolic value as a sign of resilience and resistance of the educational system itself.

Chapter 7, 'Inside the Emergency: Digital Teaching from the Point of View of Teachers' by Eduardo Barberis, Nico Bazzoli, Domenico Carbone and Joselle Dagnes, focuses on teachers' adaptation to the school lockdown in terms of the management of teaching (i.e. methods and tools used) and their representations, opinions, expectations and worries in an exceptional time. The data were collected through a web survey administered on a non-probabilistic sample of 2,274 Italian teachers (employed at every school level, from infant to upper secondary schools). The survey included information on individual and organizational practices enacted to implement emergency distance education, changes in professional routines and representations on the teaching profession. The hypothesis was that the sudden transition to remote teaching generated different ways of being teachers: some may have been favoured by the 'emergency' frame to be more willing to be part of the game; those with non-standard careers (temporary staff) and those with instrumental or accidental professional identities might have been more at risk of work-related stress; online education might have been more of a constraint than an opportunity if teachers felt that they were being stripped of their professional tools. The results show that: 1) temporary staff, especially older teachers with fixed-term contracts, and those with accidental motivations (which correlated with higher dissatisfaction) are over-represented among those who found it difficult to make it through the pandemic situation, and they felt less equipped than others to manage ICT; 2) there is a portion of staff with limited self-efficacy, regardless of the pandemic emergency, but as a problem due to the fragmented Italian recruiting system; 3) despite the fact teachers reacted quite responsively, it seems that they did so in a vacuum, given the pressing urgency to go digital without any institutional or structural help.

The view of school managers is the topic of Chapter 8, 'Distance Learning/Teaching during the Covid-19 Emergency: The Perspective of School Principals' by Stefania Capogna, Maria Chiara De Angelis and Flaminia Musella. The study focuses on the role of school principals in dealing with the organizing of schools as 'resilient organizations'. Firstly, the role of principals is deemed to be strategic in such a critical situation in order to construct and organize the techno-social space of students and their families, teachers and all the school activities. The analysis sample is based on 474 respondents. Of the surveyed schools, 83% had enacted distant teaching within a week of the lockdown decree being issued, a good performance given the fact that Italian schools lag behind other OECD countries in relation to the digitalization and integration of IT technologies for teaching purposes. A little less than 40% of the school principals interviewed claimed that it was their very first time dealing with ICT for teaching. Secondly, the main problem identified by the principals was not of an endogenous nature (i.e. internal to their organizations), but external: the relevant digital divide characterizing students and families that caused an organizational crisis in their schools. Finally, the principals complained about the lack of guidance from the ministry (and the regional school offices) on how to organize a *real* distant teaching environment; failing that, the main organizational response was to use digital platforms to deliver videoconference lessons replicating the usual face-to-face teaching. On the whole, the principals' workload grew significantly, in particular on the communicative and interactional side. Their efforts were addressed to school coordinators – a middle management role played by selected teachers – in order to mediate and negotiate between the principals and teaching staff the reorganization of the activities. Where all the efforts were aimed at re-organizing the internal-external fluxes of communication and information, schools succeeded in terms of organizational resilience.

The ninth chapter, 'The Platformization and Commodification of Italian Schools during the Covid-19 Crisis: Implications for Policy and Future Research' by Gianna Cappello, offers an overview of how the pandemic emergency has accelerated the processes of digitalization and datification of the Italian education system, with an accurate reflection on privatization. It showcases how ed-tech companies have managed to use the pandemic as a window of opportunity, expanding their role in public education. By using data coming from various sources and research, the author provides an historical reconstruction of how Italian schools and teachers have come to lock their educational practices to the services provided by private corporations and donors, while also showing the profit that has been made in this sector during the pandemic. There are two elements worth highlighting. The first is that the pandemic rushed Italian schools to strengthen their digital infrastructures and online services. However, with a lack of any relevant public investment in free and open-source solutions, the strategy of the Italian Ministry of Education has been that of suggesting a number of private solutions (such as Google Suite for Education, Microsoft and WeSchool) to the choices of schools and teachers. The result has been that of a 'patchy' situation where the differentiation of teaching/learning practices increased not only among regions, but also among schools, and classes within schools. A second issue regards the consequences of using private providers to deliver educational goals: on the one hand, the platformization of education means an increasing number of micro-data to be collected and used by private providers to generate profit; on the other, this means attributing to the market the capacity to shape pedagogy in ways that cannot be ultimately submitted to forms of democratic control. It is therefore time to question what the post-pandemic scenario is in relation to these processes and whether enough will be invested to create an institutional/public platform, along with promoting free and open-source solutions.

7   Lessons from the Emergency

Reflecting on and highlighting what such a situation produced during the hardest phase of the Covid-19 pandemic would be of great interest for academics, practitioners and policymakers who need to define guidelines to cope with traumatic situations in the future of educational systems.

The Italian case could be particularly helpful. The national education system is characterized by the strong presence of public provision, but also by a lower level of public expenditure and investment when compared to other European countries. In the field of digitalization and e-teaching, the scarce investment in ICT infrastructures and in developing the digital skills of the teaching staff have been demonstrated at every educational level. The nine essays provide an in-depth understanding of the complexities that teachers and educational institutions faced, because although the educational provision has benefited from attempts, negotiations and solutions emerging from individual teachers, head teachers and out-of-school operators, the lack of preparedness at the systemic level emerged as extremely evident.

If the lower levels of education were the most affected by this, the university system (which is spread throughout the country with significant differences between academies) put on a better performance. Overall, the volume emphasizes how the lack of prior public investment in terms of infrastructures, technologies and training – but also the lack of a clear vision of what the purposes of education are in terms of promoting democracy and social justice – has produced tensions which risk increasing teachers' disengagement, and inequalities among students and educational institutions. In the perspective developed by the sociology of education, some recommendations can be drawn from each single study and transferred to other countries and/or similar situations:

1. The pandemic magnified the importance of the socio-emotional component in educational processes. Future policies of professional development and training of all school professionals must be centred on how they can improve social and emotional skills remotely.
2. The integration between schooling and no schooling is not just a newly desired institutional configuration, nor simply a model requested by efficient practical and organizational claims. On the contrary, it takes the shape of a process of interaction, differentiation and exchange among a wide range of agencies, whose effectiveness will affect the success of policy measures in order to reconstruct a post-pandemic society.
3. The family-school relationship and parental involvement must never be neglected. The pandemic has showed us something that is often underneath and misrecognized in ordinary times. During the school closure, formal education would have been impossible without the active support and cooperation of the parents.
4. The pandemic has also shown that social inequalities among families can mark a profound impact on the students' physical well-being, so teachers

are requested to base parental involvement strategies on more knowledge about the students' conditions at home, the time availability of parents, their housing and working condition, the cultural setting, etc. These are tasks that can no longer be postponed.

5. An extensive and mass use of teaching and learning technologies at any age could generate in the students (and teachers too) a sort of alienating sense of displacement and isolation, given the lack of true face-to-face interactions and relations, along with a compression of meaning in the daily routines. If ITC applied to teaching largely sterilizes the processes of human exchange and development, there is a need for clear guidelines on how to avoid this risk.

6. The levelling out of teaching methods is one of the biggest challenges for the efficacy of teachers and schools in the post-pandemic society. The teachers' skills for innovation must be improved and they have to be prepared for a mixed teaching method. The context in which innovation is embedded also has to be improved (increasing the multilevel governance of the education system).

7. Any crisis brings disruptive aspects as well as new opportunities. The short-term organizational reaction – put in place by educational institutions during the acute phase of contagion – was by large effective, but it also calls for the importance to treasure the experiences had. This does not mean substituting in-presence teaching with distance learning, but rather to achieve an organizational configuration capable of taking advantage of the best and most effective aspects of both.

8. The Italian case represents a privileged observatory of the changes induced by the Covid-19 pandemic on the digitalization of education. The results show how the process is entering a new phase with a growing impact on the functioning of teaching, on the innovation of educational organizations as well as on the learning dynamics of the youth population. In general, young Italians welcomed the challenge with confidence and a positive attitude.

9. However, to avoid the risk of the emergency becoming chronic and of a systematic exclusion of the most disadvantaged groups from the process, an integrated planning and consolidation of innovation is needed. The balance between the progression and distribution of educational opportunities to all must be ensured.

10. The role of school principals was strategic during the emergency, to overcome any structural impediments (such as digital and/or socio-economic divides), the teachers' inadequate familiarity with digital teaching methods and the lamented lacking role of government and peripheral

governance articulations. If they must act as 'organizational pivots' capable of restoring a meaningful task environment, they also deserve particular attention and incentives from the central control of public education.
11. The penetration of ITC and private digital platforms into the school/university environment calls for policymakers, educational practitioners and students to significantly expand their understanding of the consequences of digital innovations. Data collection, student profiling and learning analytics, with their corollary of increasing personalization of educational processes, need to be discussed in their pedagogical and political goals. If it is clear how ed-tech companies can benefit of these innovations, the way they can help new generations to cope with the educational, democratic, ecological and technological challenges of the future should be a matter of urgent public concern.

8 Education and Emergency: What Is the Link? Designing a Post-Pandemic Scenario through the Lens of the Sociology of Education

This book is an attempt to use the sociology of education as a means to make sense of the 'unspeakable' experience (Frank, 2001, p. 355) we lived in 2020, with, on the one hand, a permanent state of emergency being caused by an invisible enemy (a 'risk' in actual sociological terms), with many people suffering in the uncertain present, and, on the other, a restless search to anchor our lives to public institutions. One of the main responses to address this critical situation was offered through education, whose nature is to be structured (and structuring), inclusive, while also taking care of the social needs of both single individuals and entire local communities. The question undermining this book is: Did the Italian educational institutions, as agents of education and socialization, live up to expectations? Were they up to the challenge? What remains for both the professionals and beneficiaries after the Covid-19 pandemic in terms of common goods and achieved results?

By interrogating the educational actors (teachers, parents, students, head teachers, etc.), we are able to reveal one side of the coin, the patterns of behaviours, attitudes and cultural practices through which a 'new normality' has been reconstructed, even immediately, once the schools/universities shut down. This looks like a *'pale'* routine made of almost improvised distance relationships ('screen' or 'in-cloud' interactions) and a series of instructional actions, structured as much as possible to maintain the cognitive skills of both students and teachers too, while integrating e-teaching within the traditional environment. Neither an educational revolution nor a planned reform has been attempted. On the contrary, the results of numerous empirical studies highlight, on the part of individual school/university actors, an unpredictable capability of listening-and-response that confirms the art of getting by (*'arte di arrangiarsi'*) being not only the 'typical' Italian approach to life, but also the main resource to cope with the emergency.

The other side of the coin would be the way through which the emergency impacted on the functioning of the education system at large and, as a consequence, what will be desirable in the future to enable the system not only to deal with such an emergency again but also to improve its performance. On the whole, the Italian Ministry of Education managed the situation according to legitimated principles. These included:
– precaution,
– uniformity of the imposed limitations,
– minimization of long-term damages and losses, and
– homogeneity in distribution of the resources ('a small amount of aid to a large range of beneficiaries' is better than 'a lot of aid to a selected range of beneficiaries').

The uncertainty, widespread among the decision makers in the field of education, regarding the emergency duration and the risk of contagion within the classrooms (both issues being still open when we go to print in early 2022!), has provoked diffused hesitation in the ministry. It was unable to answer crucial questions: what to recommend to teachers and how to train them to distance teach; how to reassure parents and students and involve them in learning; how to guarantee the achievement of the academic year 2018/2019 for all the students; how to prepare new ITC tools and infrastructures for 'integrated teaching' to be implemented from the academic year 2020/2021 onwards; how to include vulnerable students in distance learning, etc.

The relatively few measures implemented during the first and second waves of the pandemic by the Ministry of Education were 'emergency education policies', not a planned 'education policy in emergency'. The distinction between the two (emergency education/education in emergency) comes from the crisis contexts and is rather interesting for the rationale of this book. While *emergency education* entails 'temporary measures that accidentally turn into long-term responses to student's educational needs', *education in emergency* must exalt the protective benefits of education, creating a neutral space where the situation of emergency can be suspended with a certain quality of life being assured. Taken from a United Nations High Commissioner for Refugees (UNHCR) handbook, this sentence is illuminating: 'A key principle for education in situations of emergency and crisis is rapid response, using a community-based approach, with capacity-building through training of teachers, youth leaders and school management committees' (Sinclair, 2001). It should be sufficient to transfer this principle (and the others deriving from it) from the crisis management to the post-pandemic scenario, to understand how to give a better response to the next emergency.

In the case of Italy, during the first wave of the Covid-19 contagion teachers, school principals and academic staff all worked (individually) as 'frontline personnel' making a rapid response possible, but convinced it was only a temporary solution to the emergency. What they lacked was *capacity-building* (and they still do about two years after the initial pandemic outbreak), that is, the multifaceted process of involving the main systemic components (teachers, youth leaders, parents' representatives and school managers) in the design of a post-pandemic scenario. As Eringfeld says:

> Especially in times of crisis, when the existential questions around the purposes and practices of education become re-emphasized, the act of re-imagining educational utopias is a necessary exercise. [...] Much less researched, however, is the contribution that dystopian imagination makes to this reflective process. (2021, p. 148)

Using dystopian thinking can be a fruitful suggestion, during an emergency, when social actors find it easier (than in 'normal' times) to express their fears, suffering and hopes, and feel more legitimated in pointing out the pitfalls of the previous situation. The main concerns associated with the first wave of Covid-19 included the sense of isolation of students and teachers, the marketization and standardization of teaching and the disembedding/disembodiment of the institutional mandate of education. However, the hopes are referred to the main gains achieved during the emergency: flexibility, customization of educational provision and a sense of solidarity. It is up to the 'frontline', as well as to the 'back office', social actors to use their dystopian imagination 'not to promote pessimism but rather to energize engagement with utopianism and reinforce commitment towards positive change' (ibid.).

Authors' Note

The authorship of this Introduction is to be shared by the entire team of co-editors. For the scientific attribution, the following parts should be attributed to Maddalena Colombo: Section 1, Section 2.2 (with Vaira), 4 (with Visentin) and Section 8. To Marco Romito Section 3 (with Vaira), 5 (with Visentin). Massimiliano Vaira should be attributed Sections 2.1, 2.2 (with Colombo), and 3 (with M.

Romito). Martina Visentin should be attributed Section 4 (with M. Colombo), and Section 5 (with Romito). Sections 6–7 were written by all the authors.

Notes

1. The AIS (Italian Sociological Association) network of sociologists includes about 1,000 academic and non-academic members, of whom 15–20% are specialists in the sociology of education. The Italian Sociological Association's Sociology of Education section (AIS-EDU) has a Facebook account (with about 250 followers). Every year, the network promotes numerous scientific meetings throughout the country and since 2018, it has published a bi-annual newsletter in the education field for the AIS-EDU members. See: https://www.ais-sociologia.it/en/sociologia-delleducazione/
2. See: Prime Minister's Decree (DPCM) of March 4th 2020: https://www.governo.it/sites/new.governo.it/files/DPCM4MARZO2020.pdf
3. Since 2020, the architectural renewal of public schools has become a priority to be pursued with the future Recovery and Resilience Plan (PNRR) founded by Next Generation Italia. See: https://www.mef.gov.it/en/focus/The-Recovery-and-Resilience-Plan-Next-Generation-Italia/
4. Italy spends 4.1% of GPD, vs 5.3% UE and 5.2% OECD. See: https://databank.worldbank.org/home
5. See: https://www.drrandallcollins.com/sociological-eye/2020/7/8/sociology-of-masks-and-social-distancing

References

AGCOM. (2019). *Educare digitale. Lo stato di sviluppo della scuola digitale*. AGCOM.

Alexander, J. C. (2012). *Trauma: A social theory*. Polity.

Alexander, J. C., Eyerman, R., Giesen, B., Smelser, N. J., & Sztompka, P. (2004). *Cultural trauma and collective identity*. University of California Press.

Archer, M. S. (1979). *The social origins of educational systems*. Sage.

Avvisati, F., Hennessy, S., Kozma, R. B., & Vincent-Lancrin, S. (2013). *Review of the Italian strategy for digital schools*. OECD Education Working Papers, no. 90. OECD Publishing. https://www.oecd.org/education/ceri/Innovation%20Strategy%20Working%20Paper%2090.pdf

Banchio P., Cervella, C., Galaverna, C., & Giordano, A. M. (2021). How school has changed for 3–14-year-old students: An Italian case study. In D. Burgos, A. Tlili, & A. Tabacco (Eds.), *Radical solutions for education in a crisis context: COVID-19 as an opportunity for global learning* (pp. 273–282). Springer Nature.

Beck, U. (1992). *Risk society: Towards a new modernity*. Sage.

Bourdieu, P., et al. (1999). *The weight of the world: Social suffering in contemporary society*. Stanford University Press.

Capurso, M., Dennis, J. L., Salmi, L. P., Parrino, C., & Mazzeschi, C. (2020). Empowering children through school re-entry activities after the COVID-19 pandemic. *Continuity in Education*, *1*(1), 64–82. https://doi.org/10.5334/CIE.17

Christakis, N. A. (2020). *Apollo's arrow: The profound and enduring impact of coronavirus on the way we live*. Little, Brown Spark.

Colombo, M., & Desideri, A. (2019). School autonomy in Italy: Trends and social consequences. In S. da Cruz Martins et al. (Eds.), *School autonomy, organization and performance in Europe: A comparative analysis for the period from 2000 to 2015* (pp. 101–113). CIES-IUL editions. https://repositorio.iscte-iul.pt/bitstream/10071/19965/1/EBOOK_School%20Autonomy%20Organization%20and%20Performance%20in%20Europe_VF.pdf

Colombo, M., Poliandri, D., & Rinaldi, E. E. (2020). Gli impatti dell'emergenza COVID-19 sul sistema scolastico-formativo in Italia. *Scuola democratica*. Advance online publication. doi:10.12828/97098

Cordini, M., & De Angelis, G. (2021). Families between care, education and work: The effects of the pandemic on educational inequalities in Italy and Milan. *European Journal of Education*, *56*(4), 578–594. https://doi.org/10.1111/EJED.12483

Das, V., Kleinman A., Ramphele M., Lock, M., & Reynolds, P. (Eds.). (2001). *Re-making a world: Violence, social suffering and recovery*, University of California Press.

Dei, M. (1993). Cambiamento senza riforma: la scuola secondaria superiore negli ultimi trent'anni. In S. Soldani & G. Turi (Eds.), *Fare gli italiani. Scuola e cultura nell'Italia contemporanea*. Il Mulino.

De Mauro, T. (2017). *Storia linguistica dell'Italia unita*. Laterza.

Demertzis, N., & Eyerman, R. (2020). Covid-19 as cultural trauma. *American Journal of Cultural Sociology*, *8*(3), 428–450.

Douglas, M. (1992). *Risk and blame: Essays in cultural theory*. Routledge.

Egan, S. M., Pope, J., Moloney, M., Hoyne, C., & Beatty, C. (2021). Missing early education and care during the pandemic: The socio-emotional impact of the COVID-19 crisis on young children. *Early Childhood Education Journal*, *49*(5), 925–934. https://doi.org/10.1007/S10643-021-01193-2

Eriksen, T. H. (2021, September 23). The pandemic reminded us what really matters. *Forum: Charles University Magazine*. https://www.ukforum.cz/en/main-categories/unilife/8072-eriksen

Eringfeld, S. (2021). Higher education and its post-coronial future: Utopian hopes and dystopian fears at Cambridge University during Covid-19. *Studies in Higher Education*, *46*(1), 146–157. doi:10.1080/03075079.2020.1859681

Frank A.W. (2001), Can we research suffering? *Qualitative Health Research*, *11*(3), 353–362.

Furedi, F. (1997). *Culture of fear: Risk-taking and the morality of low expectation*. Cassell.

Furedi, F. (2018). *How fear works: Culture of fear in the twenty-first century*. Bloomsbury.

Giancola, O., & Piromalli, L. (2020). Apprendimenti a distanza a più velocità. L'impatto del COVID-19 sul sistema educativo italiano. *Scuola democratica*. Advance online publication. doi:10.12828/97097

Giarelli, G. (2018). *Sofferenza e condizione umana. Per una sociologia del negativo nella società globalizzata*. Rubbettino.

Giarelli, G. (2021, February 23–28). *From social suffering to a sociology of negative?* [Paper]. The 4th ISA forum of sociology, Porto Alegre. https://isaconf.confex.com/isaconf/forum2020/meetingapp.cgi/Session/13815

Giddens, A. (1984). *The constitution of society*. Polity.

Giddens, A. (1990). *The consequences of modernity*. Polity.

Grek, S., & Landri, P. (2021). Editorial: Education in Europe and the COVID-19 pandemic. *European Educational Research Journal, 20*(4), 393–402. https://doi.org/10.1177/14749041211024781

Gui, M. (2019). *Il digitale a scuola. Rivoluzione o abbaglio?* Il Mulino.

Gui, M., & Argentin, G. (2011). Digital skills of internet natives: Different forms of digital literacy in a random sample of northern Italian high school students. *New Media & Society, 13*(6), 963–980.

Human Rights Watch. (2021, June). *Italy: students with disabilities included in Covid-19 education plans: Examples of in-person education in pandemic offer lessons for all*. https://www.hrw.org/news/2021/06/15/italy-students-disabilities-included-covid-19-education-plans#

Istat. (2021). *Livelli di istruzione e partecipazione alla formazione*. https://www.istat.it/it/files//2021/10/REPORT-LIVELLI-DI-ISTRUZIONE-2020.pdf

Landri, P. (2009). A temporary eclipse of bureaucracy: The circulation of school autonomy in Italy. *Italian Journal of Sociology of Education, 3*, 76–93.

López, C. A., Decuypere, M., Dey, J., Gorur, R., Hamilton, M., Lundahl, C., & Sjödin, E. S. (2021). Dancing with Covid: Choreographing examinations in pandemic times. *European Educational Research Journal, 20*(4), 403–422. https://doi.org/10.1177/14749041211022130

Lupton, D., & Willis, K. (Eds.). (2021). *The Covid-19 crisis: Social perspectives*. Routledge.

Maulini, O., & Perrenoud, P. (2005). La forme scolaire de l'éducation de base: tensions internes et évolutions. In O. Maulini & C. Mondandon (Eds.), *Les formes de l'éducation: variété et variations* (pp. 147–168). De Boeck Supérieur.

Messeri, A. (2019). Un nuovo paradigma per l'educazione? Alcune ipotesi. In F. Corbo, M. Michelini, & A. F. Uricchio (Eds.), *Innovazione didattica universitaria e strategie degli atenei italiani* (pp. 467–488). Geo-Crui-UniBai.

MIUR. (2020, June 26), *Linee guida per la didattica digitale integrata* [*Guidelines for integrated digital teaching*]. Ministry of Education, University and Research. https://www.miur.gov.it/documents/20182/0/ALL.+A+_+Linee_Guida_DDI_.pdf/f0eeb0b4-bb7e-1d8e-4809-a359a8a7512f

Moretti, V., & Maturo, A. (2021). Unhome sweet home: The construction of new normalities in Italy during COVID-19. In D. Lupton & K. Willis (Eds.), *The Covid-19 crisis: Social perspectives* (pp. 90–102). Routledge.

Neill, S., & Etheridge, R. (2008). Flexible learning spaces: The integration of pedagogy, physical design, and instructional technology. *Marketing Education Review, 18*(1), 47–53.

OECD. (2013). *Education at glance 2013: OECD indicators*. OECD Publishing. https://doi.org/10.1787/eag-2013-en

Pais, I., & Stark, D. (2020). Introduction to the thematic issue on power and control in platform monopoly capitalism. *Sociologica, 14*(3), 43–46.

Pandolfini, V. (2016). Exploring the impact of ICTs in education: Controversies and challenges. *Italian Journal of Sociology of Education, 8*(2), 28–53. https://doi.org/10.14658/pupj-ijse-2016-2-3

Pavolini, E., Argentin, G., Falzetti, P., Galanti, M. T., Campodifiori, E., & Le Rose, G. (2021). Tutti a casa. Il sistema di istruzione italiano alla prova del Covid-19. *Social Policies, 8*(2), 255–280.

Pitzalis, M., Porcu, M., De Feo, A., & Giambona, F. (2016). *Innovare a scuola: Insegnanti, studenti e tecnologie digitali*. Il Mulino.

Pitzalis, M., & Spanò, E. (2021). Stay home and be unfair: The amplification of inequalities among families with young children during COVID-19. *European Journal of Education, 56*(4), 595–606. https://doi.org/10.1111/EJED.12481

Puccetti, E. C., & Luperini, V. (2020). Quale scuola dopo la pandemia?' *Lifelong Lifewide Learning, 16*(36), 93–102. doi:10.19241/LLL.V16I36.536

Reimers, F., Schleicher, A., Saavedra, J., & Tuominen, S. (2020). *Supporting the continuation of teaching and learning during the COVID-19 Pandemic: Annotated resources for online learning*. OECD Publishing. https://www.oecd.org/education/Supporting-the-continuation-of-teaching-and-learning-during-the-COVID-19-pandemic.pdf

Reimers, F. M. (2022). Learning from a pandemic: The impact of Covid-19 on education around the world. In F. M. Reimers (Ed.), *Primary and secondary education during Covid-19: Disruptions to educational opportunity during a pandemic* (pp. 1–37). Springer.

Salmieri, L. (2019). The rhetoric of digitalization in Italian educational policies: Situating reception among digitally skilled teachers. *International Journal of Sociology of Education, 11*(1), 162–183.

Saraceno, C. (2020). The impact of the COVID-19 epidemic. In C. Saraceno, D. Benassi, & E. Molicchio (Eds.), *Poverty in Italy: Features and drivers in a European perspective* (pp. 146–150). Policy Press.

Sinclair, M. (2001). Education in emergencies. In J. Crisp, C. Talbot, & D. B. Cipollone (Eds.), *Learning for a future: Refugee education in developing countries* (pp. 1–83). United Nations High Commissioner for Refugees (UNHCR).

Taglietti, D., Landri, P., & Grimaldi, E. (2021). The big acceleration in digital education in Italy: The COVID-19 pandemic and the blended-school form. *European Educational Research Journal, 20*(4), 423–441. https://doi.org/10.1177/14749041211021246

Tannert, S., & Gröschner, A. (2021). Joy of distance learning? How student self-efficacy and emotions relate to social support and school environment. *European Educational Research Journal, 20*(4), 498–519. https://doi.org/10.1177/14749041211024784

Vaira, M., & Romito, M. (2020). L'emergenza COVID-19 e la scuola. Una riflessione su alcune contraddizioni emergenti dalla crisi. *Scuola democratica*. Advance online publication. https://doi.org/10.12828/97099

Wilkinson, I. (2005, January 28–29). *From the sociology of risk to a critical sociology of suffering* [Paper]. SCARR Network. http://mastor.cl/blog/wp-content/uploads/2016/10/wilkinson.-sociological-risk-and-suffering.pdf

Williamson, B. (2021). Education technology seizes a pandemic opening. *Current History, 120*(822), 15–20. https://doi.org/10.1525/CURH.2021.120.822.15

CHAPTER 1

Challenges for Early Childhood Professionals

An Empirical Research Project on the Strategies, Practices and Effects of LEADs

Rita Bertozzi and Tatiana Saruis

1   Introduction

In Italy, the lockdown due to Covid-19 and consequent interruption of schools and services for children aged from birth to six have led early childhood educators and teachers to develop strategies for staying in contact with families remotely, in order to offer parents and children both support and educational experiences. As their work is usually strongly based on physical and emotional proximity, they had to deeply reimagine their role, aims, methods, tools and activities. In May 2020, the Italian Ministry of Education released a document aimed at recognizing these efforts and offering educational guidelines, conceptualizing them as LEADs (*legami educativi a distanza*, distance education relationships). This concept highlights the specificity of needs and actions with children aged from birth to six and the difference from the distance learning system known as DAD (*didattica a distanza*) practiced in higher levels of the school system. However, as the lockdown started in February, the first emergency had already been managed by early childhood schools and services.

Considering the weakness of the governance of the early childhood care system in Italy, our hypothesis is that the decisions on how to provide education during the pandemic were often delegated to the frontline staff of services and schools. Consequently, an extremely fragmented and heterogeneous supply may be provided to children and families, strongly influenced by the resources, skills, strategies and efforts of teachers and educators and their capacity to adapt and develop an educational dialogue with parents and children in such conditions. Furthermore, due to the fact that remote education was new for teachers and educators, we assumed that they had to make use of all possible resources in order to cope with this emergency, with the expected consequences both on the improvement of competencies and the sense of 'abandonment' within this difficult challenge.

This chapter analyses the process through which LEADs have been conceived and put into practice from the perspective of educators and teachers of children aged from birth to six. It describes the related decision-making procedures, the professional challenges and resources involved, and the kind of support provided to children and families.

The study includes: (1) an analysis of institutional documents, to shed light on the process through which LEADs were developed in the context of the pandemic; and (2) some of the results of an empirical study conducted through an online survey involving 1,086 educators and teachers of children aged from birth to six across Italy. The analysis highlights how the rapid process of adaptation and distance education strategies exposed (and often increased) the weaknesses as well as the strengths of this education segment, in terms of competences, resources, relationships and the professionals' capacity to reinterpret them under different conditions.

2 The ECEC System in Italy

In Italy, the Early Childhood Education and Care (ECEC) policy system has traditionally been structured into two segments: one providing services for children aged 0–3, and one for 3- to 6-year-olds. These two segments have different historical origins and development paths, and consequently have very different features (Mari, 2017; Sabatinelli, 2016).

The 0–3 ECEC segment consists mainly of crèches (*nidi d'infanzia*). Starting in the 1990s, supplementary services (*servizi integrativi*) were developed, providing different kinds of support in order to complement the limited provision of crèches. However, the coverage data for this segment is low: in 2017–2018 about 28.6% of children under three years old attended education services, which is below the European average of 34.2% (Istat et al., 2020). Moreover, there are wide disparities in the regional provision, with more services available in northern and central Italy. The children who do not attend the services usually remain at home with a family caregiver (often their mother or grandparents) or a babysitter, due to the parents' choice not to use the services or to their difficulty in accessing them (e.g. high cost, oversubscription, distance, hours incompatible with parent's job) (Sabatinelli, 2016).

The 0–3 segment was established as a social-educational support for children with working parents[1] in the 1970s, and has traditionally been funded by the Ministry of Social Policies, while the regions regulate, co-finance and set quality standards for these services. The municipalities are responsible for their implementation, managing the services directly or outsourcing them to Third sector or private organizations. Nowadays, a substantial part of the private provision of 0–3 services is accredited and supported by public funding. A small proportion of the private provision is not accredited and fully independent:

it only has to comply with safety requirements and does not receive public funding. The education professionals (*educatrici* and *educatori*) involved have been variously defined by the regions, based on different but growing levels of awareness of the educational value of this segment of ECEC. Crèche educators have only been required to have a degree in the last ten years, and part of the staff is still made up of non-graduates.

The 3–6 ECEC segment consists of kindergartens (*scuole d'infanzia*), i.e. preschools for children from three to six years old. Due to greater awareness of the educational value of these schools,[2] responsibility for this segment is vested in the Ministry of Education. Access to kindergartens is open to all families, although it is not compulsory. Kindergartens can be managed by the state, by municipal authorities (directly or through outsourcing to the Third sector) or by private organizations, which can be accredited or completely independent. The public-private mix differs across local areas and regions, and Catholic kindergartens are very widespread throughout Italy. Considering both the public and private provision, the coverage rate of this ECEC segment in 2017–2018 was about 90% of the target population (Istat et al., 2020). The education staff of kindergartens consists mostly of graduate teachers (*maestri e maestre*) specializing in 3- to 6-year-old children.

A recent reform, approved between 2015 and 2017, was a milestone in the regulation and organization of ECEC policies, aiming to institute an integrated system of education 'from birth to six years'.[3] The law establishes that the integrated 0–6 system must become part of the education and training policy under the responsibility of the Ministry of Education. According to this new organization, the state provides the general framework for ECEC, financing and monitoring the implementation of policies, the regions design their own regional plans and set their priorities, coordinating, regulating and co-financing their ECEC systems, and the municipalities are responsible for co-planning, organizing and managing the local services.

In practice, however, coordination and continuity between the two segments, as required by the law, is not easy to achieve. Fragmentation currently prevails, and the integrated system is expected to be implemented gradually, based on the availability of financial, human and practical resources (Mari, 2017). This framework affected the management of the ECEC provision during the lockdown.

3 Governance of the ECEC Policy System during the Pandemic Lockdown

The first health and safety measures introduced in February 2020 were applied to educational and school services in the regions of northern Italy, the hardest hit by the pandemic, but quickly spread nationwide in few weeks. The reopening of schools was postponed several times until the Prime Minister's Decree (DPCM) of May 8th 2020 announced the online ending of the school year and the scheduled reopening of schools for September 2020. No exemption was granted for early childhood education.

The general operational guidelines for DAD issued in March 2020 by the Ministry of Education only includes a few lines on early childhood education, recommending that relations with families be maintained through direct, albeit remote, contact between teachers and children, even just through simple voice or video messages, and with a focus on play activities and the education and care previously provided in the classroom. The note makes no mention whatsoever of education services for children under 3 years old. This limited attention paid to the 0–6 age group reveals the difficulty at the state level in addressing this specific segment of education, recently instituted as an 'integrated 0–6 system'.

Dedicated instructions for this age group were not issued until May 13th 2020, with the publication of the document 'Educational Guidelines for Distance Education Relationships: A Different Approach to Crèche and Preschool Education Practices' developed by the National Committee for the 'integrated 0–6 system' (Legislative Decree 65/2017, our translation). The document recognizes the specific needs of the 0–6 age group and the importance of dedicated early childhood schools and services, but also of providing support for parents and countering the risks of education poverty and inequality. It also notes the responses to the emergency already implemented at the local level and defines LEADs as providing common educational guidelines.

According to the ministry's guidelines, LEADs occur in a space that is both virtual and domestic. They are aimed at: (1) managing the relationship with children, stimulating their autonomy and focusing on play in order to convey a positive vision of the future, with due sensitivity towards their emotional experiences; (2) alternating synchronous and asynchronous activities and facilitating the engagement of all the families; (3) strengthening the education covenant by offering support and promoting the active participation of parents; and (4) underlining the value of documentation and shared planning as an educating community and being responsive to the feedback received.

However, between February and May 2020, most schools and services had already taken action with highly diversified support tools (Chieregato, 2020). This was the result of a weakly integrated governance system and an obvious disconnect between the sphere of politics and that of day-to-day practices and micro-policies (Giancola & Piromalli, 2020).

The different governance configuration of the two segments of the '0–6 system' saw different actors engaged – and likely different dynamics playing out – in the decision-making processes during the first emergency. The guidelines of the ministry had to be implemented by the public and private accredited kindergartens. The municipalities were responsible for the crèches; however, part of these services are outsourced to Third sector organizations, and in some cases the lockdown involved renegotiating the contracts. The educational activities were thus not always provided by the services' contractors, as the municipalities could decide to centralize them. Finally, the unaccredited private sector had total freedom in managing the emergency both in crèches and kindergartens, but in this case a fee renegotiation could be requested by the families, and they had to evaluate the sustainability of the remote education offering. This complex organization created an extremely variegated education offering during the pandemic, which is the focus of this chapter.

Against this background, the effects of the pandemic on Italian families and school systems gave rise to a heated debate right from the outset. For the youngest children, some Italian experts warned of the potential aggravation of educational, family-related, economic as well as health risks. They pointed to the possible harmful effects of a range of factors, including physical and social isolation, being suddenly deprived of relations with their peers and loved ones, overexposure to screens (Mantovani et al., 2020) and lack of educational experiences and spaces, with greater repercussions for disadvantaged children or those with individual or family difficulties (Save the Children, 2020; Gigli, 2020; Antonietti et al., 2020). On the other hand, they also highlighted the potential benefits to children of spending more time with their parents and of a slower pace of life (Mantovani et al., 2020; Santagati & Barabanti, 2020), despite the challenges for family organization (Manzo & Minello, 2020; Sabatinelli, 2020), as well as the potential for innovative educational methods in early childhood schools and services (Gigli, 2020), in line with some international research studies (Samuelsson et al., 2020; Barnett et al., 2020).

Some nationwide data (SIRD, 2020) show how rapidly teachers changed their teaching methods, with greater efforts made in preschools and primary schools, where teachers tried harder to reach children individually. However, the data point to low-level skills in using digital tools, particularly in early childhood education (Ranieri, 2020; SIRD, 2020), and the high uptake of training courses during the lockdown (84%) (INDIRE, 2020). Other critical areas for early childhood schools and services include the fact that they have the highest estimated number of children who could not be reached (SIRD, 2020). That said, communication with the families played a key role: when prompt, lean and continuous, it made families feel supported; when slow or absent, it compounded the sense of distance and abandonment (Gigli, 2020; Santagati & Barabanti, 2020). In many cases, the experience showed the mixed effects of technologies, 'de-demonizing' them for many teachers.

4 The Field Research: Aims, Method and Sample

Our study focuses on education professionals working in schools and services for children aged 0–6. Faced with the conditions imposed by the Covid-19 emergency, these professionals had to cope with a sudden change in the cornerstones of childhood education. Concrete experiences and direct relationships, the educational role of the environment and of the daily life routines[4] were replaced by exposure to technology, often involving screens, from which the youngest children had frequently been protected but which now became the only possible medium for re-establishing contact with them (Cino, 2020). The research seeks to examine in detail how the professional figures involved performed their roles and whether (and how) they redefined their tasks and objectives.

The hypothesis is that the decisions on how to provide distance education relationships during the pandemic were often delegated to the frontline staff of services and schools. Consequently an extremely fragmented and heterogeneous supply may be provided to children and families, strongly influenced by the resources, skills, strategies and efforts of teachers and educators and their capacity to adapt and develop an educational dialogue with parents and children in such conditions.

The research questions driving the analysis are: What was the role of early childhood education professionals in the development of LEADs? What were the challenges and difficulties they faced in adapting their role for distance education? What kinds of competences, support and resources were they or were they not able to draw upon? What did LEADs involve in practice? And what kinds of effects did they have on children and their families, but also on the professionals themselves? In sum, did LEADs work or not in the emergency context from the professionals' point of view?

In order to answer these questions, an empirical study was conducted by the University of Modena & Reggio Emilia through an online survey carried out between June and July 2020. The survey collected both quantitative and qualitative information, through 38 questions focused on decision-making processes at the beginning of the emergency, strategies for staying in contact with the families, activities for the children, workload during the pandemic, difficulties and resources in the remote education experience, and children and families reached. The questionnaire was circulated through professional and personal emailing lists and social media networks (Facebook, Telegram, LinkedIn, WhatsApp) in order to collect as many answers as possible.

The survey involved 1,086 educators and teachers in schools and services for children aged 0–6 across Italy. The sample is not based on random selection

TABLE 1.1 Type of services/schools and geographical areas in which the respondents work (% of columns)

Type of services/schools for children aged 0–6	North	Centre	Mezzogiorno[a]	Total
Kindergartens (3–6 y.o.)	55.4	62.3	77.1	61.0
Crèches (0–3 y.o.)	39.3	29.3	15.1	32.5
Supplementary services (micro-crèches, family or home crèches)	3.0	4.2	5.9	3.8
Integrated services for 0–6 y.o. children	1.7	2.5	0.0	1.6
Other services (playgrounds, etc.)	0.6	1.7	2.0	1.1
Total	100.0	100.0	100.0	100.0
No. of valid answers	641	239	205	1085

a The geographical area called the Mezzogiorno includes Italy's southern regions and islands (as in Istat et al., 2020)

SOURCE: FIELDWORK DATA

and this poses well-known limitations in terms of the representativeness of the collected data. However, it is well distributed nationwide and across types of schools and services (see Table 1.1).

We recognize the limits of the methodology used in understanding all relevant aspects of the phenomenon. Further researches can highlight other points of view, consulting other figures involved on the same processes, such as parents, children and principals. Furthermore, qualitative analysis could deepen some aspects and issues that emerge in this study, deepening the difficulties and strategies addressed during the first lockdown.

The sample consists almost entirely of women (only 4 out of the 1,086 respondents are men), reflecting the gender composition of the education staff in 0–6 early childhood schools and services. About 40% of them are over 45 years old, 36% are in the 35–45 age bracket, and 22% are under 35 years old. Almost half of them are graduates.

Educators account for 40% of the sample, teachers for 52% and special needs educators/teachers for around 5%.[5] A small percentage of coordinators (2%) and other education professionals (0.6%) make up the sample. Kindergarten staff account for 61% of the sample, crèche staff for 32% and staff in 0–6 integrated services or supplementary services for 7%.

Out of the survey participants, 59% work in the public sector (including both state and local public institutions), 15% in the private sector and 25%

in the Third sector (i.e. associations, social cooperatives, churches, foundations and so on). The majority of them (78%) have permanent employment contracts, 18% have temporary contracts (including 3% whose contracts have been 'interrupted' due to the Covid-19 emergency), a small proportion (2.6%) are owners of services/schools and self-employed professionals, and some (1.2%) are trainees or volunteers.

In terms of geographic distribution, 59% of respondents work in northern Italy, 22% in central Italy, and 19% in Italy's southern regions and islands (Mezzogiorno). It should be noted that there are more ECEC schools and services in northern and central Italy, especially for the 0–3 segment (Istat et al., 2020).

Combining the information on the sample shows that the educators are comparatively younger than the teachers (73% of educators are under 35 years old, while a similar proportion of teachers are over 45), the large majority of them work in crèches (78%), while almost all the teachers (99.5%) work in kindergartens. Educators are quite evenly spread across the three market sectors considered, with a higher proportion working in the Third sector (40%), while 82% of teachers work in the public sector; 70% of educators have permanent contracts, and for teachers that proportion increases to 88%. To sum up, the profile of educators tends to correspond to younger women working in crèches managed by the Third sector, while teachers are more often women over 45 years old working in public (state-run or locally run) kindergartens with stable jobs.

5   The Research Findings

5.1   *The Decision-Making Processes during the First Emergency*

An initial aspect of the study focuses on the decision-making processes at the beginning of the emergency regarding the possibility of continuing the relationship with the children and their families remotely. As the Prime Minister's Decree of March 2020 only required principals to ensure continuity in education, allocating resources to support staff training, the use of digital platforms and the supply of computer equipment without specific attention to the children from birth to six, the choice brought into play the potential professional contribution of educators and teachers, as well as the relevant school organizations and their capacity to support them (as explained previously). LEAD s also stress the family's participation as the basis for a solid educational partnership, given that the active engagement of parents is a necessary condition for the children's ability to access and make quality use of the education offering.

The data show a substantial difference between educators and teachers in their level of involvement in these decisions, where only 28% of the educators were involved as compared to almost half of the teachers. Coordinators were involved in 54% of cases, which seems fairly low given the specific relevance of their role. Other stakeholders also participated in the decision: organizations above the school level played a role in 10% of cases, possibly standardizing the education offering as a result, while parent representatives only participated in the decision in 12% of cases.

In just under 6 out of 10 cases, the decision was made by a solitary figure: those who found themselves making the choice alone were most frequently teachers (around 24% of the total) and coordinators (20%), while educators more rarely made the decision alone (9.4%). In around 4% of cases the choice was made exclusively by organizations above the school level (i.e. municipalities or Third sector or private organizations).

In 3 out of 10 cases, two figures were involved in the decision: teachers jointly with coordinators (12%), and educators jointly with coordinators (9.5%). The third most frequent pairing, but which only accounts for 4% of cases, was teachers and parent representatives. In only 1 out of 10 cases the figures involved were 3 or more, where the most frequent combination was between teachers, coordinator and parent representative (3.3%).

Solitary decision-making is more frequent in the Mezzogiorno regions (7 cases out of 10), and less frequent in central (6 out of 10) and northern Italy (roughly 5 out of 10). Participatory decision-making was higher in northern Italy, lower in central Italy and even lower in the Mezzogiorno regions.

No significant differences in the decision-making processes were found between the public, private and Third sectors, nor between different types of crèches and kindergartens. While there was wider participation in integrated services for children aged 0–6 (of which there are only seventeen cases), almost always involving two or three figures, the need to coordinate the 0–3 and 3–6 age segments may have entailed more complex decision-making procedures.

Lastly, parent participation in decision-making was far higher in kindergartens (15.5%) than in crèches and additional services (5%), and was also higher in the public sector (14%) compared to the Third sector (8%) and the private sector (6%). No variations in parent participation were found between geographical areas.

5.2 *The Education Offering: Contact with Families and Activities Offered*

In terms of the time taken to get into action, the findings are consistent with those of other studies (Ranieri, 2020). According to the interviewees, initial contact with families was made on average within 10 days of the school/service closure. The recorded median value was 7 days, meaning that half the families were contacted within a week. The response to the emergency was therefore very swift. In many cases, schools and services offered to provide educational support to children and their families during the lockdown right from the start, without waiting for detailed instructions or operational guidelines 'from above'. But this meant they had limited time for adapting and planning, which may be connected with the 'difficulty' described by the interviewees and the resulting quality of the offering.

The swiftest to act – in just 5 days – were supplementary services, where the staff and group of families are small. Integrated services for children aged 0–6 and kindergartens took around 9 days to act, while crèches took an average of 14 days. Differences between the public, private and Third sectors were minimal. The schools and services run by the Third sector took 9.5 days, followed by those in public sector with 10 days and those of the private sector with 12 days.

The education partnership between schools/services and families was one of the pivots of reorganization during the emergency. Education professionals had to adapt the times and modalities of their education offering, devising various ways of establishing and re-establishing their relationship with the families and children.

Looking at the features of the education offering, the first aspect we investigated was its continuity. 70% of the interviewees stayed constantly in contact with the families, while around 27% went through periods with variably intensive or discontinuous contact. Only 2.5% stated that the school or service ceased all contact with the families during the lockdown. Kindergartens kept constantly in contact with families in 80% of cases, with supplementary and integrated 0–6 services following well behind at 60%, while in crèches contact with families was less constant (54% of cases).

The public service stayed constantly in contact with families more frequently than did the private and Third sectors: 77% in the former case and around 60% in the latter two. Consistently with this, kindergarten teachers and older teachers, public sector staff and those with greater job stability report greater continuity. These data suggest that stability of services and job stability influenced the system's capacity to support families during the emergency compared to more flexible situations. The private and Third sectors may also have had to consider availability of resources and personnel, and assess costs, benefits and business risk in the strategy they pursued. Whatever the case, the families using public services probably received a steadier and also, as we shall see later, a more intensive flow of education actions during this period.

With regards to frequency, contact with families occurred twice or more times a week in around half the cases. In 30% of cases contact was weekly, in 15% it was daily and in the remaining 4% or so cases it was generally rare or occasional. The findings show significant differences between the children's age groups. Contact took place daily or more than twice a week in 70% of kindergartens, compared to 56% for crèches. Greater frequency was also found in public sector services (68%) compared to Third (62%) and private (59%) sector services.

The activities offered usually involved a mix of different modes of communication, the predominant of which was asynchronous communication (Figure 1.1). Phone and video calls were used 'frequently' to communicate with the children by slightly over one-third (35%) of the interviewees. In around 83% of cases, contact with children was based on video and audio recordings made by the teachers/educators themselves. Although the children involved are in the pre-school age group, frequent use was also made of written text, a communication mode that requires more active engagement from the parents as 'mediators' of the message. Lastly, audio and video materials created by other parties were used less frequently.

The frequent use of synchronous communication rises to 41% in kindergartens, where the children are older and better able to interact in this way. This percentage falls to around 23% in crèches, where in addition to the fact that infants and toddlers are less able to communicate, their daily routines are also more diversified and unpredictable, making it more difficult to plan a convenient time for the family. For the segment from birth to six, video or

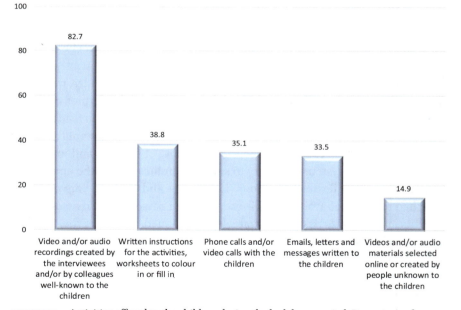

FIGURE 1.1   Activities offered to the children during the lockdown period: Percentage of respondents who answered 'Frequently' (Source: Fieldwork data)

audio recordings made by the educators are thus by far the main mode of communication (increasing to around 86%).

The educators and teachers had two different strategies for managing the emotional aspects. Some tried to address negative emotions, such as concern about the pandemic underway, while others focused more on fun and light-hearted activities to help families 'escape' from the climate of isolation and concern about what was happening across the country.

The topic of Covid-19 was introduced by teachers especially in southern and central Italy (47% and 34% respectively), or was addressed in response to prompting from the children (24% in both areas). In northern Italy, by contrast, the teachers' prevailing approach was not to address the topic (53%), although some offered activities on their own initiative (25%) or in response to prompting from the children (24%) or at the parents' request (2%). Similarly, while the topic was introduced by children in 57% of cases, there were significant differences between geographical areas, with a higher frequency in southern (77%) and central Italy (61%) and a lower frequency in northern Italy (49%). We can suppose that this lower frequency may be due to two factors: the more severe effects of the pandemic in the northern regions and therefore the possibility of greater difficulty in tackling the topic, and the larger presence of 0–3 services in the northern Italy sample that could explain the greater difficulty in addressing a similar topic with the youngest children. Indeed, it was addressed more frequently in kindergartens (74%), where the children could deal with the situation with greater awareness, than in crèches (25%).

The activities carried out involved not just the children but the parents as well, with parental support actions being provided in 80% of cases. In over half the cases (52.6%) educators and teachers also played an active role with the parents by sending them suggestions as well as through phone calls/video calls/chats with them, individually or in a group. In just over 17% of cases the actions were entrusted to external figures, either exclusively or concurrently with those of the educators and teachers.

Lastly, the data describe the workload for educators and teachers in terms of the time they spent on planning, organizing and performing the activities and staying in contact with the families. Over half of the teachers/educators (54%) worked less than eight hours per week, while the remaining 46% worked more than eight hours per week, although less than 60 out of the total number stated that they worked all or even over their contracted hours. Thus, when looking at time spent on the activities, the workload does not appear to have been particularly heavy. As will be seen later, the main challenge was the need to rethink their profession, using different and not always familiar modalities and tools, and working in conditions of physical isolation and individual responsibility.

5.3 The Ability to Reach Families and Children

Against the background of these efforts, the interviewees expressed their perception of the ability to reach the children. More than half of them (55%) stated that all or almost all the children in their class participated in the activities offered, while 17% reported that many children (more than half) did so, and a further 17% said almost half the children did. Only 6% stated that participation was very low. However, some interviewees (4%) said they are unable to answer the question, reflecting one-directional or interrupted communication, which made it impossible to reach the children and adapt the activities offered based on their feedback as envisaged by LEADs.

Northern Italy and Mezzogiorno report similar percentages of children reached, while central Italy recorded a higher participation rate. Counterintuitively, given that younger children would seem to be more difficult to engage with using remote modalities, higher participation was reported in crèches (58%) than in kindergartens (53%). Lastly, the private sector seems to have been less effective (48%) in attracting wider participation than the public (57%) and the Third sector (56%).

Independently of the efforts made by schools and services, according to the interviewees, the factors impacting negatively on participation are: the parents' worries or busy schedules (51%), the parents' lack of interest in the activities offered by the schools (48%), lack of adequate IT skills and resources (32%), language difficulties (16%) and children's health/disability issues (4%). While the impact of technology issues and language difficulties is perceived as being greater on families of lower social status and public service users, the lack of interest in the activities offered seems to apply across the board. However, the feedback from those who participated is perceived as positive in the majority of cases (77%), even though not all the families provided feedback (13%), or their feedback tailed off over time (9%).

5.4 The School-Family Connection

The collected data show a different capacity of educators and teachers to stay in contact with children and parents, but also the heterogeneity of the educational offer in terms of both activities and targets. Considering the frequency of contact between teachers/educators and children/families, the offering of activities mainly addressed to children but also for supporting parents, and the feedback from parents, a typological index of school-family connection[6] was constructed which allowed four profiles to be identified (Table 1.2).

The most common profile is 'family-oriented and intensive' (54.2%), i.e. those who built a relationship aimed at keeping frequent contact with the children (thanks to the necessary collaboration of the parents) and who, at the same time, tried to offer targeted parental support.

TABLE 1.2　Index of the school-family connection

	%
Family-oriented and intensive	54.2
Family-oriented and occasional	26.0
Child-oriented and intensive	11.5
Child-oriented and occasional	8.3
Total	100.0
N	942

The 'family-oriented and occasional' profile (26%) represents those who maintained more occasional contact with children and families, but also aimed at parental support. In both of these first two profiles, direct engagement of teachers/educators in creating parental support activities and positive feedback from parents prevail.

The 'child-oriented and intensive' profile (11.5%) represents those professionals who have built a connection with families centred on children, therefore without specific parental support activities, with frequent and intensive contacts. The profile 'child-oriented and occasional' (8.3%) represents those who had more occasional and less frequent contacts, without parental support activities. This profile has the lowest level of positive feedback from parents.

The 'family-oriented and intensive' profile is the most widespread across the three geographical areas, even though in the north the second profile, 'family-oriented and occasional', has a much higher incidence than in the centre and the south (Table 1.3). On the whole, the professionals in the northern regions have built a family connection more oriented towards combining attention to children with support for parents. The frequency of contact in the north,

TABLE 1.3　Index of school-family connection by geographical areas

	North	Centre	Mezzogiorno
Family-oriented and intensive	51.2	59.5	57.5
Family-oriented and occasional	31.2	18.8	19.2
Child-oriented and intensive	9.7	11.4	17.0
Child-oriented and occasional	8.2	10.3	6.4
Total	100.0	100.0	100.0
N	550	203	188

TABLE 1.4   Index of school-family connection by type of services

	Crèches	Supplementary services	Integrated services for 0–6	Kindergartens	Other services
Family-oriented and intensive	51.1	54	66.6	55.5	55.5
Family-oriented and occasional	35.5	29.7	33.3	20.6	33.3
Child-oriented and intensive	5.9	5.4	0.0	15.1	11.1
Child-oriented and occasional	7.5	10.8	0.0	8.8	0.0
Total	100.0	100.0	100.0	100.0	100.0
N	305	37	9	582	9

however, is more occasional, perhaps because it was the first area in the country to be hit by the pandemic and therefore the teachers may have encountered greater difficulties or had chosen specifically not to be too intrusive or to overload families already put to the test.

In kindergartens, an intense school-family connection prevails, while in crèches there is an occasional and more sporadic connection, although educators and teachers in the 0–3 segment are more involved in providing advice and support to parents (Table 1.4).

5.5   *Difficulties, Relations and Resources of the Education Staff during the Emergency*

Reconfiguring the educational settings was obviously a challenge for the education staff's ability to adapt their role to online education, highlighting the difficulties (Table 1.5) faced by educators and teachers but also the resources they managed to find. The first difficulty they encountered involved reconfiguring their profession in terms of combining physical distance with emotional closeness. For a large majority of them, i.e. 3 out of 5 interviewees (62.7%), this was particularly challenging.

Almost 3 out of 10 respondents (28.7%) found it hard to reconcile their work with their own difficult family situations. Since the vast majority of respondents are women (Colombo & Barabanti, 2020), this finding is not surprising in view of Italy's well-known and continuing gender inequality when it comes

TABLE 1.5 Difficulties experienced by teachers/educators in carrying out online activities

Difficulties	% on respondents[a]
Difficulty in rethinking their profession in remote modality	62.7
Family difficulties (managing children, dependent persons, the home, etc.)	28.7
Personal problems that made it difficult to concentrate (worries, sadness, etc.)	21.0
Difficulty in using technologies	20.2
Lack of/inadequate IT resources (PC, tablet, internet connection)	15.2
Other difficulties	4.7
No difficulties	4.4
Total answers	1,060

a   The sum of percentage values is higher than 100% because each interviewee could provide more than one answer.
SOURCE: FIELDWORK DATA

to household chores and family care, which the pandemic has exacerbated (Manzo & Minello, 2020; Santagati & Barabanti, 2020). Interviewees from the intermediate (36–45) age group had the greatest difficulties in this respect.

One interviewee out of five said they found it difficult to concentrate on their work for personal reasons, such as worry and sadness. Some of them may well have been affected by illness and bereavement, as well as by the impact of isolation.

Difficulties in using technology were reported by 20% of the interviewees, with a further 15% lacking adequate IT resources or internet access. The greatest difficulties in this regard were experienced by respondents over 45 years old, special needs educators and teachers, high school diploma holders and those working in the public sector.

Around 5% reported other problems, including the ability to reach all or some of the families effectively or getting feedback from them, managing relations with their colleagues and/or superiors and sourcing useful teaching materials for the activities (in view of the closure of services, schools, stationery stores, bookshops and libraries). Conversely, only 4% experienced no difficulties.

We then asked who they received support from in coping with these difficulties, with the possibility of mentioning more than one person. Colleagues provided the most important support networks, with 85% of the interviewees turning to their class or school/service colleagues, and a further 18% relying on colleagues in other schools/services. A fairly significant proportion found support through the virtual community, with 18% getting help from colleagues or experts contacted through the internet or social media networks, or by participating in online meetings.

The percentage of those who mentioned coordinators from their own school/service (e.g. teaching coordinators, school heads or principals) as significant sources of help was not very high, with less than 1 interviewee out of 4 selecting this answer. This signals the weakness of 'vertical' relations, raising questions as to the ability of these professional figures to play a pivotal role in supporting educators and teachers both during and beyond the emergency. Lastly, roughly 5% indicated other support figures, such as their family members (children, partners, etc.) or lack thereof, or said they did not need any.

Overall, the prevailing feeling among the interviewees is that they were supported within their own organization during the pandemic: 45% said they felt fully supported, 39% said they felt reasonably supported, while 12% did not feel supported. Those who felt least supported, though not always with marked differences, were the younger educators and teachers, the interviewees working in crèches compared to kindergartens, and in the Mezzogiorno area and the Third sector.

5.6 Perception of the Effects of the Lockdown on Professional Competences

One of the key aspects of the reflection was the impact that the LEAD experience had and is going to have on the profession of educators and teachers. Overall, the experience seems to be regarded as positive: 60% of the interviewees stated that they had learned a great deal and improved their professional competences from the experience, while for over 7% it had more positive than negative effects. A significant proportion of the sample thus see it as having positive spinoffs for their work, which could also be beneficial when the children go back to school. By contrast, 17% believe the experience had more negative than positive effects, and 6% think it should be completely forgotten. The remaining 10% of the interviewees answered 'other', pointing to the emergency nature of remote modalities and suggesting that LEADs should be seen as a temporary digression to get past completely, highlighting the dangers of excessive exposure to screens, which they disapprove of, and underscoring the importance of direct contact in early childhood education.

The perception of a very positive impact on their professional competences is higher among teachers in kindergartens and integrated services for children aged 0–6, in the public sector and in Italy's Mezzogiorno, and it rises as the respondents' age increases. The perception of improvement is lower among interviewees with an academic background in education and pedagogy.

One of the reasons for the perceived improvement of professional competences may be the fact that many of the interviewees participated in training activities during the lockdown. Around 82% took part in online training courses or events, some found independently online (45%), others offered by the organization they work for (33%), or both (4%).

We also asked the interviewees whether and how their relationship with IT tools changed with the experience of LEADs: 52% of them said the experience bolstered the good relationship they already had with these tools before the lockdown; 25% already used them before, and the experience did not increase their appreciation; and 18% had avoided them before, but their experience of

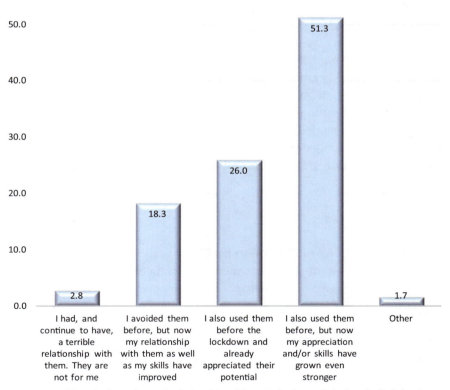

FIGURE 1.2 How the interviewees' relationship with IT tools changed during the lockdown (Source: Fieldwork data)

working remotely improved their relationship with digital tools and their skill in using them. For 3% of respondents IT tools remain something alien and to be avoided.

The interviewees' reflections on the impact of the lockdown show a polarized response between, on the one hand, those who had a positive experience and are optimistic and, on the other, those who suffered through this period, with knock-on effects also for the children's return to the classroom. Middle-ground positions appear to be a minority.

Thus, at one end, there are those who successfully overcame physical distance from the families and children as well as from their colleagues. While they point to the difficulties and the efforts made, these are compensated by the sharing of a complex experience that strengthened relationships, particularly when the educators and teachers with stronger skills made them available to the group. While they are aware that there will be a new stage of readjustment when the children return to school, they are also conscious of the additional resources developed during the months of closure.

At the other end, some stress the difficulties faced in reaching the families and in managing change jointly with their colleagues. They feel concerned about the children's return to school due to the disruption of relationships during the lockdown. They are afraid of being exposed to the virus due to the parents' presumed irresponsibility in assessing risks, and added to this is the expectation of the children's loss of autonomy. There is widespread concern about the reorganization of schools and services when in-person attendance is resumed, compounded by strong diffidence towards those in top positions within the relevant organizations. Lastly, the study revealed the financial worries of those working in the private and Third sectors, who risk losing their job.

6   Conclusions

The emergency due to the Covid-19 pandemic made it necessary to rapidly experiment with strategies for remote contact between children, parents and education personnel, disrupting the ordinary routine based on in-person encounters.

The empirical data presented above enabled us to analyse how education professionals built and managed distance education relationships even before these were formalized. Comparing the evidence emerging from the professionals we interviewed with subsequent ministerial guidelines, we can identify both consistencies and divergences.

In the contexts analysed, LEADs were based on asynchronous activities, which are more flexible in relation to the parents' needs, although some synchronous activities were carried out, especially in kindergartens, and this finding is consistent with the general educational guidelines. Thus, for teachers/educators of children aged from birth to six the main challenge was to adopt an alternative (and totally new) professional approach, requiring them to deploy creative and improvisational skills. At the same time, the general educational guidelines encourage careful planning of the activities to avoid them becoming improvised ways of entertaining the children; they also encourage the teaching team to plan shared programmes, with possible assistance from coordinators and principals.

The data collected at the outset, however, show some inconsistencies, because decision-making processes were more frequently solitary rather than collegial, and teachers and educators were not always involved in decisions on how to deal with the emergency (with some differences among geographical areas and type of services/schools). Professionals perceived weak support from coordinators, principals and institutions. However, the practical effort to manage the activities and contact the families were often left to them, and their creativity was crucial in implementing new practices. Indeed, the interviewees actively sought support and ideas through online contact with peers and online professional communities and experts, as well as from family members, showing the importance of horizontal networks. In order to re-establish and maintain an educational relationship between teachers, children and parents, LEAD s necessarily require the parents' mediation and engagement, from planning to the moment of contact, so as to jointly identify the most accessible tools and activities. However, parents were only marginally consulted in decision-making processes and thus had little impact on planning.

An important point is that LEAD s are constructed in a virtual environment, as an 'online physical presence' that requires a familiarity with digital technologies, given their potential in this respect. The findings confirm that the relationship with digital technologies is still a challenge for Italian teachers/educators of children aged from birth to six, in terms of the required skills and their use as educational tools, pointing out the limitations of school policies that have invested in 'digitalisation at school' in recent decades (Gui, 2019). The interviewees' uptake of a multiplicity of online training activities suggests they feel a need to fill gaps in their skills and also perhaps to use the unusual situation as an opportunity for professional development.

Regarding the relationship with the children, the data show that around 60% of teachers expressly asked for feedback from the children. Also with respect to relationships, the findings evince the efforts made to combine attention to emotions with practical activities and parental support actions. The topic of Covid-19 was introduced intentionally by kindergarten teachers especially, but more frequently in southern Italy than northern Italy, while in the 0–6 services it was addressed primarily in response to prompting from the children. The importance of getting feedback from children and of talking to parents about what is happening and how it is being addressed is explicitly highlighted by the educational guidelines.

At the same time, the data confirm the hypothesis of the different capacity of the professionals to adapt to the new situation and develop a different educational dialogue with the families. Some professionals were able to maintain a dialogue remotely and an emotional connection with the families, leading among other things to a greater sense of their effectiveness, with positive spin-offs in terms of their professional competences over the long term as well. By contrast, other professionals did not manage to have an educational dialogue with the families, and this weakened the activities and the capacity to keep the children and their families connected.

Looking at the school-family connection, there are clear suggestions in the LEAD guidelines for a non-intrusive teachers' presence, active listening and offering trust without feeding illusions. The link between teachers and parents is suggested both as a way of renegotiating the forms of collaboration and to provide support and a point of reference at a time of great uncertainty. The school-family connection index makes it possible to capture both of these dimensions: the forms of collaboration with parents that have made it possible to renegotiate activities aimed at children, and those that, in addition to this aspect, have taken on forms of parental support.

The LEADs guidelines stress the key goal of reaching everyone, tracing those with whom contact is lost and using feedback to redesign the actions. In the contexts analysed, not all the families were reached and the most vulnerable were likely 'lost', without the opportunity to redesign the education offering in the light of their feedback. In the sample, the education offering was not the same for all: continuity of contact was influenced by stability of services and employment contracts (greater in the public sector) compared to flexibility and intermittence (in the private and Third sectors). Differences emerged also between crèches and kindergartens in the northern and southern or central regions. In this respect, the study confirms the expected heterogeneity and the governance challenges of this – as yet still wholly unaccomplished – integrated system.

Thus, the delay in providing guidelines on how to deal with the pandemic crisis in the 0–6 education system caused a sense of abandonment and disorientation among teachers and educators. Nevertheless it did not prevent many professionals from exercising agency.

The pandemic magnified the importance of the socio-emotional component in educational processes, of which this sector in particular is strongly aware. The work needed for refocusing on and improving social and emotional skills remotely, which these professionals saw as requiring the greatest effort, can offer a significant contribution in the wider perspective of professional development and training policies, where this is becoming a key topic (Kankaraš & Suarez-Alvarez, 2019; Chernyshenko et al., 2018). This study shows that emotional connection was frequently the basis for successful relationships, but also the goal of the implemented actions. In this context, the skills present in the 0–6 segment and the adaptation measures taken could provide interesting insights for higher levels of the school system as well, highlighting areas of skills improvement on which to focus greater attention, including in terms of professional training and of the new scenarios that are opening up.

Notes

1. See Italian Law no. 1044/1971 (NL1044/1971).
2. See Italian Law no. 444/1968 (NL 444/1968).
3. See Italian Law no. 107/2015 (NL 107/2015) and Legislative Decree 65/2017 (NLgsD 65/2017).
4. See Ministero dell'Istruzione – Commissione nazionale per il Sistema integrato di educazione e di istruzione [Ministry of Education – National Committee for the Integrated System of Education and Training], Art. 10, Legislative Decree no. 65, 13/4/2017, Documento base linee pedagogiche per il sistema integrato 'zerosei' [Basic document: Educational Guidelines for the integrated 0–6 system].
5. In Italy, children with disabilities attend the same schools and classes as their peers in both ECEC segments, facilitated by special needs teachers (*insegnanti di sostegno*) who help them with learning and integration.
6. The school-family connection typological index synthesizes the information collected on three different variables: how frequent the contact with families or the sending of activities was, whether or not parental support activities were planned, and parental feedback. In order to arrive at the construction of the typological index, these three variables were first recoded, dichotomizing them. The combination of the three variables generated eight profiles of situations, which were then reduced to four categories in the final index.

References

Antonietti, M., Guerra, M., & Luciano, E. (2020). Servizi 0/6 nell'emergenza e famiglie con bambini/e in condizione di bisogno educativo speciale: prove di relazione da un'indagine in tempi di pandemia. *Nuova Secondaria, 2*, 365–378.

Barnett, S., Jung, K., & Nores, M. (2020). *Young children's home learning and preschool participation experiences during the pandemic: NIEER 2020 preschool learning activities survey: Technical report and selected findings.* National Institute for Early Education Research.

Chernyshenko, O., Kankaraš, M., & Drasgow, F. (2018). *Social and emotional skills for student success and well-being: Conceptual framework for the OECD study on social and emotional skills*. OECD Education Working Papers, no. 173. OECD Publishing. https://doi.org/10.1787/db1d8e59-en

Chieregato, N. (2020). L'educazione ai tempi del Coronavirus (e dopo): risultati preliminari di una ricerca qualitativa condotta con i professionisti dell'educazione. Focus sull'alleanza educativa nella fascia 0–6 anni. In A. Gigli (Ed.), *Infanzia, famiglie, servizi educativi e scolastici nel Covid-19. Riflessioni pedagogiche sugli effetti del lockdown e della prima fase di riapertura* (pp. 40–47). Centro di Ricerche Educative su Infanzia e Famiglie (CREIF). https://edu.unibo.it/it/terza-missione/formazione/dossier-creif

Cino, D. (2020). Ripensare il concetto di 'screen time' nel contesto del Covid-19: un riposizionamento epistemologico. In A. Gigli (Ed.), *Infanzia, famiglie, servizi educativi e scolastici nel Covid-19. Riflessioni pedagogiche sugli effetti del lockdown e della prima fase di riapertura* (pp. 35–39). Centro di Ricerche Educative su Infanzia e Famiglie (CREIF). https://edu.unibo.it/it/terza-missione/formazione/dossier-creif

Colombo, M., & Barabanti, P. (2020). Female hegemony among Italian educational professionals. In M. Colombo & L. Salmieri (Eds.), *The education of gender: The gender of education: Sociological research in Italy* (pp. 43–60). Associazione per Scuola Democratica.

Giancola, O., & Piromalli, L. (2020). Apprendimenti a distanza a più velocità. L'impatto del COVID-19 sul sistema educativo italiano. *Scuola democratica*. Advance online publication. doi:10.12828/97097

Gigli, A. (Ed.). (2020). *Infanzia, famiglie, servizi educativi e scolastici nel Covid-19. Riflessioni pedagogiche sugli effetti del lockdown e della prima fase di riapertura.* Centro di Ricerche Educative su Infanzia e Famiglie (CREIF). https://edu.unibo.it/it/terza-missione/formazione/dossier-creif

Gui, M. (2019). *Il digitale a scuola*. Il Mulino.

INDIRE. (2020, July 20). *Indagine tra i docenti italiani pratiche didattiche durante il lockdown. Report preliminare.* Istituto nazionale di documentazione innovazione e ricerca educativa. https://www.indire.it/wp-content/uploads/2020/07/Pratiche-didattiche-durante-il-lockdown-Report-2.pdf

Istat, Università Ca' Foscari, & Consorzio Mipa. (2020, June). *Nidi e servizi educativi per l'infanzia, Stato dell'arte, criticità e sviluppi del sistema educativo integrato 0–6.* Dipartimento delle Politiche per la famiglia. https://www.istat.it/it/files//2020/06/report-infanzia_def.pdf

Kankaraš, M., & Suarez-Alvarez, J. (2019). *Assessment framework of the OECD study on social and emotional skills*. OECD Education Working Papers, no. 207. OECD Publishing. https://doi.org/10.1787/5007adef-en

Mantovani, S., Picca, M., Ferri, P., Bove, C., Ripamonti, D., Manzoni, P., Cesa Bianchi, A., & Mezzopane, A. (2020, August). *Bambini e lockdown. La parola ai genitori*. Università degli Studi di Milano Bicocca. https://www.unimib.it/sites/default/files/Report_Bambini_e_lockdown.pdf

Manzo, L. K. C., & Minello, A. (2020). Mothers, childcare duties, and remote working under COVID-19 lockdown in Italy: Cultivating communities of care. *Dialogues in Human Geography, 10*(2), 120–123. https://doi.org/10.1177/2043820620934268

Mari, A. (2017). *Il sistema integrato di educazione e di istruzione dell'infanzia. Un ordinamento ad assetto variabile*. Aracne.

Ranieri, M. (2020). La scuola dopo la DAD. Riflessioni intorno alle sfide del digitale in educazione. *Studi sulla Formazione, 23*(2), 69–76.

Sabatinelli, S. (2016). *Politiche per Crescere. La prima infanzia tra cura e investimento sociale*. Il Mulino.

Sabatinelli, S. (2020, March 24). Famiglie diseguali anche di fronte al virus. *Welforum*. https://welforum.it/il-punto/emergenza-coronavirus-tempi-di-precarieta/tempi-di-precarieta/famiglie-diseguali-anche-di-fronte-al-virus/

Samuelsson, I. P., Wagner, J. T., & Odegaard, E. E. (2020). The coronavirus pandemic and lessons learned in preschools in Norway, Sweden and the United States: OMEP policy forum. *International Journal of Early Childhood, 52*(2), 129–144.

Santagati, M., & Barabanti, P. (2020). (Dis)connessi? Alunni, genitori e insegnanti di fronte all'emergenza Covid-19. *Media Education, 11*(2), 109–125. https://doi.org/10.36253/me-9646

Save the Children. (2020). *Riscriviamo il futuro. L'impatto del coronavirus sulla povertà educative*. https://s3.savethechildren.it/public/files/uploads/pubblicazioni/limpatto-del-coronavirus-sulla-poverta-educativa_0.pdf

SIRD. (2020). *Per un confronto sulle modalità di didattica a distanza adottate nelle scuole italiane nel periodo di emergenza COVID-19*. Società Italiana di Ricerca Didattica. https://www.sird.it/wp-content/uploads/2020/07/Una_prima_panoramica_dei_dati.pdf

CHAPTER 2

Rethinking the Role of No Schooling during the Pandemic

Maurizio Merico and Fausta Scardigno

1 (Re)emergence: The No Schooling during Pandemic Time

What we propose in this chapter could appear as a play on words, built by shifting from one letter to another: from emergen*cy* to emergen*ce*, and adding the prefix 're' to the latter (and back). There is this understanding in our proposal. However, the main aim of our discourse is to stress how the *emergency* that Italy and the entire world has been going through since the end of 2019, with the terrifying experience of a global pandemic, produced – together with other more or less (un)predictable effects – the *(re)emergence* of an issue that has crossed the sociology of education since its foundation: the critical relationship between schooling and no schooling, or between the educational processes that take place in formal contexts and those that occur 'outside', in non-formal and informal contexts.[1]

Looking at the public debate that has developed since the first months of the pandemic, it is easy to recognize that what on January 30th 2020 the WHO declared to be a 'public health *emergency* of international concern' (emphasis added) sparked an intense debate among educational agencies, which, however, was riven with questions concerning the responses and solutions managed by institutions towards an 'unpredictable' crisis, the needs and contradictions of distance learning, the digital divides that affect – in different manners – people along the social stratification and the different local contexts, and so on.

All these aspects seem to reveal a kind of debate that relies on a model of education based entirely on formal institutions, where the school appears as the only agency able to respond – whether with innovation or tradition does not matter – to the challenges with which educational systems are confronted. As testified by Save the Children (2020), also in this framework, it is possible to easily recognize problems and contradictions, mainly connected to the risks of a dramatic increasing in educational poverty, school dropout and – not least – the so-called 'learning loss'.[2]

The same research clearly shows how these effects become more intense when considering that, because of the subsequent lockdowns, children, adolescents and young people not only have experienced the lack of (formal) educational opportunities (as described in the other chapters of this volume) but have also undergone the plunder of all these occasions connected – to name but a few – to physical, recreational and, more generally, extracurricular activities (Save the Children, 2020).

Moving on from this point, what seems to be dramatically lacking in the discourse on educational processes that have developed during the pandemic is the carefulness towards the wide variety of educational opportunities – both non-formal and informal – of which people – in particular children, adolescents and youngsters – have been silently expropriated. Nevertheless, focusing on just schooling, there is clear evidence of how, on the one hand, non-formal and informal activities produce lasting positive effects on the learning process (Alexander et al., 2007) and, on the other hand, of how school dropout and the gaps in educational attainment can produce 'scarring effect(s)'[3] (Musella & D'Isanto, 2018).

It is from this extensive background that our proposal develops: Looking beyond the mainstream debate, is it possible to recognize how the Covid-19 *emergency* produced the *(re)emergence* of the (apparently old-fashioned) critical issues underlying no schooling and, more generally, the need for conceiving an integrated educational system?

The same issues could be further explained by asking whether it is possible to think of an educational system pivoting around the solely formal dimension (as in the Parsonsian model), or in which schooling and no schooling retain – to recall another word that has recently acquired an everyday use – a substantial 'distancing'. Or whether it is finally imperative, also as a consequence of the emergency we are still facing, to start seriously to link the corners of the educational triangle (Chisholm, 2008). This is a process that needs, as a first step, to better define, as we will try to do in what follows, the borders and the contents of a magmatic and porous reality, whose premise and promise have always been to widen – at the intersection between the non-formal and the informal – educational opportunities, times and spaces (Giovannini, 1997).

2   Notes for a Genealogy

There seems to be an association among the *(re)emergence* of the debate on the links between schooling and no schooling and the experiencing of a period of profound social change and crisis. Within a wider itinerary, almost as if taking snapshots, in what follows we will recall some key illustrations, each one representing different periods and perspectives of analysis, while also trying to grasp some major themes useful to trace a (short) genealogy of the contemporary debate.

2.1 The Chicago Tradition

In the sociological tradition, the recognition of the educational relevance of no schooling (and of its link with formal education) can be traced back in the debate that arose in Chicago at the beginning of the twentieth century on the basis of George H. Mead's contribution (Mead, 1999). The debate developed from two different, albeit converging, standpoints. The first one was based on Jane Addams' *applied sociology*. If schools can be criticized, as contexts that had become detached from people's experience (Sayles, 2005), Addams insisted on 'educational methods' able to bridge the relevance of moral education with the adventurous '*spirit of youth*', as well as to recognize recreation as a public function in urban communities (Addams, 1909, 1994). The second standpoint can be identified in the field researches carried out by the youth scholars working in the Department of Sociology at the University of Chicago. To consider the main account developed in Chicago, when analysing youth gangs in the mid-1920s, Frederic Thrasher (1927, p. 190) recognized how 'the effective education of the boy [...] takes place far more vitally outside the schoolroom in those informal contacts which escape conventional supervision'. He further extended this analysis during later projects he coordinated in New York on Boys' Clubs and on 'motion pictures and youth' (Merico, 2015, 2016). Here, Thrasher (1934, p. 471) asserted the need to pay specific attention to 'informal educative processes' that were 'so effective that the personality and character of the child are shaped by them in a thousand different ways'. As far as we are concerned here, in both Addams' and Thrasher's analyses, there is a tension linking the different educational agencies (Dimitriadis, 2006). To mention two illustrations that sound dramatically lively even today: on the one hand, Addams thought 'that public schools should be neighborhood centers, connecting people to each other [...] rather than functioning as a place apart' (Fischer, 2003, p. 44). On the other, throughout his sociological engagement, Thrasher recurrently insisted on the need to coordinate youth social services in the community, with a specific attention to the interplay between the 'the school system' and the 'spare-time needs of children and young people' (Thrasher, 1945, p. 399).

2.2 Mannheim's Influence

The debate on the interplay between schooling and no schooling will find a relevant turning point in Karl Mannheim's definition of education. Moving from recalling that 'the main educative agent is the community', in sharp contrast to the functionalist theory, Mannheim's main argument is the distinction between the 'formal, institutionalized aspects of education such as are to be found in the schools, and the *broader* more generalized notion of social education': two components which can no longer – according to the Hungarian-born sociologist – be thought of 'in terms of compartments' (Mannheim & Stewart, 1962, pp. 19–20, emphasis added). Within the analysis we are developing here, it is vital to recall that Mannheim's goal was – in the context of the last phase of his intellectual career – to identify, through the sociological lens, the 'fundamental educational kit for a citizen in democratic society' that, in turn, wanted to *reconstruct* and *revitalize* itself (Casavecchia, 2017, p. 259). In this respect, the earlier educational processes and techniques had to be replaced by a wide integral youth policy (Remmling, 2015; Merico, 2019), able – as Mannheim (1943, p. 47) had already pointed out in the early 1940s – 'to affect our whole educational system, as the latter will have to assist in educating a whole generation for entirely new tasks'. Consistently with the aspects recalled above, after a long and gruelling crisis, this requires the recognition and the enhancement of cooperation between formal educational agencies (with the school playing the pivotal role) and the wide range of actors and contexts, such as primary and informal groups (home, church and public life), in which what he defined as 'social education' takes place. At the same time, according to Mannheim (1943), such a process enables the achievement of a twofold goal: on the one hand, it provides younger generations with the knowledge and tools necessary for them to consciously tackle the changing situation; on the other hand, it shapes the personalities most suitable to social change, thus supporting youthful 'latent resources' to assume an active role in social change (Canta, 2006; Merico, 2019).

2.3 *The Lifelong Learning Perspective*

The period between the 1970s and the early 1980s represent a crucial moment for the development of the international debate on no schooling and its effect on economic and social development. The debate took place in a scenario marked by a twofold goal: first, the definition of international policies for developing countries; second, the search for an alternative to formal education (Simkins, 1977). In such a scenario, the idea of 'open' education seemed to be the most suitable answer to respond – from the micro to the macro level – not only to the dilemma of the educational systems' crisis, but also to the social and economic development of the Global South (Rogers, 2007). It is not by chance, we assume, that in the same period they developed the works that constitute the main theoretical foundations of the modern debate on no schooling: to mention but a few, the well-known UNESCO report *Learning to Be: The World of Education Today and Tomorrow*, in which a specific light was shed on lifelong education (UNESCO, 1972), as well as the contributions of Philip Coombs and Manzoor Ahmed (1974) and Thomas La Belle (1982). While from different perspectives, all these inputs stressed the need to pay specific attention to the peculiarities of no schooling, meant as a complement to the formal dimension, as well as to their mutual integration, considered as the 'effort' that best responds to the challenges of social crisis and changes (Coombs & Ahmed, 1974). In brief, we can argue that the debate on the integration between formal, non-formal and informal education found its most innovative expansion in the climate of the 'emergency' of the mid-1970s, when it led to the need to innovate, within the global context, in educational systems in order to support disadvantaged countries. It is clear, however, that these initiatives were not radically new. The relevant novelty relies on the fact that in the 1970s the issues we are concerned with here were finally 'discovered' (La Belle, 1982): in other words, they received for the first time a specific 'label' and widely recognized scientific attention.

2.4   On 'Educational Polycentrism'

Turning our attention to the Italian debate, we can recognize that during the 1960s and the 1970s someone criticized the school system (Ribolzi, 2012), but in the following decades a new conception of educational processes developed (Besozzi, 2017). This conception was based on the recognition of the multidimensionality of educational processes, with a specific focus on the role of meanings and inter-subjectivity (Besozzi, 2009). The overcoming of the school-centred perspective led a group of scholars to introduce the concept of 'educational polycentrism', which entails the recognition of the plurality of educational trajectories, with reference either to educational spaces, times, beneficiaries, agencies and opportunities (Cesareo, 1976; Giovannini, 1997). It then takes shape a new, more horizontal, image of the educational system, to which corresponds a strong attention towards the enhancement of the individual choice's skills. The pluralization of socialization agencies puts the individual agency at the core, in a process in which the subject is requested to take the responsibility for its choices within a series of opportunities emerging in structural and environmental interstices (Merico & Scardigno, 2009; Spanò, 2018). Therefore, at the core of this polycentric scenario, there is a cultural and social model that revolves around self-expression, self-fulfilment and the multiplicity of options and experiences. At the same time, the shaping of a polycentric reality underlines the need to build links and synergies between differentiated formal, non-formal and informal contexts of experience (Giovannini, 1997; Mongelli, 2006). The theoretical perspective that underpins the concept of 'educational polycentrism' has not found a general consensus (most scholars have mainly focused on its formal dimension). However, the attention paid to no schooling seems to have reached a mature stage (Colombo & Censi, 2010). This has intertwined with the growing interest in lifelong learning (Mongelli, 2006), thus opening a relevant space for approaching – from a wide range of points of view – the links between schooling and no schooling, but also emotions, motivations and forms of engagement (Ribolzi, 2012).

2.5 *The European Perspective*

All these inputs have found an ongoing constructive synthesis in the policies, programmes and measures implemented by the Council of Europe and the European Commission, either individually or in cooperation through youth partnership (Lauritzen, 2008). Over the last three decades, these European institutions have elaborated – within the wider framework of *lifelong* and *lifewide learning* – a perspective aiming at promoting an inclusive relationship among the different youth educational agencies that focus on the pivotal role of non-formal education (Tuschling & Engemann, 2006; Merico et al., 2015). This has increasingly included a specific emphasis on the validation of non-formal learning and the recognition of the actors involved in the field (Chisholm et al., 2011; SALTO-Youth, 2016). Clearly, over time the two European institutions have assumed a perspective that has given priority sometimes to the 'learning' dimension, in other cases to the 'educational' one. Whatever the case, with the new century, the issue of the relationship between schooling and no schooling has become a central focus of European youth and educational policies. To take but a few emblematical examples, it is possible to refer to:

- the *Memorandum on lifelong learning*, issued in 2000 by the European Commission, in which formal, non-formal and informal learning are finally 'institutionally' defined and the awareness that 'the different levels and sectors of education and training systems [...] must work in close *concertation with each other*' affirmed (EC, 2000, p. 10, emphasis added);
- the Council of Europe's Recommendation no. 1437 on '*Non-formal education*', issued in the same year, which encouraged 'all those who will shape educational policies to acknowledge that non-formal education is an essential part of the educational process', as well to recognize the contribution made by NGOs and youth work(ers); and, not least,
- the European Commission white paper *A New Impetus for European Youth*, in which, moving from the recognition of 'the complementary character of formal and non-formal learning', the Commission called for a 'joint strategies on the part of the various organisations providing education (schools, training centres, enterprises, communities, youth work)' (EC, 2002, pp. 33–34).

With the process described in this last snapshot, the recognition of the interplay between schooling and no schooling becomes – as we have tried to point out – institutionally recognized. However, it is worth noting how the theoretical and political principles and accounts have mostly remained on paper, revealing not a few contradictions in being translated into practice. It is exactly to practices that we now shift our attention, looking at some experiences developed during the last year.

3 Shy Attempts of Dialogue: Experiences and Practices during Pandemic Times

In this section, we will present and discuss the main results from an exploratory study conducted between March 2020 and April 2021, with the main aim of identifying a series of national and European good practices adopted on no schooling and in outdoor education contexts, with particular attention to the opportunities, spaces and social actors involved in those experiences.

Observing the experiences of dialogue between schooling and no schooling during 2020, we immediately notice how the pandemic emergency was, first of all, an opportunity to develop a greater sensitivity towards the issues of sustainability promoted by the United Nations 2030 Agenda for Sustainable Development, but also of the relevance of nature and respect for the relationship between well-being and health.

In this sense, the experiences of the so-called 'natural schools', based on the idea of a learning process able to connect the members of the educating community and not just the pupils, have been very relevant. In Italy, a network of projects financed by the Fondazione con i Bambini is also moving from the bottom, supporting innovative partnerships between schools and the non-formal world, with the aim of promoting not only cognitive skills, but also soft skills and an understanding of how to achieve community well-being. The Reggio Emilia experience of the Diffused School model (Paolella, 2013) is also extremely significant, with an important commitment to new spaces, mainly public, intended for teaching, along with a substantial organizational mobilization as well as a substantial economic commitment to return to the classroom after the acute phase of the Covid-19 pandemic, in compliance with health and social safety measures.

Other examples of the alliance between school and family designed during the health emergency come from the outskirts of Naples, with the story of Maestro Tonino Stornaiuolo, as well as from those of the Esquilino neighbourhood in Rome. In these cases, the school network has become a support system for the whole neighbourhood; the most disadvantaged families have been reached by the Maestro, by the associations as well as by other families who have acted as intermediaries for the services. In some situations 'bubbles' were set up as an experiment, such as in the case of 22 young people aged sixteen to eighteen who continued to engage in sport, prayer, online school lessons and all the restricted sociality they had been deprived of during the lockdown inside an oratory in northern Italy.

In the town of Ivrea, in the Piedmont, a twentieth-century industrial city and a UNESCO world heritage site, an outdoor education project was promoted during the pandemic that offered educational activities for children between three and six years old. The initiative was set up as an experimental project and initially aimed to include 20 pupils from the Sant'Antonio Nursery School and the Don Milani Kindergarten. The programme was subsequently extended for another two weeks and involved up to 30 children from the municipal schools. Also in the town of Ivrea, thanks to funding from a private foundation, the Onlus Alce Rosso, and in collaboration with schools, outdoor education experiences were carried out at Villa Girelli, a large park built for the children of workers from the nearby Olivetti production centre, creating a summer camp for over 40 children under the age of three in the summer of 2020.

As a part of the National Network of Outdoor Schools, about 40 public primary and lower secondary schools tried to deliver interdisciplinary open-air lessons with children aged between nine and ten years, offering them a series of activities to stimulate creativity and participation.

In Rome, in the autumn of 2019, a few months before the pandemic, a 'forestry school' was opened at the Marymount International School, a private school that offers an educational path of excellence for students aged two to eighteen, and which, due to its large space, is immersed in the natural reserve of Monte Mario, a protected area near Rome. The opening of the 'forestry school' was inspired by a widespread practice in England, which led to the preparation and carrying out of lessons safely even during the pandemic.

The Scuole che Promuovono Salute Lombardia (Schools That Promote Health – Lombardia) network and the homonymous programme of the Regional Prevention Plan are examples of intersectoral collaboration involving the worlds of health and education inspired by the practices adopted in some European countries of the Schools for Health in Europe (SHE) Network, whose aim is to make each school a context that supports the importance of health, implementing it both at a regional and local level.

Shifting our attention to the international context, among the countries that were the first to plan a steady reopening of primary and secondary schools in 2020, there is Denmark, which, together with Estonia, the United Kingdom and the United States, stood out during the pandemic for having implemented outdoor learning practices in the contexts of no schooling. In Denmark, education outside the classroom (EOtC) is configured as a set of curricular activities carried out outside of the school and sets out that during the school year at least 300 minutes a week are dedicated to carrying out these activities, with it being used mainly in primary schools that have more practical spaces and are predisposed to the development of manual and creative skills, developing the senses and creating games and group work that stimulate mutual cooperation (Schneller et al., 2017; Bentsen et al., 2018; Mygind et al., 2019).

Denmark reopened nursery schools, kindergartens and elementary schools as early as April 2020, solving the problem of social distancing through temporarily holding outdoor lessons in larger spaces, such as amusement parks, zoos and museums, closed to the public. The reopening ensured compliance with the anti-Covid protocol – in which each of the classes of the Danish schools involved was divided in two so as to maintain the necessary safety distance between one child and another – by adopting a rigorous sanitation regime that did not lead to an increase in infections among school staff with the reopening.

Building on the Danish experience (Waite et al., 2016), British architecture firm Curl la Tourelle Head built the first social distance tent, a pop-up school at London's Manorfield Primary School designed to optimize social distance between pupils and teachers during the post-Covid-19 period, creating an environment capable of safely hosting as many students as possible, and at the same time allowing for compliance with social distancing rules. In spring 2020, Learning through Landscapes, a UK charity specializing in outdoor learning, play and education, partnered with the National Lottery Heritage Fund to create 'My School, My Planet', an innovative outdoor education programme across the UK, which supports disadvantaged students to improve their knowledge, physical activity and sense of well-being, in the belief that outdoor learning should be integrated into every child's school day. In England, between September and November 2020, more than 1,000 children enrolled in 49 schools (in some areas at risk of social exclusion) benefited from outdoor learning. To allow the educational programme to have a greater impact and involvement on the groups of pupils from disadvantaged and ethnically diverse backgrounds, learning focused on topics such as climate change, soil enhancement, biodiversity, etc.

In Scotland, in the outdoor learning activities promoted during the first phase of the pandemic, there is an implicit awareness that children and their families can benefit from being in an external environment in which a guide involves the pupils both in learning activities and in play (Thorburn & Allison, 2010). The Virtual Nature School (VNS) programme is widespread in the country. Thanks to recent funding received to support the resumption (in total safety) of its educational activities, it has proposed to provide an adequate kit of work tools and a professional training path to the staff involved in the initiative, so as to allow their students to play outdoors. The VNS is a non-profit programme created in response to the needs of children and families during the Covid-19 pandemic by Living Classrooms, a community interest company. In 2016 it established the International Association of Nature Pedagogy, a professional organization which aims to promote and support different activities and forms of education that take place in nature as well as spread them all over the world. The programme provides home learning support to families (most of them from the Auchlone Nursery) who need help to carry out the initiatives included in the project, so as to evaluate the learning acquired during these activities.

Estonia has also joined the Schools in Motion educational programme by committing to reduce the negative impact that the pandemic has had on the well-being of pupils (Mooses et al., 2021). The programme focuses on the diversification of distance learning and the integration of traditional school learning with outdoor learning. The educational programme was launched about five years ago and over time has expanded to 148 schools with a total of 63,000 students participating. This is a research-based programme initiated by the University of Tartu's Move Lab (Research Group of Physical Activity for Health), which has turned its attention to the effects produced on the situation experienced following the health emergency. Among the schools participating in the programme, it is worth mentioning the Sõmeru Basic School, which carried out outdoor learning activities, involving pupils in the construction of a planetarium in the snow, thus integrating English lessons with those of natural sciences and developing new forms of learning outdoors. The Move Lab is committed to developing new solutions to support both face-to-face learning in the school context and distance learning at home. Among the objectives, there is the importance of increasing the level of learning in contexts outside the school, favouring the acquisition of learning contents through the integration between the different subjects proposed, and at the same time guaranteeing pupils the possibility to perform more physical activity (Tuuling et al., 2019; Mishra et al., 2020).

In the United States, the Inside-Outside Network of Educators and Educational Institutions, which advocates the importance of promoting teaching and learning in nature for pupils, has supported schools in Maine, New Hampshire and Vermont in spreading examples of good educational practices of outdoor learning implemented by elementary schools during the health emergency. These are clear examples of an open-air educational approach incorporated into the planning of the school week to take place in pre-arranged locations, such as school courtyards, nearby open areas and public spaces.

Examples of good practices include those implemented by schools in Moretown, Vermont (where teachers designed and set up classrooms with stumps for seats, pine needles for carpets and the sun as natural light), and in schools in the towns of Stacyville in Maine, which involved the installation of two additional pavilions to the existing ones and the creation of five classrooms in the area outside the school, thanks to the help of a team of volunteers who contributed to the organization of these activities. According to the school protocol, each class spends from three to five hours a day outdoors, and the programme includes reading texts, mathematics, science, art and music exercises, along with visits to local farms and manual activities. Participation in these activities is based on the importance of recognizing equal access to safe and suitable environments for the development of each pupil, including outdoor spaces, as well as the possibility of benefiting from flexible paths, responding to cultural contexts and the specific needs of each family, thus offering effective support to their children's learning.

There are also European countries where some research-action experiences have been consolidated between fields, places and systems of education. In Germany, the Sport and Health Education Chair of the University of Munich, in collaboration with the health insurance company AOK Baden-Württemberg, is carrying out a research project on outdoor teaching at the Anna-Essinger-Gymnasium in Ulm entitled 'Learning in Nature: Aspects of Physical and Mental Health, Motivation to Learn, Learning Performance and Reference to Nature in Regular Outdoor Lessons'. The project, launched in 2019, will end in the first half of 2021. The aim of the study is to understand the effects of EOtC at the German Higher Institute, evaluating different parameters such as the physical activity of students, satisfaction of basic psychological needs, health-related quality of life and proximity to the natural environment. The study affirmed how it is possible to adopt the practice of outdoor learning in the current pandemic context, taking as an example the management of a class at the Ulm Institute, which has a lesson in the forest once a week, integrating into the programme the study of subjects planned for the school year, such as German, biology, mathematics and geography. The research also argues that there are clear indications that lead to affirm that the intrinsic motivation of pupils to learn increases in outdoor contexts such as woods and forests. Therefore, it is possible to say that the schools that have already implemented these activities can leverage the examples of good practices and adopt and implement them even in a period such as the current pandemic. In addition, further development projects on the subject are planned in Germany and will be implemented in the coming years, so as to expand and develop the research and studies on EOtC (Sahrakhiz et al., 2018).

In Scandinavia the term *udeskole* (which means 'outdoor school') is used to indicate a particular form of learning widespread in the Denmark, which involves children aged between seven and sixteen in educational contexts other than traditional school environments, as external environments that are an 'integrated part of the school system' (Bentsen et al., 2010, p. 236). This practice, although widespread mainly in natural environments such as forests and parks, also refers to other more traditional contexts and constitutes an innovative and effective system, capable of simplifying learning, motivation and understanding of the topics covered. Studies by Bentsen et al. (2009, 2010) have stated that '*udeskole* can contribute to the realisation of the overall aims of the Danish school system, especially its impact on health, well-being, and social competencies was emphasised' (Bentsen et al., 2009, p. 35). Greater attention to these practices would help to make the dialogue between the adoption of classroom teaching systems and students' outdoor learning more productive.

In the Czech Republic, the Faculty of Education of Masaryk University carried out a study in 2020 to understand how outdoor education (OE) was widespread in some primary and lower secondary education institutions in the urban and rural area. The first phase of the study involved a specific analysis aimed at knowing the level of learning in the school education programmes (SEPs) in the different school contexts involved, to then integrate the data with qualitative research in which interviews with a small sample of eighteen teachers from nine model schools were carried out. From the research, it emerged that the practice of OE in the territory of the Czech Republic was based not only on 'traditional' educational contexts such as the countryside and the school yard, but also activities such as excursions, educational visits (with specific programmes aimed at pupils) and sports courses and activities (Svobodová et al., 2020).

In preschools in the province of Liège, Belgium, OE is based on the carrying out of activities that take place in extracurricular settings, capable of promoting, through self-directed or guided play, the experiential learning of pupils. The activities are practiced in both urban and rural areas, such as schoolyards or woods, undertaking 'activities that stimulate body movement, manipulation and interaction with environment and peers' (Jidovtseff et al., 2021, p. 530).

The attention to these issues was the subject of a study by the Childhood Research Unit of the Belgian University of Liège, which in the first months of 2021 carried out a study to investigate how the practice of OE was developed within some kindergartens where it was widespread, and what were the environmental factors and the attitude of teachers towards this practice. The aim of the study was to investigate the practice of OE in some Belgian preschools and the relationships between intervening environmental factors and the attitude of teachers in adopting this innovative practice. The study, therefore, directly involved kindergarten teachers, who were invited to participate in an online survey with semi-structured interviews aimed at capturing the perceptions experienced by the teachers themselves regarding the possible advantages and disadvantages regarding this activity, as well as any suggestions they might have towards its improvement (Jidovtseff et al., 2021).

From the collection of the experiences that have developed, especially in Italy, during the lockdown, it is evident that the prevailing characteristic is an imbalance, especially on the aspects related to the management of spaces (indoor/outdoor) and times (synchronous/asynchronous) of the initiatives of dialogue between schooling and no schooling. We are still perhaps in the context of an 'extended system' rather than an 'integrated system', which would need a step forward, in a period of severe health crisis, towards systemic communication, but which still has a long way to go towards integration intended above all as the co-planning and co-construction of new teaching-learning environments in which the non-formal and the informal play the same game together with the formal: that of education.

In other words, while being aware of the limits of a pilot exploratory study on the topic, the analysis of the collection of practices discussed above seems to be capable of offering an input into the need to rethink the educational practices and experiences implemented in other European countries, restoring the value of the whole learning processes back into the core of the academic, institutional and political debate. Once again, the challenge seems to be that of recognizing the 'polycentric' and integrated structure of the spaces and times of educational action.

4   Beyond the Pandemic: Towards a Renewed Framework?

It is evident that during the (first) lockdown(s), especially in Italy, no schooling played a residual role in the public debate. However, the least offer of non-formal and informal educational opportunities produced relevant effects on the lives of (young) people, and families in particular. During the #stayhome period, the latter have carried the greatest burden, being asked to redefine times, spaces and borders, both internally and externally (Giaccardi & Magatti, 2020).

By contrast, it is possible to claim that, during the long emergency, the informal contexts, NGOs, the composite world of organizations dealing with sport and physical activities, the spare time groups, and so on, have experienced an ambivalent involvement. On the one hand, they have been forced into a sort of (indefinite) deferral, due to the need for 'social distancing', being thus situated in a non-place and a non-time which have, in a sense, deprived people of that 'spirit of community' that would have probably been vital in such a phase (Aime et al., 2020). On the other, as we have tried to support in the previous pages, a consistent part of them have tried –through a sometimes unsystematic process – to engage in dynamic and proactive pilot experimentations, which have shown, on the whole, how the strength of the interaction between schooling and no schooling might have lessened the centrifugal forces of the polarized debate between face-to-face and distance learning at school.

In this respect, Christoph Mall (2020) has claimed the relevance of 'education outside the classroom' (EOtC), experiences in which, 'on a regular and long-term basis, learning environments are deliberately moved outside the regular classroom setting', which easily becomes 'a health-related intervention in terms of a teaching concept which aims to counteract the [...] health risks and further support the fight against the Covid-19 pandemic'. In the same way, it is also possible to read the 'unusual' collection of 20 statements on the way the pandemic is impacting the educational practices, prepared by the editorial board of the *Journal of Outdoor and Environmental Education* (Quay et al., 2020): the voices collected from scholars working from all over the world (Australia, Canada, Denmark, Japan, New Zealand, Norway, Singapore, the United Kingdom and the United States) clearly show the benefits of this kind of education, thus highlighting not only what currently takes place, but also what can be learned from the Covid-19 experience. We must take into careful consideration two aspects. On the one hand, it is worth remembering the need for a thoughtful analysis on the balance between the contributions to social well-being offered by the activities carried out in outdoor (recreational) spaces and the needs of implementing actions to minimize the risk of disease transmission (Freeman & Eykelbosh, 2020). On the other, the evidence of several scholars suggests that there are 'lasting impacts' on a wide range of outcomes produced by the wide range of no schooling settings and environments (James & Williams, 2017; Prince, 2020).[4]

In this direction, the Covid-19 emergency could be considered – we suggest – as an occasion to definitively overcome the school-centred model. The proposal outlined by Lynne Chisholm (2008) now acquires a renewed relevance. In it she called for a re-contextualization of educational processes that need to be approached from three standpoints: 'deconstruction-decoding' of learning practices, 'refocusing-repositioning' learning sites and 'reconstruction-recoding' the educational discourse within what she refers to as the 'educational continuum', bringing together its own tensions and contradictions.

If, then, the perspective is that of recovering from this last emergency, it seems vital to move from the debate and the experiences we have outlined so far, that is, from those contributions that have contended the possibility of a positive and necessary integration among the polycentric educational times and spaces. However, this challenge has to be dealt in a very different way: on the one hand, avoiding both a scattered logic and a perspective based on an ongoing experimentation; on the other, ensuring that the different educational agencies proceed from a common screenplay, shared by all those who animate both the formal, non-formal and informal dimensions. This also means engaging in a cooperative dialogue, either internally and externally.

If we now look at what has happened since the beginning of the pandemic, we can identify some illustrations useful for the future. First of all, keeping to the reference point mentioned above, the perspective of outdoor education developed by the Italian government within the Piano per l'Infanzia e l'Adolescenza (National plan for childhood and adolescence) and then assumed as the starting point in the so-called *decreto rilancio*[5] (decree relaunch): these documents pointed out explicitly – in the short term – the need for a dialogue between schooling and no schooling during the summer after the first long lockdown. Secondly, still at a governmental level, it is possible to refer to the ongoing ministerial project about the *patti educativi di comunità* (community educational agreements): these are agreements between local authorities, schools, public and private institutions, and NGOs aimed at strengthening – at the local level – educational alliances, to improve the education on offer and to lower the dropout rate. This relies on making open spaces, parks, theatres, libraries and so on available to young students. Connected to the latter, it is worth mentioning the initiative promoted by 'Save the Children – Italia'[6]: according to this proposal, it is vital to open the schools, transforming green areas, libraries, sport facilities and other services into new spaces and make them available to networks engaged in a completely new educational effort which make children and youth core players of their own growing up.

Finally, it is worth referring to the development that involved, since the very beginning of the pandemic, the composite world of Italian youth workers, who found in the limitations imposed on their projects and activities (in particular, those connected to international mobility) the trigger for an inclusive debate that allowed them to share experiences and contradictions, but chiefly to start to rethink their role, training, professionalization and recognition as collective actors.[7]

In the perspective developed by the sociology of education, the integration between schooling and no schooling is not just a newly desired institutional configuration, nor simply a model requested by efficient practical and organizational claims. On the contrary, it takes the shape of a process of interaction, differentiation and exchange among a wide range of agencies, whose effectiveness will affect the success of policy measures and projects with which – again our metaphor – the society re-emerging from this unpredictable emergency wants to educate its young citizens for completely new tasks. Formal education alone cannot recognize these new citizenship skills. In this perspective, there is a profound need for open spaces, challenging situations and horizontal relationships, in which these skills can be tested. In other words, we can consider the integration between schooling and no schooling as a generative 'mechanism of outcomes' (Pawson & Tilley, 1997), or even as the chance to recognize the autopoietic ability of polycentric educational processes in informal and non-formal contexts: a resource that seems to be vital in a context of fear, anxiety for the future and a lack of confidence.

Beyond the urgency of the emergency, all the no schooling initiatives experienced over time must be reconsidered as educational opportunities, times and spaces that can – with competence and professionalism – encompass the massive void left empty by the deferral of school life. Obviously, this recognition does not refer to them alone, but 'in dialogue' with the formal dimension. In this sense, as we have tried to clarify, the issue is not simply that – however pivotal – of opening schools or other kinds of educational space. More accurately, the challenge is that of considering this (new) emergency as an extraordinary opportunity to outline a new, richer, more plural, heterogeneous time for education. A time refunded to children and young people (as well as their families), but also to the educational actors running non-formal and informal contexts and experiences, whose agency is no longer configured as a substitute (or simply as a compensation) of teachers, but definitely complementary to schooling. Summing up, the Covid-19 pandemic represents a critical chance to activate new processes of reflective learning and innovation, both in order to limit potential damages and to take advantage of the opportunities occurred during the emergency, as well as to proactively address such a scenario of continuous pressure towards changes, thus supporting the emergence and the genuine recognition of the 'polycentric' and integrated structure of the educational system.

Acknowledgements

This chapter builds on a common reflection presented in a previous paper (Merico & Scardigno, 2020). We wish to thank Marianna Colosimo and Nadia Crescenzo for their significant support in retrieving and collecting the national and international experiences documented in the chapter.

Notes

1 According to international literature and European official documents, *formal education* usually refers to the processes which take place in structured environments, organized in a vertical and intentional form, and leading to certification; *non-formal education* refers to the learning which takes place through planned activities and structured from the learner's perspective, which usually does not lead to certification; finally, *informal education* consists of all those (non-intentional) educational situations resulting from daily activities, which however are not organized in terms of objectives, time or learning support, as well as not leading to certification (see in particular: Mongelli, 2006; Chisholm, 2008; European Union, 2012).
2 The term refers to any loss of knowledge and skills – as well as to a reversal in school or university progress – generally caused by discontinuities or extended gaps in a student's career. The MILO study, supported by UNESCO, offers an interesting illustration on the impact of Covid-19 in terms of learning loss at the end of primary schooling in six African countries (see: https://covid19.uis.unesco.org/learning-loss/).
3 The 'scarring effect' consists in the consequences of youth unemployment over working life, in terms of increasing the probability of being unemployed in the future, as well as on negative effects on earnings prospects and chances of obtaining a decent job in the longer term.
4 This second aspect being also linked to core curriculum subjects (Becker et al., 2017) and students' school motivation (Bølling et al., 2018).
5 Cf. the Law Decree issued on May 19th 2020, n. 34 (art. 105).
6 We refer here to the series of webinars on 'Tutti a scuola: metodi e strategie per ricominciare ad innovare la didattica' ['All at school: Methods and strategies to restart at innovating teaching']. Cf. https://www.savethechildren.it/blog-notizie/corsi-online-gratis-docenti-strumenti-la-didattica-digitale
7 Cf. in particular the initiative 'Youth worker, come stai?'

References

Addams, J. (1909). *The spirit of youth and the city streets.* Macmillan.
Addams, J. (1994). *On education.* Routledge.
Aime, M., Favole, A., & Remotti, F. (2020). *Il mondo che avrete. Virus, antropocene, rivoluzione.* UTET.
Alexander, K. L., Entwisle, D. R., & Olson, L. S. (2007). Lasting consequences of the summer learning gap. *American Sociological Review, 72*(2), 167–180.
Becker, C., et al. (2017).Effects of regular classes in outdoor education settings: A systematic review on students' learning, social and health dimensions. *International Journal of Environmental Research and Public Health, 14*(5). doi:10.3390/ijerph14050485
Bentsen, P., et al. (2010). The extent and dissemination of *udeskole* in Danish schools. *Urban Forestry and Urban Greening, 9*(3), 235–243.

Bentsen, P., et al. (2018). *Udeskole*: Education outside the classroom in a Danish context. In M. T. Huang & Y. C. J. Ho (Eds.), *The budding and blooming of outdoor education in diverse global contexts* (pp. 81–114). National Academy for Educational Research.

Bentsen, P., Mygind, E., & Randrup, B. T. (2009). Towards an understanding of udeskole: Education outside the classroom in a Danish context. *Education 3–13: International Journal of Primary, Elementary and Early Years Education, 37*(1), 29–44.

Besozzi, E. (2009). Students and the meaning of education. *Italian Journal of Sociology of Education, 1*(1), 50–67.

Besozzi, E. (2017). *Società, cultura, educazione. Teorie, contesti e processi*. Carocci.

Bølling, M., et al. (2018). The association between education outside the classroom and students' school motivation: Results from a one-school-year quasi-experiment. *International Journal of Educational Research, 89*, 22–35.

Canta, C. C. (2006). *Ricostruire la società. Teoria del mutamento sociale in Karl Mannheim*. FrancoAngeli.

Casavecchia, A. (2017). Connecting education to society through Karl Mannheim's approach. *Italian Journal of Sociology of Education, 9*(3), 256–264.

Cesareo V. (1976). *La scuola tra crisi e utopia*. La Scuola.

Chisholm, L. A. C. (2008). Re-contextualising learning in second modernity. *Research in Post-Compulsory Education, 13*(2), 139–147.

Chisholm, L., Kovacheva, S., & Merico, M. (2011). *European youth studies: Integrating research, policy and practice*. M. A. EYS Consortium.

Colombo, M., & Censi, A. (2010), Il policentrismo formativo. In Associazione Italiana di Sociologia (Ed.), *Mosaico Italia. Lo stato del Paese agli inizi del XXI secolo* (pp. 141–146). FrancoAngeli.

Coombs, P. H., & Ahmed, M. (1974). *Attacking rural poverty: How non-formal education can help*. Johns Hopkins University Press.

Dimitriadis, G. (2006). The situation complex: Revisiting Frederic Thrasher's the gang: A study of 1,313 gangs in Chicago. *Cultural Studies – Critical Methodologies, 6*(3), 335–353.

EC. (2000). *A memorandum on lifelong learning*. European Commission. Office for Official Publications of the European Communities.

EC. (2002). *A new impetus for European youth*. European Commission, White Paper. Office for Official Publications of the European Communities.

EU. (2012, December 20). Council recommendation of 20 December 2012 on the validation of non-formal and informal learning (2012/C 398/01). *Official Journal of the European Union*. https://eur-lex.europa.eu/legal-content/EN/TXT/PDF/?uri=CELEX:32012H1222(01)&from=EN

Fischer, M. (2003). *On Addams*. Wadsworth.

Freeman, S., & Eykelbosh, A. (2020). *COVID-19 and outdoor safety: Considerations for use of outdoor recreational spaces*. National Collaborating Centre for Environmental Health.

Giaccardi, C., & Magatti, M. (2020, April 26). Per la famiglia bene comune. Ciò che ancora manca per la ripartenza. *L'Avvenire*, pp. 1–2.

Giovannini, G. (1997). I molti tempi, luoghi, attori della formazione: un'analisi del policentrismo a partire dall'offerta. In E. Morgagni & A. Russo (Eds.), *L'educazione in sociologia: testi scelti* (pp. 393–410). CLUEB.

James, J. K., & Williams, T. (2017). School-based experiential outdoor education: A neglected necessity. *Journal of Experiential Education, 40*(1), 58–71.

Jidovtseff, B., et al. (2021). Outdoor education practices in Belgian preschools and relationships with both environmental and personal factors. *Journal of Physical Education and Sport, 21* (Supplement issue 1), 530–536.

La Belle, T. J. (1982). Formal, nonformal and informal education: A holistic perspective on lifelong learning. *International Review of Education, 28*(2), 159–175.

Lauritzen, P. (2008). *Eggs in a pan: Speeches, writings and reflections*. Council of Europe Publishing.

Mall, C. (2020). *Education outside the classroom: An innovative teaching concept during COVID-19*. EERA Blog: European Educational Research Association. https://blog.eera-ecer.de/education-outside-the-classroom/

Mannheim, K. (1943). *Diagnosis of our time. Wartime essays of a sociologist*. Kegan Paul, Trench, Trubner & Co.

Mannheim, K., & Stewart, W. A. C. (1962). *Introduction to the sociology of education*. Humanities Press.

Mead, G. H. (1999). *Play, school, and society*. Peter Lang.

Merico, M. (2015). Giovani e processi educativi nelle ricerche di Frederic M. Thrasher. *Sociologia, 49*(1), 35–41.

Merico, M. (2016). La (controversa) partecipazione di Paul G. Cressey ai Payne Fund Studies. In P. G. Cressey (Ed.), *Giovani, cinema, educazione* (pp. 7–28). Mimesis.

Merico, M. (2019). Introduzione. In K. Mannheim (Ed.), *Giovani e generazioni* (pp. 9–44). Meltemi.

Merico, M., Morciano, D., & Scardigno, F. (Eds.). (2015). *Youth work, non-formal education and youth participation. Special section in Italian Journal of Sociology of Education, 7*(1).

Merico, M., & Scardigno, F. (2009). Adolescenti del Nord e del Sud Italia. In E. Besozzi (Ed.), *Tra sogni e realtà. Gli adolescenti e la transizione alla vita adulta* (pp. 113–125). Carocci.

Merico, M., & Scardigno, F. (2020). Ri-emergenze. Il no schooling ai tempi del COVID-19. *Scuola democratica*. Advance online publication. doi:10.12828/97101

Mishra, B., Bell, S., & Mishra, H. S. (2020). An exploration of how playground design affects the play behaviour of kindergarten children in Tartu, Estonia. In M. Khan, S. Bell, & J. Wood (Eds.), *Place, pedagogy and play* (pp. 41–62). Routledge.

Mongelli, A. (2006). Il non schooling nel quadro del policentrismo formativo. In M. Colombo, G. Giovannini, & P. Landri (Eds.), *Sociologia delle politiche e dei processi formativi* (pp. 369–394). Guerini.

Mooses, K., et al. (2021). Developing a comprehensive school-based physical activity program with flexible design – from pilot to national program. *BMC Public Health, 21*(1), 1–14.

Musella, M., & D'Isanto, F. (2018). Povertà Minorile, abbandono scolastico e disoccupazione: Un'estensione ulteriore dello scarring effect. In M. Musella, & S. Capasso (Eds.), *La povertà minorile ed educativa. Dinamiche territoriali, politiche di contrasto, esperienze sul campo* (pp. 129–140). Giannini.

Mygind, E., Bølling, M., & Seierøe Barfod, K. (2019). Primary teachers' experiences with weekly education outside the classroom during a year. *Education 3–13: International Journal of Primary, Elementary and Early Years Education, 47*(5), 599–611.

Paolella, F. (2013). La pedagogia di Loris Malaguzzi. Per una storia del Reggio Emilia approach. *Rivista sperimentale di freniatria, 1*, 95–112.

Pawson, R., & Tilley, N. (1997). *Realistic evaluation*. Sage.

Prince, H. E. (2020). The lasting impacts of outdoor adventure residential experiences on young. *Journal of Adventure Education and Outdoor Learning, 21*(3), 261–276. doi:10.1080/14729679.2020.1784764

Quay, J., et al. (2020). What future/s for outdoor and environmental education in a world that has contended with COVID-19? *Journal of Outdoor and Environmental Education, 23*, 93–117.

Remmling, G. W. (2015). *The sociology of Karl Mannheim*. Routledge.

Ribolzi, L. (2012). *Società, persona e processi formativi. Manuale di sociologia dell'educazione*. Mondadori.

Rogers, A. (2007). *Looking again at non-formal and informal education towards a new paradigm*. CRICED.

Sahrakhiz, S., Harring, M., & Witte, M. D. (2018). Learning opportunities in the outdoor school: Empirical findings on outdoor school in Germany from the children's perspective. *Journal of Adventure Education and Outdoor Learning, 18*(3), 214–226.

SALTO-Youth. (2016). *Recognition of youth work and of non-formal and informal learning within youth work*. SALTO Training and Cooperation Resource Centre.

Save the Children. (2020). *La scuola che verrà*. Save the Children Italia Onlus.

Sayles, S. (2005). Education for democracy: Discovering civic engagement. *McNair Scholars Journal, 9*(1), article 14. https://scholarworks.gvsu.edu/cgi/viewcontent.cgi?article=1056&context=mcnair

Schneller, M. B., et al. (2017). Children's physical activity during a segmented school week: Results from a quasi-experimental education outside the classroom intervention. *International Journal of Behavioral Nutrition and Physical Activity, 14*, 80. https://doi.org/10.1186/s12966-017-0534-7

Simkins, T. (1977). *Non-formal education and development: Some critical issues*. Department of Adult and Higher Education, the University of Manchester.

Spanò, A. (2018). *Studiare i giovani nel mondo che cambia. Concetti, temi e prospettive negli Youth Studies*, FrancoAngeli.

Svobodová, H., et al. (2020). A proposal of a concept of outdoor education for primary and lower secondary schools: The case of the Czech Republic. *Journal of Adventure Education and Outdoor Learning, 21*(4), 336–356. doi:10.1080/14729679.2020.1830138

Thorburn, M., & Allison, P. (2010). Are we ready to go outdoors now? The prospects for outdoor education during a period of curriculum renewal in Scotland. *The Curriculum Journal, 21*(1), 97–108.

Thrasher, F. M. (1927). *The gang: A study of 1,313 gangs in Chicago*. University of Chicago Press.

Thrasher, F. M. (1934). Social backgrounds and informal education. *Journal of Educational Sociology, 7*(8), 470–484.

Thrasher, F. M. (1945). Some principles underlying community coordination. *Journal of Educational Sociology, 18*(7), 387–400.

Tuschling, A., & Engemann, C. (2006). From education to lifelong learning: The emerging regime of learning in the European Union. *Educational Philosophy and Theory, 38*(4), 451–469.

Tuuling, L., Õun, T., & Ugaste, A. (2019). Teachers' opinions on utilizing outdoor learning in the preschools of Estonia. *Journal of Adventure Education and Outdoor Learning, 19*(4), 358–370.

UNESCO. (1972). *Learning to be: The world of education today and tomorrow*. UNESCO.

Waite, S., Bølling, M., & Bentsen, P. (2016). Comparing apples and pears? A conceptual framework for understanding forms of outdoor learning through comparison of English forest schools and Danish *udeskole*. *Environmental Education Research, 22*(6), 868–892.

CHAPTER 3

Rhetoric, Problem or Necessity?
A Study of Parental Involvement during Covid-19

Mariagrazia Santagati and Paolo Barabanti

1   Introduction

Even if Covid-19 in Italy appeared first and foremost to be a public health emergency, it soon became apparent that there would be spillover effects in other fields. Schools were swift to react and adapt: they have thus begun to build new ways of schooling in order to ensure education and teaching continuity and continuous contact with students and families (Colombo et al., 2020). Teachers were immediately tasked to implement distance learning modalities in order not to interrupt the curriculum learning path, but also to bridge the social distance and to introduce new ways of interacting in the educational field.

The first national school closure in Italy due to the pandemic (March 2020) represented a turning point for school experiences. Emergency education highlighted the relevance of parental involvement for the success of remote learning, especially for pupils attending kindergarten and primary schools, as the help of parents became necessary to conduct distance learning and their physical presence close to children was, sometimes, the only way to enable teachers' activities to be carried out at home (Di Pietro et al., 2020; Lagomarsino et al., 2020).

In this scenario the Covid-19 emergency can be considered a stress test for the Italian educational system and both for teachers and for families. In this chapter we will use parental involvement as a lens through which to take an in-depth look at school-family relationships. This chapter aims at looking inside the black box of parental involvement, deconstructing the rhetoric of school-family relationships as a crucial key to enhance the school success of the students, and providing a more complex picture of the dynamics occurring in this relation. Furthermore, it aims to analyse the relational and educational problems deriving from the asymmetric school-family relation and from the disadvantaged conditions of some parents and to identify cooperation strategies between parents and teachers developed during the time of the pandemic.

To reach these aims, the chapter investigates the lockdown effects on the school-family relationship in Italy, a country that could be considered a privileged case for this analysis. Italy has been among the most affected countries by the virus in Europe and it was the first Western country to close all kinds of educational institutions (at the end of February 2020). Even if parental involvement is recognized and supported by Italian legislation, research shows that school-family relationships continue to be problematic and complex (Pitzalis & Spanò, 2022). Qualitative data collected by the Vo.Ca.Le. project, involving parents and teachers of compulsory education, will allow us to outline the school experience and the transformation of the school-family relationship during this extraordinary time.

After a review of the main current definitions of parental involvement in Section 2, we will analyse how parental involvement was implemented in the Italian education system under the conditions created by the closure due to the Covid-19 pandemic in Sections 3 and 4. Section 5 will present the methodological approach used to collect qualitative data and to recruit the participants of the Vo.Ca.Le. project. Finally, data concerning parental involvement will be analysed in Section 6, identifying some interpretative key concepts in order to explore different experiences of parental involvement during the emergency situation.

2   Parental Involvement, an Ambivalent Concept: Definition and State of the Art

In theory, parental involvement represents 'a powerful and potentially vital mechanism with which to enhance the relationships between home and school' (Smrekar & Cohen-Vogel, 2001, p. 79). In practice, it reveals a negative side, because it is clearly linked to educational inequalities (Lareau, 1989): family characteristics, especially socio-economic circumstances and migrant status, may interact with the school organization to determine the nature and quality of family-school relationships. Since the Coleman Report (Coleman et al., 1966) found that family social background was the most important predictor of children's academic success in the United States, parental involvement in children's education has become a more and more interesting topic for researchers, initially at international level and, more recently, in Italy (Dusi, 2012).

As the most recent literature points out, on the one hand, the alliance between school and family is considered a key contribution to children's school performance, to motivate their achievement and their discipline, to improve their social skills, health conditions and self-esteem (Àlvarez-Àlvarez,

2020). On the other hand, the lack of parental involvement produces negative effects on students' learning: sometimes many obstacles prevent the school-family collaboration and increase the likelihood of parent-teacher disagreement and conflict, especially in conditions marked by challenging parents and scarce teacher training – which have been found to be the main barriers to the building of effective family-school partnerships (Lasater, 2016).

Despite a significant amount of research on parental involvement, a unique, delimited and shared definition of the concept does not exist: Grolnick and Slowiaczek (1994), for example, refer to 'the dedication of resources by the parent to the child within a given domain'; Borgonovi and Montt (2012) focus on the 'parents' active commitment to spend time to assist in the academic and general development of their children'. Beyond definitions, contemporary scholars are aware that parental involvement consists of a multitude of experiences and activities located both at school and at home, involving the commitment of parents' resources to the academic arena of children's lives (Pomerantz et al., 2007).

Epstein (2016), one of the leading researchers on this topic, developed the most influential and widely cited classification which identifies six distinct types of parental involvement: (1) parenting (family practices and home environments which could support their children as students); (2) communicating (when the school is asked to inform the parents about the school curriculum and children's learning in a manner which is comprehensible to all parents, the parents, at the same time, should be open to such communication); (3) volunteering (when parents help and support school activities, such as parties, workshops, celebrations); (4) learning at home (helping students at home with homework and other curriculum-related activities); (5) decision-making (including parents in school decisions and developing parent leaders and representatives); and (6) collaborating with the educational institution (to strengthen school programmes, family practices, and student learning and development).

Even if family involvement in schools is a complex and multidimensional phenomenon (Epstein, 2016), it is possible to simplify it within a conceptual framework referring to two different forms of involvement: school-based and home-based. The first is characterized by direct contacts between parents and schools, most typically teachers, and consists in talking with teachers, taking part in school meetings and events, volunteering at school (Comer, 1995; Epstein, 2001; Hill & Taylor, 2004). The second refers to parental children support which takes shape, for instance, in helping with their homework, providing resources, talking about kids' school experiences and transmitting the values of education (Cooper, 1989; Fan & Chen, 2001).

Research shows that the degree and quality of parental involvement is ambiguous and also heavily influenced by several factors regarding, for instance, the characteristics of parents and teachers.

On the family side, highly educated parents appear more involved (Crozier, 1999; Potvin et al., 1999; Peña, 2000; Jordan et al., 2001; Lee & Bowen, 2006) but, at the same time, they may have less time to dedicate to their children's education (Bæck, 2010). Lareau (1987, 1989, 2011) applies Bourdieu's theory to understand the variation in parent involvement among social classes, finding a 'concerted cultivation' typical of middle-class parents, as opposed to the 'accomplishment of natural growth', more prevalent among working-class families. She shows an association between parental practices and family socio-economic status, remarking that if the parents are familiar with the language and style of the educational discourses, they are more inclined to participate and negotiate with the school regarding their children's growth. Also, parents with an immigrant background are more likely to have difficulties in being involved, for example, because of a lack of both linguistic proficiency and school system knowledge (Chiswick & DeBurman, 2004; Glenn, 2004; Kristen & Granato, 2007; Kristen et al., 2008). The interactions of these families, and of socio-economically and culturally disadvantaged families in general, with the educational institutions continue to be problematic at all educational levels. These problems derive, on the one hand, from the parents' passive behaviours and attitudes and from their difficulties that become obstacles to school participation, and, on the other hand, from the widespread absence of an explicit project for the improvement of school-family relationships and the lack of a clear institutional strategy (Santagati, 2021; Stevens & Dworkin, 2019).

On the school side, Dusi (2012) reports that parental involvement depends on the teachers' commitment and desire to involve parents, and on their knowledge of concrete strategies aimed at increasing parental collaboration. Swap (1993) showed that, even if schools are formally open and supportive, parents continue to be kept at a distance, as there are still significant barriers. In practice, school managers and teachers can take advantage of the parents' lack of knowledge about school life and organizational matters because parents and students are not helped in understanding them and so make only small requests to the school actors (Meyer & Rowan, 1977; Dornbusch & Glasgow, 1996). Further research revealed that teachers tend not to encourage the involvement of parents when they belong to low-income classes and/or are members of a minority, as they are perceived as being part of the problem rather than a resource (Mac Ruairc, 2011; Palaiologu et al., 2011). Sometimes, teachers seek parental collaboration when problems occur, or when difficulties regarding disciplinary issues or learning matters appear (Papazoglou, 1984).

3 The Covid-19 Pandemic as a Stress Test for Educational Systems

Home-based involvement became a crucial point when the school began to be affected by the Covid-19 emergency: a positive and trustworthy school-family relationship became an essential key to ensure the success of distance learning, as parents were, especially for younger learners, necessary to making sure teachers' activities were carried out at home.

Even if parental involvement appeared indispensable for schools at the time of Covid-19, school-family relationships showed their known limitations, especially for disadvantaged families (Macià Bordalba & Llevot Calvet, 2019). Furthermore, educational activities carried out by 'forced distance learning' by means of ICT and various e-learning environments accelerated the (debate on) digitization of teaching and learning (Decuypere et al., 2021) and reshaped the socio-educational world, encouraging schools and families to adopt new ways to communicate as well as to ensure learning and relationship-building opportunities. This unexpected situation, however, emphasized some critical issues which have always characterized the school-family alliance, such as communication difficulties and lack of mutual understanding and shared educational objectives.

Starting with the first school closure (March 2020) and the activation of distance learning, teachers (and their principals) requested, explicitly or implicitly, the parents' collaboration and active participation to fill the gaps with home-based educational activities, as well as the parents' moral support. However, teachers and principals failed to consider how parents would and could fulfil those demands, in terms of digital skills, methodological teaching knowledge and time. As research has highlighted (Ardizzoni et al., 2020; Gigli, 2020), many teachers have complained to their colleagues about the lack of parental engagement during distance learning. Several parents pointed out the failure of some teachers to provide support and understanding when pupils were not able to keep up with the activities to be carried out. An empirical study commissioned by the European Union (Vuorikari et al., 2020) remarked that families need to be better supported for remote schooling, for instance: possibilities for children to do online educational activities with their classmates, ideas for extracurricular activities to be done at home, guidelines on how to support children with distance education activities and homework, and psychological support for children confined to the home.

However, this school-family relationship was not always a problem, and in some cases, it became stronger and more cooperative. Actually, some parents reported that teachers did their best to overcome difficulties in order to preserve a good relationship with pupils (Mantovani et al., 2020). In addition, the lockdown allowed parents to acquire a greater awareness of the complexity and difficulty of the teachers' work, as well as a stock of teaching and relational skills (Maglia, 2020). Many parents became conscious of this and appreciated the fact that teachers strove to reinvent their working practices, sometimes going beyond their formal role, and were doing this out of a strong sense of duty (International Commission on the Futures of Education, 2020).

4 The Study: The Voice Care Learning (Vo.Ca.Le.) Project

4.1 Parental Involvement in an Emergency

Italy represents a special case for the analysis of family-school relationships and parental involvement during Covid-19. It was one the most affected countries in Europe by the pandemic, it was the first Western country to close all educational institutions nationwide (at the end of February 2020) and it implemented drastic mitigation measures against the Covid-19 epidemic. This scenario lasted until the end of the 2019/2020 school year (June 2020) and students, teachers and families, and their reciprocal relationships were affected by this sudden transformation of learning and teaching, and by the shift of all relations that it entailed.

Parental involvement is recognized and supported by Italian legislation, as a result of a long historical process aimed at facilitating parental participation in the co-management of schools starting in the mid-1990s. The creation of participatory bodies in the mid-1990s transformed the schools into more open and democratic arenas (Colombo, 2019). The decision-making process, which up until then had been led by school managers and teachers, began to be shared with representatives of parents and students, raising questions about how to foster parents' involvement. Another step, in the late 2000s, was marked by the mandatory introduction in each school of 'co-responsibility agreements' between the school, the student and their parents, in order to make everyone aware of their own responsibilities and duties in the children's education process. Finally, with the 2015 school reform, the central role of parents as co-builders of the educational process and co-beneficiaries of the school service was reaffirmed. Thus, parents acquired the right to be informed and the right to participate, due to: shared planning and frequent interactions with teachers, strategies for interactions developed and promoted by the schools, opportunities to participate in parents' associations and the freedom to make proposals for cultural, sport and entertainment activities.

Despite the formal promotion of parental involvement, there is still a gap between 'rhetoric' and 'reality' (Hornby & Lafaele, 2011). Actually, although several policies are trying to encourage parents' participation in schools, stimulating forms of partnership and collaboration (Galli, 2000; Eurydice, 2005), the school-family relationship continues to be problematic and complex, and it is characterized by little parental participation, interference, confusion between roles, a lack of adequate forms of home-school communication and the need to make investments in parents' and teachers' training (Censi, 2009; Dusi, 2012). There are also social and cultural factors which inhibit the engagement of disadvantaged parents – such as: parents' low level of education, low socio-economic status, working time constraints, poor knowledge of the education system – in a scenario of crisis of the school-family alliance in the education of new generations (Colombo, 2016; Maccarini, 2019). The school-family relationship, therefore, during the Covid-19 pandemic highlighted problems that were, to an extent, pre-existing.

4.2   *Research Aims and Method*

In order to observe the school-family relationships during the time of Covid-19, we used data collected through the Voice Care Learning (Vo.Ca.Le.) project, a study carried out in the middle of the pandemic and in one of the areas most affected by the virus in Europe. The research was aimed at investigating 'in real time' the effects of the first school closure (from February to June 2020) on parents' and children's experiences of schooling and in particular on the school-family relationship, a crucial and risky resource in the managing of this emergency.

The research questions were: (1) What kind of school-family relationships were experienced during the first school closure (February–June 2020) and to what extent did agreement or disagreement between teachers and parents emerge? (2) Which problems interfered with the school-family interaction during lockdown? (3) Which strategies were being used by teachers and parents to support and develop collaboration and mutual trust at a distance? (4) How has this relationship been reinvented, re-actualized or transformed in the emergency context?

We chose a methodological approach based on involving the main players in the school experience, trying to give voice to each of their stories, feelings and relational dynamics in order to explore what had happened or was happening and to monitor what kind of change was taking place. In fact, the project aimed to cover school experiences from kindergarten to lower secondary school, gathering students', parents' and teachers' voice messages by WhatsApp and taking advantage of the mobile instant messaging interview (MIMI) methodology during a time of social distancing (Kaufmann & Peil, 2019).[1] Participants in the project were asked to send a voice message to respond to a brief interview drafted around four open-ended macro-themes[2]: (1) school reaction to the closure due to the Covid-19 emergency; (2) positive and negative aspects of distance teaching and learning; (3) positive and negative aspects of distance relationships; and (4) fears, worries and priorities about the future.

Voice messages were preferred to remote interviews for many reasons. At the beginning of the pandemic, WhatsApp was already a very common application, used in everyday life and in various milieus (job, family, friends, etc.), and it lent itself to creating a friendly environment and an unintrusive and undemanding interaction with unknown respondents. Voice messages enabled interviewers to get in touch quickly with a large number of subjects, through snowball sampling, in a social distancing situation, easily reaching parents and teachers confined at home and shocked for the amount of time, effort and energy needed to support their children in their everyday activities from home.[3] The adults, moreover, simply involved their children in their accounts through WhatsApp.

In this sense, this methodological approach allowed the acquisition of qualitative data 'at a distance' during the emergency pandemic, collecting the various school stakeholders' voices and leaving them the freedom of answering if and when they could and wanted. Furthermore, voice messages gave school players the opportunity to express experiences and feelings and to take stock in a particularly chaotic and uncertain moment. It was also a way to put to the test a new and easy-to-use tool to monitor stakeholders' thoughts.

Finally, the interviews through voice messages were integrated by a web questionnaire on Qualtrics, which gathered socio-demographic details of the interviewed people and information about the school organization and activities during the lockdown.

A total of more than 160 voice messages were collected during lockdown and in the following summer (from April to August 2020) in some of the cities most affected by the virus (especially Bergamo, Brescia, Milan and Turin). In this chapter we want to focus our analysis on what has emerged from teachers and parents of primary and lower secondary school students. The sample included 62 teachers and parents in primary school and 37 in lower secondary school (Table 3.1).

5   Results

In the following analysis, the Covid-19 emergency is considered a stress test for the educational system and its functioning. We use parental involvement as a 'mirror' to gain an in-depth insight into school-family relationships, organizing the data analysis in three parts. First, in Section 5.1, school-family relationships experienced during the first closure (February-June 2020) are described, reconstructing positive and negative narratives offered by teachers and

TABLE 3.1 Participating sample in Vo.Ca.Le. project (absolute values)

	Students	Parents	Teachers
Gender			
Male	21	11	6
Female	25	68	35
School order			
Kindergarten	–	23	6
Primary school	37	40	21
Lower secondary school	9	16	14
Province of residence			
Brescia	19	32	22
Milan	8	17	10
Turin	9	15	5
Other provinces	10	15	4
Participants (a.v.) – Total: 166	*46*	*79*	*41*

SOURCE: DATA FROM VO.CA.LE. PROJECT

parents, considering the complex and ambivalent dynamics occurring in this relation, and discussing the rhetoric of parental involvement as a fundamental (but often only formal) aspect to enhance students' learning.

The second step of the analysis, in Section 5.2, concerns the understanding of problems, tensions or conflicts in the school-family relationships, affected by the different conditions of the families or from temporary conditions created by the pandemic, highlighting difficulties for parental involvement during lockdown.

Finally, in Section 5.3, strategies used by schools, teachers and parents to deal with the emergency and to guarantee didactic continuity through family-school collaboration are identified, evaluating whether family-school relationships were transformed and fostered in the emergency context, because they were perceived as necessary and indispensable, or remained unchanged from the period before the pandemic.

5.1 *Between Rhetoric and Reality: School-Family Relationships during Lockdown*

What kind of school-family relationships were experienced during the first school closure in Italy? How did parents and teachers describe the dynamics occurring in this relation? To what extent did agreement or disagreement between teachers and parents emerge?

In a previous analysis (Santagati & Barabanti, 2020), we pointed out that the main narrative about distance learning – made by pupils, teachers and parents of the Vo.Ca.Le. project – was quite negative. In particular, the analysis of their voice messages shed light on unusual situations as possible sources of learning problems, highlighting how different kinds of distancing between pupils and teachers (for example, technological, relational, emotional and educational), impacted on disadvantaged groups.

How did teachers and parents describe in their messages their relationship during the first lockdown? The first reaction to the general lockdown was a sort of paralysis of the school system: teachers and school principals were unable, at first, to react promptly to the government's decision to close all schools nationwide. How could all students be reached? What kind of learning methods could be implemented? How long would the situation last? What had to come first: learning or socialization? After the unexpected closure, each school, albeit with different response times, realized that the first thing to do was to begin contacting the families, using both formal and informal ways. Schools tried to cope differently; teachers (and headmasters) tried to deal with the emergency through different means: through learning content, teaching methods, interpersonal techniques and ways and opportunities to involve stakeholders.

The electronic class register (Table 3.2) was the formal method most commonly chosen; in addition to that, email and learning platforms were widely

TABLE 3.2   Ways used by schools to inform parents about school activities organization in March–May 2020 (answers 'Often' + 'Always or Nearly Always' by parents and teachers, in percentages)

	Parents		Teachers	
	Primary	Lower secondary	Primary	Lower secondary
WhatsApp groups among parents	68	42	68	15
WhatsApp messages from teachers to parents	13	11	44	17
Electronic class register	69	100	90	79
Emails	45	36	58	36
Word of mouth from parent to parent	24	14	21	31
Learning platforms	58	43	55	46

SOURCE: DATA FROM VO.CA.LE. PROJECT

used. Regarding less formal ways, WhatsApp played a central role, especially among parents and at primary school level, as it ensured circulation of information to all members.

A centralized and only partial participatory decision-making style was the most frequently adopted strategy by schools concerning distance learning (Table 3.3). The school digital teams played a key role, as they trained and supported all teachers to cope with the emergency, providing new teaching strategies by means of ICTs. One of the most striking findings is the one about the low involvement of class councils, teaching staffs (school principal and all teachers) and school staffs (school principal and teachers with strategic roles). The school board (composed of the school principal with members representing teachers, parents and technical and caretaking personnel) was the only group which included parents and it was the least consulted. Here is the first home truth: families were not very much involved in the decision-making process.

However, not all schools had a centralized and unified way to contact families and occasionally it was left to teachers to adopt the best solutions according to their pupils' characteristics and their class context.

> Schools had different timings to react as they weren't prepared for the emergency. [...] They had to reinvent themselves in no time. [...] Initially, a shared planning [process] was missing, and the idea of letting teachers be more autonomous to face the issue individually, pursuing the most suitable choices according to their pupils seemed preferable. [...] But there could be the risk of giving precedence to a single point of view. [...] and this is not necessarily the best one. (57, PR-T)[4]

Even if families were not generally involved in the decision-making process, after the first ups and downs, teachers started assigning homework, requesting

TABLE 3.3   School collective bodies involved in decision-making about distance learning in March–May 2020 (teachers' answers, in percentages)

	Primary	Lower secondary
Digital team	62	71
Class council	57	57
Teaching staff	48	50
School staff	43	71
School board	33	29

SOURCE: DATA FROM VO.CA.LE. PROJECT

participation in online activities (such as video lessons) and expecting deadlines to be met. The opinions about school-family relationships held by the teacher participants in the Vo.Ca.Le. project were very dependent on how the parents (and pupils) respected the tasks that the teachers allocated. Nearly all the primary school teachers gave a positive account of their relationship with their pupils' parents. The relation was seen as 'quite good'. It involved constant dialogue and support as well as mediation by representatives of the class council to ensure that the parents understood and accepted the learning proposal. This relationship of trust and active cooperation was furthered or, at times, initiated during this period marked by Covid-19.

> Parents have been of crucial importance; there has been a very positive collaboration: without them, we, as teachers, would not have been able to do anything with 6- or 7-year-old children. (102, PR-T)

There were obviously some exceptions to this positive narrative because the relationship was changing, and parents at times seemed dissatisfied not seeing their children engaged for eight hours a day as was the case with school in normal times. Only one teacher underlined the lack of willingness of parents to collaborate and proposed a counternarrative about parents' excessive delegation to teachers in the learning process.

> Distance learning needs a lot of collaboration with the parents. Sometimes they have real difficulties, [but] sometimes they have no desire to collaborate with the school. They delegate a lot to the teachers and the children are not helped at home to do what is required. [...] They delegate a lot to the school, pretending not to have to do anything at home. (28, PR-T)

Teachers in lower secondary school, as their colleagues of primary school, described their good relationships with parents: parents' representatives and teachers with the role of class coordinator were the key actors to support contacts, communication and personal interviews at a distance with all parents. In some cases, school-family relationships seemed almost to improve – if compared to the phase before the school closure – because parents began to recognize and value the teachers' efforts in maintaining contact and in continuing the learning process. Both parents and teachers had an attitude of mutual patience to get through a school year so severely affected by Covid-19. Distant learning enhanced collaboration with all the people involved in order to deal with different problems and worries.

> Every parent was great with us, especially class representatives. They helped us a lot. (94, LS-T)

> Distance learning has fostered the cooperation with all the stakeholders involved. (98, LS-T)

For the majority of parents with children attending primary school, close and caring relationships were maintained during distance education: many of the interviewed parents highlighted an intense and frequent contact with their teachers. They appreciated these new ways of communicating and a kind of relationship able to go beyond the educational and professional sphere. Even if they felt secretly observed by the parents, teachers were able to show their best side: they were, for instance, patient, available, welcoming, proactive, comprehensive, friendly, attentive to parents' and pupils' needs. Consequently, parents never felt alone during the home-schooling experience.

> We notice the teachers are very patient, welcoming and helpful. We watched them as if they were in the classroom. They seemed very natural, and they did not suffer from being spied on by us. [...] We liked the way they built the relationship. They were available, friendly, attentive to children. They were patient with parents, too. (79, PR-P)

Some parents reported some difficulties in their relations with the teachers: they complained of the teachers' excessive focus on pupils' learning and on homework, and of their inability to empathize and to build harmony with parents and children. In five cases, parents pointed out they had no contacts with their children's teachers: a mother described the disastrous situation of her daughter whose 'appalling' teachers had not been seen or heard from by families for months.

> My daughter attended fifth grade, and it was a disaster. Her teachers disappeared for two months. One even had the excuse that she had gone to Sicily, and she was stuck there without a computer. These teachers were really dreadful. They only assigned tasks and they had no direct contact with parents. (90, PR-P)

> The relationship between pupils and teachers does not exist. [...] There is no more the human connection as when they were physically at school. (6, PR-P)

> The relationship between pupils and teachers continues to have ups and downs. [...] Some teachers have never had a live lesson and always sent worksheets and web videos. [...] Now they are testing pupils' knowledge. [...] I find it incredibly insensitive. (48, PR-P)

Parents of students attending lower secondary school showed more ambivalent opinions toward school-family relationships during the lockdown. Some parents gave a positive evaluation, emphasizing that the parents' representatives and the class coordinators were supportive intermediaries and appreciating the increased time and opportunities to interact with teachers. However, if some teachers were described as 'wonderful and professional people', others were viewed as 'inhuman beings' who completely avoided any direct contact with the students.

> There have been wonderful teachers, ready to listen to and to talk with the children. [...] Then there have been other ones who never directly contacted the children, but only sent homework and videos downloaded from the web. They are now in charge of the learning evaluation of our children, without ever having seen them. I find this really inhumane. (48, LS-P)

5.2   Role Conflicts and Educational Disorder

What kind of tensions and conflicts in the school-family relationships were either created or exacerbated by the e-learning experience? And were the problems caused by teachers and/or parents?

Let us focus, at first, on the difficulty encountered by parents and teachers with reference to their respective roles. In the last decades school and family have been affected by radical transformations that have undermined their respective roles, functions, and authority: the mutual delegation of responsibilities has provoked negative interferences and confusion between roles, messages and behaviours (Getzels, 1972; Censi, 2009). Moreover, the 'forced' home-schooling – especially in its first phase marked by uncertainty, hesitation, unclear indications and sudden changes of plan – represented a condition that exacerbated existing problems about the definition of role boundaries. This view emerged from the adults' voice messages in our research.

Both teachers and parents of primary school students perceived the risk of confusion in the definition of roles and the danger of role shifts. On the one hand, the parents of primary school children manifested different attitudes. Some mothers refused the role of teacher for themselves (they had neither the formal nor the informal skills necessary to fulfil this role); other mothers acted as if they were teachers – clarifying children's doubts, answering questions, explaining new topics, simplifying contents for children with special needs, tutoring them in the use of digital devices, etc. There were also parents who enjoyed this process, realizing the possibility of being at the same time parent and teacher.

> As a parent, I'm aware that I cannot also be a teacher. [...] I don't have the patience, the right vocabulary, the right determination to teach him new topics. (26, PR-P)

> The positive side of distance learning is the pleasure of staying with your children and sharing their school experience. It is a duty, but it is also a pleasure to be a parent as well as a teacher, or a tutor, supporting my daughter in her first grade of primary school. (79, PR-P)

A second kind of problem emerged from the didactic organization. Actually, parents described the redundant, disordered and contradictory communication of teachers, their lack of digital competence and their poor organizational skills (for example, in proposing and keeping a timetable and in creating and managing files). Another difficulty was due to the confusion caused by the simultaneous use of many communication tools or channels (WhatsApp, electronic register, Google Classroom, etc.) and platforms (Meet, Zoom, Skype, Teams, etc.), creating disorientation and stress in the families. Parents of pupils in primary school also mentioned a certain resistance of the educational institutions towards using synchronous/live lessons, which began to be scheduled only months after the school closure. Primary school teachers seemed to prefer sending homework by WhatsApp, providing activities on worksheets to be printed and filled in, videos, etc. In contrast to what has been underlined in Section 5.1, in which parents focused on the positive aspects of the school-family relationship, here the parents listed the many problems they encountered. Some of them even reported being abandoned by the teachers and the schools, which focused on bureaucratic matters and unloaded the responsibility of teaching the children on to the parents' shoulders.

> Learning is completely dumped on the parents' shoulders because children at this age are not autonomous, neither in downloading materials from the platform nor in doing their homework. We disagree with the teachers' choice of not doing video lessons. (60, PR-P)

> Some difficulties are related to the fact that teachers have some ICT deficits and they provide redundant and contradictory information – even if that's forgivable. Another negative aspect is the tendency to manage live

> video lessons as if they were in class. [...] It seems they are not aware that children are in another environment and that it is necessary to mediate between home and school needs. (55, PR-P)

These difficulties resulting from e-learning had an impact on the daily life of the families. They complained they had to dedicate too much time, effort and energy to support their children's engagement in school activities. This level of participation and attention to the children's school experience, as well as the related physical and mental stress of the parents, could be considered an effective reaction and response to the emergency in the short term, even if it could not be easily sustainable for families in the medium and long term (cf. Cordini & De Angelis, 2021). It entailed managing spaces for work and study, ensuring all children had access to a device and a reliable internet connection, organizing materials, checking the assignment deadlines and delivering them in the required ways and on time and catching up on any unfulfilled assignments over the weekends. The responsibility hit parents like a never-ending, relentless task. This heavy organizational and managerial load was a burden especially for mothers, who found themselves at home, having taken leave from work or working from home in order to look after school-age offspring. Their workload was aggravated by the need to provide constant school supervision of the children. They had to juggle all the domestic tasks (house cleaning, cooking, laundry, etc.) and the wider problems of family-work balance with the constant and urgent need to manage children who could be nervous, lazy, unfocused, struggling with learning difficulties, etc.

> My little child has many difficulties following lessons because distance learning can bring many distractions. Teachers require a lot of collaboration, a lot of effort, but.... Also, not all parents are in the position to follow their children's lessons and to give them explanations. [...] There are some parents, like me, who have to carry on working from home and are not available – neither to teach their children nor to support them in doing homework. (71, PR-P)

> I was alone at home because his father has always out at work. So I had to manage all these moments of video lessons and homework, except for the weekends. Managing this was complicated because I also had to work from home. (80, PR-P)

> It is difficult to balance school, work, and family. If you work, you cannot control and support your children adequately. [...] I keep repeating all the

time: 'Have you done everything? Have you read, studied, sent, seen...?' This is a heavy refrain for the whole family. (39, LS-P)

5.3 Strengthening a Necessary Link: Cooperation Strategies between Teachers and Parents

Despite continuous complaints from Vo.Ca.Le. participants about the shortcomings, confusion and disorganization resulting from the school closures, teachers were well aware that distance learning could not take place without the collaboration of the families. They considered it necessary to keep in touch with pupils and carry out some educational activities. The school closure represented, in the voice messages of many teachers, a turning point in their teaching experience in which the importance of parental involvement to guarantee compulsory educational continuity clearly emerged, especially for the youngest pupils or for pupils with special needs. In particular, formal and informal cooperative strategies between teachers and families were reinforced or invented to cope with the educational emergency, trying to respond to the different needs of families and pupils.

The first kind of strategy highlighted in the voice messages concerned the *organizational choices* made by the educational institutions *to guarantee distance learning with the collaboration of the families*. This strategy was implemented in order to combine the requirement of learning continuity with the distinctive needs and conditions of the parents. To avoid placing an excessive burden on families with many children of different ages, for example, the use of a unique platform for the whole institute and of the same teaching tools for all the classes was recommended by some school leaders. Paying attention to the needs of working parents (whether or not they were working remotely), teachers also proposed flexible, simple, negotiable and adaptable solutions. Sometimes, asynchronous lessons and videos made by teachers were preferred by the class community as they were available regardless of time and space constraints, considering the requirement for parents to mediate the ICTs access for younger children. In other cases, synchronous video lessons were chosen: this decision was not imposed by the teaching staff but resulted from a negotiation between teachers and parents to reach an agreement on the school timetable.

> The school leader gave an indication to the institute by trying to share the use of the same tools and asking teachers to use the same methods in order not to create problems for families who have several children. (11, PR-T)

> We held many meetings with parents to try to meet their remote working needs and to decide the most suitable times for video lessons. (84, PR-T)

> We recently had a meeting with the parents to understand the current situation, plan ahead the next steps and, above all, discuss with them some initiatives. (41, PR-T)

> The class coordinator immediately tried to give a signal, to organize Skype video conferences every day, trying to find innovative ways to go on. These lessons were organized in a family-friendly manner – that is, when the families were more available and they were free from work. (39, LS-P)

Informal strategies linked to the initiative of individual teachers were also reported. For example, in order to maintain the learning path thanks to direct school-family contact, some teachers called the parents to book ad hoc teacher-student meetings if the pupils did not have the ability to follow the live video lessons. If a pupil had not submitted their homework, the teachers did all they could to connect with the 'lost student', sometimes identifying their difficulties in cooperation with their parents.

> The teacher of Italian was very helpful. She called me at home. We solved many problems because, sometimes, I could not connect. So, we made connections and meetings at other times, even outside working hours. (36, PR-P)

> This morning, I called the parents of a pupil of mine, because she is not sending me any homework. So, as I have the possibility to talk to her parents, I think I should do that, even if it means more work for me. (9, LS-T)

The second kind of strategy referred to *formal channels of communication* that were *maintained, extended* and sometimes *renewed*. The school-family relationships were kept open through communication, exchange and dialogue that were mediated by class representatives (of parents) in primary school and teachers, with the role of class coordinators, in lower secondary school. These key actors were crucial in fostering the school-family collaboration, facilitating two-way communication and parents' participation.

> Thanks to the parents we were able to start with distance learning, especially through the mediation of the class representatives. With the sudden school closure, an important and trusting relationship has developed. Parents got active and were very supportive. (40, PR-T)

> The relationship with the parents is more than positive. There is continuous feedback, especially with the class representative. (52, PR-T)

As it was already the case before the school closure, school-family communication was carried out through the electronic register, to which new functions were added to facilitate the collaboration in some cases. The use of email increased in order to deal with doubts and problems emerging from distance learning.

> The relationship with the teachers was great, incredible. New ways of communicating have been acquired. A new part headed 'Collaborate' was added to the electronic register. All tasks and messages have been loaded in this part. (26, PR-P)

> The relationship with parents has changed. They can get in touch with you by email. I have given my personal email address, so that parents can send me messages with a list of questions and difficulties encountered by their children while listening to the online lessons. (11, PR-T)

Moreover, in some schools the online teacher-parent interviews, ad hoc or periodic one-to-one or class meetings, were maintained and intensified, representing a wide range of possibilities to contact and be contacted, to ensure a dialogue in case of specific problems, to have a concerted time to discuss, and to reflect together on problems and opportunities during this critical time. WhatsApp groups involving parents and organized by class representatives existed before Covid-19, and they were extended to include teachers, as a way to communicate swiftly and easily and transmit important information and news in real time, as required by the emergency situation.

> There was a continuous exchange of emails and messages. We've had no difficulty in reaching anyone and we also have periodically collected voices and feedback from parents, through parents' interviews, class meetings and questionnaires. (102, PR-T)

> The meetings with the parents at a distance has worked out well. We established slots for the meetings and the parents participated by being on time and by respecting the [parameters of the] appointment, and not going overtime, as usually happens in in-person meetings. (101, LS-T)

> We immediately created a WhatsApp group for the class with the parents, and we exchanged emails continuously. We also held a class meeting with an educationalist to talk about the opportunities we have found in this time of crisis. (96, PR-T)

The third kind of strategy pertained to *informal channels of communication*, rarely used before the emergency but very useful to verify the effectiveness of communicative and didactic strategies. In fact, video calls, phone calls and chats between families and school representatives allowed the teachers to better assess the reception and the understanding of the messages sent to the parents.

> I appreciated the phone call from the Italian teacher, made to us after the first weeks of closure, to find out how my daughter was doing and how she reacted to this phase. I felt this was a form of closeness in the school-family relationship. (30, PR-P)

> The Italian teacher does not require contact through official channels (mail, classroom) only. We can call her or write to her on WhatsApp about any difficulties. She has always been extremely helpful, and this has greatly comforted us. We never felt abandoned, absolutely. (76, PR-P)

Furthermore, these communication tools enabled direct contact with parents of pupils with special needs or with parents whose children did not take part in distance learning. Informal and constant communication with families, through different and mixed ways, compensated for the distance and the school closure and represented a valuable solution to fill the lack of closeness and face-to-face interaction. A lesson taught by this pandemic is that the systematic and periodic collection of feedback from parents is a key strategy to guarantee the educational routine in emergency situations and it could bring very positive results in an ordinary times, too.

> Teachers were very helpful about getting in touch (with phone calls and emails) with children and families who had difficulties, due to special needs, family issues or socio-economic disadvantage. We are using two channels: the lesson, with almost no dialogue, and the chat channel or private phone calls, for personal support. (32, LS-P)

> The school considers being truly in contact with families, regardless of presence or distance, to be a necessary strategy. (77, PR-T)

> A positive aspect is precisely this way of reaching everyone with mobile phones or emails, but above all the idea of a school that is remote but always present. (89, PR-T)

> Thinking about a school that needs to be rethought in its overall setting, a school that is effective in its relationship with families in person as well as at a distance. (69, PR-T)

The teacher-parent relationship appeared to be 'remote' during the emergency (due to the constraints imposed by the physical separation), but parents and teachers found they were very connected in many ways, in a constant and continuous communicative flow and sharing/working towards a school vision that needed to be rethought as always present and effective when using remote channels as much as when people are physically at school. In this renewed framework, the school-family relationship appeared to be good and, perhaps, was even improved. Parents fully recognized the role, skills and competencies of the teachers, and felt free to seek their support and assistance, only after their children were learning from home.

> The parents were wonderful. The class representatives helped us a lot in maintaining relationships. Those parents who were not able to use ICTs were helped by more expert parents. The parents were patient, and we tried to be patient with them. I, as a class coordinator, really worked closely with them and I must say that they were wonderful. I also received many thanks at the end on behalf of all our colleagues. (94, LS-T)

> Relations with parents are really good – maybe they have [even] improved during this period. Parents recognize the efforts made to maintain contact with the children. Sometimes parents look for the teacher's support; they look for psychological assistance for this moment in which children are at home with them. (33, LS-T)

6 Conclusions

This analysis of the school-family relationship during the coronavirus emergency has highlighted that distance relationships and learning are experiences heavily dependent on the quality of the 'teamwork' of teachers and parents. From the examination of the voice messages collected, the school-family relationships are interpreted using some keywords as synthetic categories which refer to different ways to look at the formal, problematic or necessary role of parental involvement.

1. With some exceptions, the teachers and parents of our sample developed a positive narrative of school-family relationships during Covid-19. However, parental involvement was rare in practice and often seems more a rhetorical discourse than a concrete experience. Without asking the parents' opinions or feedback on the situation at home, the teachers who were interviewed expected a great deal of collaboration from parents to lay the groundwork for distance learning.
2. Furthermore, the analysis of the voice messages highlighted a degree of educational disorganization and blurring of the traditional separation of roles between teachers and parents, exacerbated by the school closures. Unusual situations emerged and became possible instances of misunderstanding and conflict. Parents complained about the ways of managing distance learning in which roles were distorted, and they had to shoulder an increasing workload to support and monitor their children's activities, as well as to invest a lot of time and energy and to cope with a lot of stress. This level of parental involvement could be considered an effective short-term reaction and response to an emergency such as Covid-19, as least initially, but it would not be sustainable for families in the medium and long term.
3. As a degree of school-family cooperation was indispensable to guarantee the continuity of compulsory education during the school closure, at the same time, many strategies of collaboration were maintained, extended or introduced, providing ICT connections which were able to recreate a new kind of direct sociality with and among parents, in a school which was trying to be 'present at a distance'. The strategies adopted by schools and families in order to solve the learning and social problems emerged with the school closure and the consequent distance learning were focused on bridging this distance gap. The educational institutions proposed unconventional strategies that reveal an unexpected attention to avoiding an excessive burden on vulnerable families, families with many children and families with children with special needs, learning or relational difficulties, etc.

Through these strategic organizational choices and through several formal and informal ways to communicate and cooperate, the teachers were looking for direct and immediate contact with parents, negotiation and agreement with them on the school timetable and activities, and cooperation between key actors (parents' representatives, class coordinators, etc.). The systematic and periodic collection of feedback from parents is a key strategy to guarantee the educational routine in emergency situations: this strategy is a very important lesson learned by all players during the pandemic and it could have positive effects also when applied in ordinary conditions, especially with disadvantaged pupils and families.

Notes

1. WhatsApp is the most prevalent mobile messaging app, free of charge and advertising free, available for all major mobile platforms, which has more than one billion users in 180 countries (cf. https://www.whatsapp.com/about): it allows users to have both one-to-one and group chats, ensuring a wide range of multimedia functions, including audio messages. This app and (generally all) other mobile instant messaging apps are attracting more and more methodological interest in the field of social sciences, even if their capabilities have not been fully exploited (Maeng et al., 2016; Kaufman & Peil, 2019; Jailobaev et al., 2021).
2. Participants were sampled by snowball sampling and reached using researchers' personal contacts, through work colleagues and university students in the education sciences. Thanks to a special mobile number set up for this research, potential interviewees received a message on their personal phone number. The receipt of voice messages occurred in asynchronous mode and did not provide further interactions but the request for a reply to a brief web questionnaire (through a link sent by WhatsApp) did. The questionnaire integrated the research, collecting background information (such as gender, age, level of the school attended, province of residence, parental working conditions) and some data, from parents and teachers, about the activities proposed to pupils by the school, the ways used by the school to inform parents about school activities and to involve them in the decision-making process.
3. Despite a certain number of advantages, the downside of using WhatsApp is that it is not yet possible to guarantee data security on the part of the platform provider as participants were also subject to WhatsApp's terms of usage and had passed over their data rights when initially setting up their WhatsApp account (Gergle & Hargittai, 2018). Moreover, from an ethical point of view, as mobile messaging apps are usually part of privately owned corporations it is questionable whether, and to what extent, academic research should use commercial software based on private interests.
4. Voice messages have been codified in the following quotes by number, school level (PR for primary school; LS for lower secondary school), and type of interviewee (T for teacher; P for parent).

References

Àlvarez-Àlvarez, C. (2020). Parental involvement in Spanish schools: The role of parents' associations. *Improving Schools, 23*(2), 125–139.

Ardizzoni, S., Bolognesi, I., Salinaro, M., & Scarpini, M. (2020). *Didattica a distanza con le famiglie: l'esperienza di insegnanti e genitori, in Italia e in Cina, durante l'emergenza sanitaria 2020. Uno studio preliminare.* Università di Bologna.

Baeck, U. K. (2010). Parental involvement practices in formalized home-school cooperation. *Scandinavian Journal of Educational Research, 54*(6), 549–563.

Borgonovi, F., & Montt, G. (2012). *Parental involvement in selected PISA countries and economies*. OECD Education Working Papers, no. 73. OECD Publishing. https://doi.org/10.1787/5k990rkojsjj-en

Censi, A. (2009). School and family: Values and relations. *Italian Journal of Sociology of Education, 1*, 85–96.

Chiswick, B., & DeBurman, N. (2004). Educational attainment: Analysis by immigrant generation. *Economics of Education Review, 23*, 361–379.

Coleman, J. S., Campbell, E. Q., Hobson, C. J., McPartland, J., Mood, A. M., Weinfield, F. D., & York, R. L. (1966). *Equality of educational opportunity*. US Government Printing Office.

Colombo, M. (2016). Education and citizenship between decline of charisma and need of educational anchoring. *Italian Journal of Sociology of Education, 8*(1), 87–101.

Colombo, M. (2019), *National Policy Legislation On Parental Involvement in Italian Schools* In M. M. Bordalba & N. L. Calvet (Eds.), *Families and Schools. The involvement of foreign families in schools,* Edicions de la Universitat de Lleida, Lleida (pp. 133–139). doi:10.21001/families.2019

Colombo, M., Rinaldi, E., & Poliandri, D. (2020). Gli impatti dell'emergenza COVID-19 sul sistema scolastico-formativo in Italia. *Scuola democratica*. Advance online publication. doi:10.12828/97098

Comer, D. R. (1995). A model of social loafing in real work groups. *Human Relations, 48*(6), 647–667.

Cooper, H. (1989). *Homework*. Longman.

Cordini, M., & De Angelis, G. (2021). Families between care, education and work: The effects of the pandemic on educational inequalities in Italy and Milan. *European Journal of Education, 56*(4), 578–594. https://doi.org/10.1111/ejed.12483

Crozier, G. (1999). Parental involvement: Who wants it? *International Studies in Sociology of Education, 9*(3), 219–238.

Decuypere, M., Grimaldi, E., & Landri, P. (2021). Introduction: Critical studies of digital education platforms. *Critical Studies in Education, 62*(1), 1–16.

Di Pietro, G., Biagi, F., Costa, P., Karpiński, Z., & Mazza, J. (2020). *The likely impact of COVID-19 on education: Reflections based on the existing literature and recent international datasets*. Publications Office of the European Union. doi:10.2760/126686

Dornbusch, S. M., & Glasgow, K. L. (1996). The structural context of family-school relations. In A. Booth & J. F. Dunn (Eds.), *Family-school links: How do they affect educational outcomes?* (pp. 35–44). Lawrence Erlbaum Associates.

Dusi, P. (2012). The family-school relationship in Europe: A research review. *CEPS Journal, 2*(1), 13–34.

Epstein, J. L. (2001). *School, family, and community partnerships: Preparing educators and improving schools*. Westview Press.

Epstein, J. L. (2016). Framework of six types of involvement. In D. Couchenour & J. K. Chrisman (Eds.), *The Sage encyclopedia of contemporary early childhood education*. Sage.

Eurydice. (2005). *Citizenship education at school in Europe*. http://eacea.ec.europa.eu/ressources/eurydice/pdf/0_integral/055EN.pdf

Fan, X., & Chen, M. (2001). Parental involvement and students' academic achievement: A meta-analysis. *Educational Psychology Review, 13*(1), 1–22.

Galli, N. (2000). *Pedagogia della famiglia ed educazione degli adulti*. Vita e Pensiero.

Gergle, D., & Hargittai, E. (2018). A methodological pilot for gathering data through text-messaging to study question-asking in everyday life. *Mobile Media & Communication, 6*(2), 197–214.

Getzels, J. W. (1972). Comportamento e conflitti di ruolo nell'ambiente scolastico. In V. Cesareo (Ed.), *Sociologia dell'educazione. Testi e documenti*. Hoepli.

Gigli, A. (Ed.). (2020). *Infanzia, famiglie, servizi educativi e scolastici nel Covid-19. Riflessioni pedagogiche sugli effetti del lockdown e della prima fase di riapertura*. Centro di Ricerche Educative su Infanzia e Famiglie (CREIF). https://edu.unibo.it/it/terza-missione/formazione/dossier-creif

Glenn, C. (2004). I figli degli immigrati a scuola. In M. Ambrosini & S. Molina (Eds.), *Seconde generazioni. Un'introduzione al futuro dell'immigrazione in Italia* (pp. 169–183). Fondazione Giovanni Agnelli.

Grolnick, W., & Slowiaczek, M. L. (2008). Parents' involvement in children's schooling: A multidimensional conceptualization and motivational model. *Child Development, 65*(1), 237–252.

Hill, N. E., & Taylor, L. (2004). Parental school involvement and children's academic achievement: Pragmatics and issues. *Current Directions in Psychological Science, 13*(4).

Hornby, G., & Lafaele, R. (2011). Barriers to parental involvement in education: An explanatory model. *Educational Review, 63*(1), 37–52.

International Commission on the Futures of Education. (2020). *Education in a post-Covid world: Nine ideas for public action*. UNESCO. https://unesdoc.unesco.org/ark:/48223/pf0000373717/PDF/373717eng.pdf.multi

Jailobaev, T., Jailobaeva, K., Baialieva, M., Baialieva, G., & Asilbekova, G. (2021). WhatsApp groups in social research: New opportunities for fieldwork communication and management. *Bulletin de Methodologie Sociologique, 149*, 60–82.

Jordan, C., Orozco, E., & Averett, A. (2001). *Emerging issues in school, family, & community connections: Annual synthesis*. Southwest Educational Development Lab. http://files.eric.ed.gov/fulltext/ED464411.pdf

Kaufmann, K., & Peil, C. (2019). The mobile instant messaging interview (MIMI): Using WhatsApp to enhance self-reporting and explore media usage in situ. *Mobile Media & Communication, 8*(2), 1–18.

Kristen, C., Reimer, D., & Kogan, I. (2008). Higher education entry of Turkish immigrant youth in Germany. *International Journal of Comparative Sociology, 49*(2–3), 127–151.

Kristen, C., & Granato, N. (2007). The educational attainment of the second generation in Germany. *Ethnicities, 7*(3), 343–366.

Lagomarsino, F., Coppola, I., Parisi, R., & Rania, N. (2020). Care tasks and new routines for Italian families during the COVID-19 pandemic: Perspectives from women. *Italian Sociological Review, 10*(3S), 847–868.

Lareau, A. (1987). Social class differences in family-school relationships: The importance of cultural capital. *Sociology of Education, 60*, 73–85.

Lareau, A. (1989). Family-school relationships: A view from the classroom. *Educational Policy, 3*(3), 245–259.

Lareau, A. (2011). *Unequal childhoods: Class, race, and family life*. University of California Press.

Lasater, K. (2016). Parent-teacher conflict related to student abilities: The impact on students and the family-school partnership. *School Community Journal, 26*(2), 237–262.

Lee, J., & Bowen, N. K. (2006). Parent involvement, cultural capital, and the achievement gap among elementary school children. *American Educational Research Journal, 43*(2), 193–218.

Maccarini, A. (2019). *Deep change and emergent structures in global society*. Springer.

Macià Bordalba, M., & Llevot Calvet, N. (Eds.). (2019). *Families and schools: The involvement of foreign families in schools*. Edicions de la Universitat de Lleida. https://repositori.udl.cat/handle/10459.1/67580

Mac Ruairc, G. (2011). No parents beyond this point. Una riflessione critica sulla partecipazione parentale nella scuola primaria in Irlanda. In P. Dusi & L. Pati (Eds.), *Corresponsabilità educativa. Scuola e famiglia nella sfida multiculturale: una prospettiva europea* (pp. 141–172). La Scuola.

Maeng, W., Ahn, H., Yoon, J., & Lee, J. (2016). Can mobile instant messaging be a useful interviewing tool? A comparative analysis of phone use, instant messaging, and mobile instant messaging. *Proceedings of HCI Korea 2016* (pp. 45–49). Hanbit Media, Inc.

Maglia, E. (2020). COVID-19, decreti governativi ed effetti di genere. *Politiche Sociali, 2*, 315–318.

Mantovani, S., Picca, M., Ferri, P., Bove, C., & Manzoni, P. (2020). *Bambini e lockdown. La parola ai genitori*. Università degli Studi di Milano Bicocca.

Meyer, J. W., & Rowan, B. (1977). Institutionalized organizations: Formal structure as myth and ceremony. *American Journal of Sociology, 83*(2), 340–363.

Palaiologou, N., Evangelou, O., & Tsapakidou, A. (2011). Le famiglie immigrate trovano ascolto negli spazi scolastici? Il caso della Grecia. In P. Dusi & L. Pati (Eds.),

Corresponsabilità educativa. Scuola e famiglia nella sfida multiculturale: una prospettiva europea (pp. 141–172). La Scuola.

Papazoglou, N. (1984). *School-family relations: Teachers, parents and pupils' rights*. Ed. Epikerotita.

Pena, D. C. (2000). Parent involvement: Influencing factors and implications. *Journal of Educational Research, 94*(1), 42–54.

Pitzalis, M., & Spanò, E. (2022). Il corpo assente: riflessioni sulla scuola ri-materializzata. *Scuola democratica* (forthcoming).

Pomerantz, E. M., Moorman E. A., & Litwack, S. D. (2007). The how, whom, and why of parents' involvement in children's academic lives: More is not always better. *Review of Educational Research, 77*(3), 373–410.

Potvin, P., Deslandes, R., & Leclerc, D. (1999). Family characteristics as predictors of school achievement: Parental involvement as a mediator. *McGill Journal of Education, 34*(2), 135–153.

Santagati, M. (2021). Writing educational success. The strategies of immigrant-origin students in Italian secondary schools. *Social Sciences, 10*(180), 1–18.

Santagati, M., & Barabanti, P. (2020). (Dis)connessi? Alunni, genitori e insegnanti di fronte all'emergenza Covid-19. *Media Education, 11*(2), 109–125. https://doi.org/10.36253/me-9646

Smrekar, C., & Cohen-Vogel, L. (2001). The voices of parents: Rethinking the intersection of family and school. *Peabody Journal of Education, 76*(2), 75–100.

Stanzani, S. (2020). Trust and civic engagement in the Italian COVID-19 lockdown. *Italian Sociological Review, 10*(3S), 917–935.

Stevens, P. A. J., & Dworkin, G. A. (Eds.). (2019). *The Palgrave handbook of race and ethnic inequalities in education* (2nd ed.). Palgrave Macmillan.

Swap, S. M. (1993). *Developing home-school partnerships: From concept to practice*. Teachers College Press.

Vuorikari, R., Velicu, A., Chaudron, S., Cachia, R., & Di Gioia, R. (2020). *How families handled emergency remote schooling during the COVID-19 lockdown in spring 2020: Summary of key findings from families with children in 11 European countries*. Publications Office of the European Union.

CHAPTER 4

From Classroom to Screen

An Exploratory Study of University Students in Sicily during the Covid-19 Lockdown

Umberto Di Maggio

1   Introduction: The Pandemic Scenario and the Sociological
          Perspective of Distance Learning

This contribution highlights the preliminary results of an exploratory analysis, 'Stay Home & Keep in Touch', conducted by the LUMSA University of Rome and the Institute for Educational Technology of the National Research Council of Italy (CNR-ITD) during the Covid-19 pandemic. It explicitly concerns 'social distancing' (SD) and 'distance learning' (DL). Without making concrete assertions, aware of the study's many limitations and recognizing that we are in an initial and exploratory phase of inquiry, we believe that our study can contribute cognitive elements to the great effort being made by the social sciences to understand the social changes resulting from the Covid pandemic.

As already mentioned, this study specifically concerns SD and DL. We purposely used the words 'distancing' and 'distance' as we realize that the spread of the virus has inducted us into a new way of experiencing space and relationships. Therefore, we are not convinced that what we have called 'SD' or 'staying at home' over the past months has been a complete relational distancing. Nor are we convinced that what we call 'distance learning' keeps students apart from each other and teachers. '*Io resto a casa*' ('I stay at home') is the slogan used by the Italian government during the lockdown to invite the population to embrace home isolation and SD in order to cope with the first wave of the coronavirus pandemic in spring 2020.

'I stay at home' is not just a slogan: it is a message of crucial semantic relevance. It is indicative because this exhortation towards physical distance and relegation into the domestic space could cognitively and socially change our way of perceiving our sense of a 'safe distance' in the context of relationships with others. In this scheme, technology is of great importance.

Even before the Covid pandemic, digital technologies were powerful tools. Now they have become even more indispensable because they have made it possible to stay connected while maintaining the security offered by one's own home. With specific reference to students and teachers, the technologies used for DL have been the tools that have allowed lessons to continue without interrupting didactic activities. (These tools have also become a new space for relationships, which we will discuss more in the course of this contribution.) What is the price of this great advantage?

1.1 *Digital Exclusion and the Rhetoric of the Technological Panacea*

Today, after more than a year of SARS-CoV-2 spreading worldwide and causing countless deaths, a radical change in lifestyle is still underway. Some talk about the victory of disaster capitalism (Klein, 2007) and surveillance (Zuboff, 2019). Others, taking up risk society theories (Beck, 1992), hypothesize that the current state of risk and exception may become the new norm.

Therefore, the current pandemic is a living laboratory, a never before seen social experiment (Matthewman & Huppatz, 2020) and a fertile ground for the social sciences (Hanafi, 2020). We specifically refer to the disease not as a generic event. Together with medicine it must be considered, taking up Durkheim (1897, 1952), and as in the case of a pandemic such as Covid-19, a collective phenomenon. These 'social facts' effect 'imbalances' that invade all areas of life: work, family, affections, etc.

The coronavirus has also imposed teaching reorganization. DL has become the mandatory solution, probably the only possible one. The impact on educational and training processes has been considerable (UNICEF, 2020). We do not know when the pandemic state of emergency will end: we are still experiencing this exceptional state. We do not know when classrooms will be attended again by students and professors as before the virus spread worldwide. Some countries – usually those with more advanced economies – that are pushing for mass vaccination are the ones that will undoubtedly stop using DL as the only solution. Perhaps they will revert to in-presence lessons or most likely will adopt blended modes. Many other countries, considered the 'Third World', where vaccination is slow and which deal with many other problems besides Covid, will have to organize themselves differently. Therefore, we are certain that schools and universities are compelled to reorganize both teaching methods and contents notwithstanding the persisting of the pandemic situation and the latitude it has required.

1.2 *From the Classroom to the Screen: Is a New Educational Dimension Emerging?*

The implementation of DL during the first phase of the Covid-19 pandemic, aside from the digital divide (Van Dijk, 2020; Vaira & Romito, 2020; Adnan & Anwar, 2020), the unpreparedness of the educational and training systems

(OECD, 2020) and pedagogical, technical, financial and organizational obstacles (Lassoued et al., 2020; Sokolovskaya, 2020; Mascheroni et al., 2021) has been an adaptive (Annisa et al., 2020) and reflective experience, for teachers, students, families and educational institutions (Dhawan, 2020). They all have had to reset their lifestyles or strategies to cope with a new educational environment that has inevitably become domestic and digital.

In the new pandemic scenario, teachers are compelled to undertake a rapid and radical change in their activities. They have reset the teaching content with new educational practices (Ramella & Rostan, 2020; Dietrich, 2020) and new communication codes.

We hypothesize that DL and, more generally, the massive use of digital technologies have significantly contributed to the restructuring and compression of personal and social space-time and the general change of behavioural rituals, linguistic styles and everyday habits that constitute the general architecture of our lives. The didactic experience has moved from the classroom to the screen. In the educational process, stage and backstage – two of Goffman's concepts (1959, 1963) – have been compressed.

The lessons moved from the blackboard to the screen have significantly modified the interactive rituals of daily life and the rules of conduct. Teachers and students have abolished the distinctions between the time of work and the place of work.

Thus we can say that DL has been an exceptional opportunity (Gurajena et al., 2021) for both teaching and learning. First and foremost it has been a new tool to temporarily resolve the social distancing prescribed to contain the spread of the pandemic. Nevertheless, from our perspective, DL has also been a means for sharing emotions, maintaining contacts, building new relationships and participating in the collective commitment to cope with the epidemic crisis.

In the next section, we will outline a theoretical background to these issues. We will do so by reasoning about space, time, routine and social distance. Our work will proceed using the sociological prism created by Simmel, Durkheim and, above all, Giddens and his perspective on the social construction of time and daily routine.

2   Space, Time, Distance and Routine through the Sociological Prism

This section proposes a brief and certainly not exhaustive discussion of the concept of 'distance', taking as reference some crucial sociological theory contributions. The guiding hypothesis is that the so-called social distancing recommended and practised during the pandemic is just a re-conceptualization of social actors' space-time relationships. So social distancing has affected some relationships, specifically those involving physical proximity and specific social spaces. However, government regulations requiring social distancing have activated the amplification of other online relationships that have grown and changed along with routines. The massive use of digital technologies have played a significant role, especially in the pandemic.

These relationships have changed along with everyone's routine. This change is due to the massive use of digital technologies (Bonini, 2020, pp. 16–19) which have played an essential role in the pandemic. We consider the space as a portion of reality where meaningful social actions take place. Space is variable; it depends on one's relative perception. Space is composed of the interweaving of distant and interconnected points within which several forces are exerted.

The use of technologies (such as those used in DL), as we will see, further accentuates the concept of proximity and distance. Simmel highlighted this concept when he stressed the relativity between proximity and distance in each person's relative perception of space. Simmel refers to frames and their socio-spatial properties. Precisely, space cannot be perceived without the senses. Senses are the channels through which a specific reciprocal social interaction is planned, takes shape, develops, characterizes and distinguishes itself, or is homologated with other interactions. The relationship of distance-proximity is perceived through the senses and it takes on meaning, becoming a stimulus for reciprocal action (Simmel, 2009). Simmel added that the perception of reciprocity concerning space also derives from the proximity-distance relation and the relative belonging-separation relation. It is then possible for a developed intelligence to perceive both the common belonging to what is spatially separated and the absence of what is spatially close (ibid.). Hence, a kind of closeness and concordance is possible for subjects in a condition of distance. At the same time, it is also possible for there to be a sort of estrangement for those subjects in a close condition.

In our view, these Simmelian emphases are interesting because they allow us to consider the student-teacher and student-student relationships developed within DL platforms during the pandemic, as relationships that were not necessarily 'at a distance'. On the contrary, these relationships are stimulated through virtual closeness despite the physical distance, in many cases. They have helped to reinterpret and not only reduce the SD and the emotional stress related to domestic isolation and, more generally, to the pandemic situation. However, the perspective of another classical sociologist will further help explain the theoretical frame of our research. According to Durkheim, the spatial representations of a given civilization are of social origin. Moreover, spatial organization reproduces social organization as a model (Durkheim, 1912). Therefore, space perception is a social issue since it refers to the internalization and relative representation of the properties of space itself, which takes on meaning within the reference group. Thus, space is fundamental because social life depends on it and vice versa. So, can we say that the DL in the pandemic has been transformed from a simple learning solution into a real relational space?

Before Covid-19 the 'First World' developed itself through a rough division between space zones and temporal rhythms. Time for study, free time, time for work, friendship and affection, although interconnected, could be roughly distinguished. Covid-19 and digital technology have accelerated an already significant change that perhaps today we can consider irreversible. Nevertheless, even before the pandemic, we realized that technology could compress or expand the space-time relationship.

As we anticipated, space determines the temporal planning and the overall organization of society. Space, therefore, also has a social and not a purely mechanical nature. In this pandemic, the area of relationships has been remodulated. Due to home lockdowns and quarantines, domestic, public, work, learning, physical, and virtual spaces have collapsed into one new space, that of the digital platforms. For example, we have spent – and are still spending – our lives with new routines in rooms created by Zoom. In those rooms we studied, worked, had aperitifs with friends, celebrated birthdays, held condominium and party meetings. They became our agoras for discussion and, at the same time, private spaces for intimate relations. However, the setting has always remained the same: that of our homes.

However, beyond that, it is necessary to refer more precisely to the sudden changes in educational and training processes. We must refer to what happened in the part of the world that has the means and structures to connect to the internet without particular problems and which has been able to recalibrate, more or less quickly, the entire educational paths for both schools and universities. In this chapter we want to specify this issue and are not interested in highlighting the performance of educational processes. Regardless of the performative aspect of the DL, we want to understand instead, if the DL has influenced social relations more overall, even those that go beyond the student-teacher and student-student relationship. For example:

– Has the use of DL contributed to the increased stress caused by pandemic isolation?
– Or on the contrary, has it solved the stress caused by the obligation of SD prescribed by the authorities to reduce the coronavirus infection?
– Has DL been transformed to a real relational space in the pandemic?

– Is the massive use of DL consistent with a new social organization model of companies dealing with Covid-19, which, to contain the contagion, have moved a large part of their activities to the digital channel (without considering it 'un-real')?

In the case of DL, virtual classrooms have not been the mere online replication of school classrooms. Nevertheless, at the same time, they did not become the mere sum of the places where people connected for lessons. Everyone remained in their own homes and inhabited, in parallel, virtual spaces in which to attend classes – as well as to connect in other ways. Students and teachers lived their 'non-virtual' domestic space-time and, at the same time, lived in another 'virtual' space-time that we can therefore consider 'virtual-enhanced'. They were allowed to revolutionize routines and behavioural codes because in this new space the codes of the 'real' world were relatively valid. For example, one could wear pyjamas or comfortable clothes and thus change the dramaturgy of habitual relationships involving specific behavioural codes. The novelty of the pandemic was that it forced us to adopt SD to contain the virus and that this virtual rapprochement – new and full of new social practices to experiment with – resolved, at least in part, 'physical distancing'. This rapprochement was made possible by implementing another space-time dimension that mixed the virtual and the non-virtual. We cannot consider this dimension 'un-real'. The relationships are differently 'real'. The new daily lessons, work meetings, family and friends in the digital platforms were concrete and produced a new routine. However, what has been the price of this significant change?

At this point we can affirm that the most critical consequence of this pandemic, in which technology at many levels is omnipresent more than in the past, is the restructuring of relationships in an indefinite space-time. The new pandemic time, in its social meaning, is no longer simply *chronos* (χρόνος) and therefore just astronomical time, quantitatively sequential, chronological and 'unstoppable'. On the contrary, 'social time is not continuous but is interrupted by critical dates' (Sorokin & Merton, 1937, p. 615). In the new pandemic time, personal life cycles become collective life cycles of 'waiting'. We refer to the end of the epidemic emergency that becomes a new normality. On the other side, the new social space becomes a pandemic space where virtual and non-virtual spaces are always interconnected, almost indistinguishably.

We can decode this new space-time relationship and the invasive use of digital technologies in everyday life, referring to the Simmelian concept of 'intensification of nervous life'. This intensification occurs when external and internal impressions meet rapidly and intermittently (Simmel, 2012). This overload often inhibits action and renders subjects unable to react. Therefore, we can analyse DL as the originator of a new 'blasé' condition (Simmel, 2012, p. 14). We can explain it as an additional dimension of pandemic fatigue (WHO, 2020) and Covid-19 exhaustion. We refer precisely to the feeling of tiredness and exhaustion caused by a prolonged state of crisis. Pandemic fatigue is also related to the sudden change in habits and the sense of loss of control of one's life. We refer precisely to the feeling of tiredness and exhaustion caused by a prolonged state of crisis. Who among teachers and students (this also applies to other social actors who have done smart working, for example) did not feel frustration and therefore loss of control, when the internet connection fell, the microphone or the webcam did not work or when the didactic rhythms were so 'different', and therefore uncontrollable, compared to in-presence learning?

This brief review of sociological literature that we have used together with some of our preliminary considerations, is crucial for investigating the effects of social distancing in the new daily routine. It is essential to understand the new conception of space and time of digital platforms for DL power.

As we have stated, the use of these technological tools is relevant to our research. It is not for the effectiveness or ineffectiveness of the transmission of training and educational contents. We are interested in understanding whether DL could reduce or amplify the fatigue – and therefore the emotional stress – caused by the social distancing imposed by pandemic blocks and restrictions. Through the DL platforms we hypothesize that new forms of sociality can develop. At the same time, we hypothesize how DL can exacerbate the condition of social isolation and loneliness. We are not digitally enthusiastic about technology, but we are not neo-Luddites, either: we see the need to analyse DL critically. Especially in times of pandemic emergencies, it can certainly help solve some problems.

Of course, we do not consider DL as a panacea for solving the more general issues facing education systems – regardless of epidemics – which, as is often said, require constant innovation.

We will try to confirm these hypotheses in the next section by presenting and discussing the data collected from the exploratory research 'Stay Home & Keep in Touch', which has the university students of the LUMSA of Palermo as its reference population.

3 Empirical Analysis

3.1 *Objectives*

The main objective of this exploratory research was to study the effects of social distance in the students' new daily routine and verify the contribution of DL platforms to increase or decrease stress, fatigue and the perception of SD due to Covid lockdowns.

We based our research hypotheses on Giddens' theory of space-time and routine as social construction and deconstruction of daily life (1984). With specific reference to the school and university daily routine, especially in the first phase of the coronavirus spread in spring 2020, we can affirm that it has radically changed, requiring a great effort by teachers, students and families to adapt. The change has also affected the way people interact socially beyond education and training systems. The massive use of digital technologies has accelerated this process, which has also influenced the contents, methods and codes implemented with the new pandemic DL.

Nevertheless, again a clarification is mandatory: we are not interested in underlining whether the DL has improved or worsened the quality of educational processes. Instead, we are interested in understanding if DL could be considered an overall relational social space to spend this suspended time of the pandemic and, therefore, living a new space-time dimension of relational life.

3.2 *Hypothesis*

The following hypothesis guided this exploratory research: the pandemic SD needs to re-conceptualize the space-time relationship between social actors and relational environments. Digital technologies, especially in times of crisis, are the authors of a rapid (and perhaps irreversible) change in the perception of time and space. This change has consequences for the social relations between actors and institutions such as the educational system we are talking about in this research.

The specific working hypothesis was the following: with specific reference to the daily university routine, the digital platforms used by DL were not only a tool to continue teaching in an emergency condition. DL platforms have also become a relational space that partially resolved the condition of isolation, fatigue and uncertainty generated by the health emergency and exacerbated by SD. However, DL has not been a panacea to the health and relational emergency because, on the contrary, it has often exacerbated emotional fragility and generated a 'Covid blasé' condition, which we can consider as a form of 'pandemic fatigue'.

3.3 *Target Population*

We collected the data starting from March 2020 through a semi-structured questionnaire administered online (via Google Forms) to students of the Social Service, Education and Training, Economics and Law courses of the LUMSA

University of Palermo. Students in the academic year 2019–2020 attending the five degree courses in the Legal and Economic area and the Social and Educational area are the target population: 1,412 students constitute the entire target population of enrolled students (849 females and 563 males) and 449 are the attending students. We got answers from 261 subjects (203 females and 58 males) that are those attending and directly interested in the DL topic.

3.4   Limits of the Survey

We are aware of the small number of respondents. Despite this limitation, 'Stay Home & Keep in Touch' can lead to an understanding the dynamics related to DL in small groups. In any case, to solve the problem of sample size we will try to probe the data in depth and then longitudinally. For this reason we will collect information that will involve the same target population until the end of the health emergency in Sicily, presumably at the end of 2022, to test our hypotheses both in a pandemic and post-pandemic scenario.

3.5   Survey Instrument

As anticipated, we distributed to university students of LUMSA in Palermo a semi-structured questionnaire consisting of three sections. The first section collected personal information; the second, consisting of four close-ended questions, sought opinions on DL; the third and final section had two open-ended questions regarding SD and the university in pre-Covid routines and the lockdown scenario.

We performed an unvaried analysis of the information collected in the first and second sections, referring to the issues concerning the effectiveness of DL with in-presence learning, and the feelings experienced during DL in lockdown.

The qualitative data in the corpus of texts collected by the open questions in the third section, which addressed changes of routine as a result of the pandemic and concerned the massive use of technology in DL, were analysed with the multidimensional lexical analysis software IRaMuTeq.

Specifically in the first socio-demographic section we asked the LUMSA students of Palermo to identify their degree course, year of study, gender and age. The classes of the latter variable are 19 to 29 years old, 30 to 50 years old and over 50 years old.

In the thematic section on DL, we asked the respondents to indicate:
1. Teaching methods used by the student with the possible options: lessons on Google Meet platform, Google Suite apps, e-learning platform, didactical materials on the teacher's page, video lessons and/or podcasts set up by the teacher;

2. Effectiveness of the preferred didactic mode (DL/Lessons in Presence (LP)/both solutions);
3. Whether DL supplements or replaces LP;
4. Sensations experienced during the distance lessons. Students could indicate different pairs of answers simultaneously, only pleasant, only unpleasant or both. The pairs are: Closeness, Proximity; Loneliness, Solitary confinement; Stress, Fatigue; Engagement, Sharing, Anxiety, Nervousness; Wellness, Satisfaction, Other: specify.
5. Finally, in the thematic section regarding SD and the new Covid-19 routine, we asked 'What was missing?' and 'What was not missing?' from university life due to the lockdown.

3.6 *First Results*

Respondents indicate that DL is mainly considered a substitute for in-presence learning (54.4%) and not a complementary tool (43.3%). We believe that students refer to this specific emergency DL implemented during the pandemic and we assume that their statement is particularly critical. We also interpret this value as a concerned response to the possibility that all teaching might move online. Respondents also indicated a greater preference for in-presence learning (80.8%) and a lower preference for DL (11.8%). Only 6.12% consider both solutions effective. We therefore interpret these data by underlining how, for LUMSA students, the use of DL is perceived as a support tool that is valid in case of emergency, but that cannot entirely replace the educational and relational needs that LP offers. Information of this kind can be interpolated by referring to the SD questions which we will discuss later.

The variable 'Felt sensations in DL…' operationalized the concept of 'pandemic emotivity' relating to the use of DL in a pandemic and therefore to what concerns the new 'blasé' condition deriving from the massive use of technologies. The properties were collected from the answers received with the multiple-choice question 'During DL I felt sensations…'. Firstly we classified the answers to the question aggregated into five classes of sensations experienced during DL: Unpleasant (33.3%) and Mostly unpleasant (8.05%), Pleasant and unpleasant (20.69%), Mostly pleasant (4.9%) and Pleasant (32.9%).[1] By aggregating the first two categories, the substantial prevalence of unpleasant sensations emerges (41.38%). Regarding the age groups, unpleasant feelings are more recurrent among young people aged 19–29, who constitute the largest share of students. These data confirm that DL was experienced by the students as a stressful experience rather than a pleasant one. This confirms what has also been found in other studies of teachers. These studies on the population of Italian university academics show that those who would like to switch permanently to distance learning represent a small minority of respondents – just 2%. On the other hand, 54% would like at least part of their teaching to be carried out in 'mixed form', integrating face-to-face lessons with online activities. Instead, 44% would like to return to the pre-emergency situation as soon as possible (Ramella & Rostan, 2020).

The last answers that should be analysed concern the question: 'What do you miss from your college life routine before Covid?' It is interesting to note that

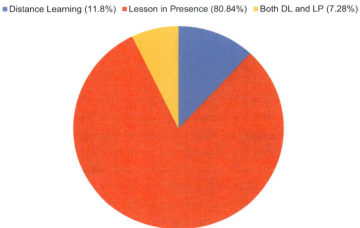

FIGURE 4.1 Question: 'Do you prefer DL, LP or both solutions?' (% value) (Source: 'Stay Home & Keep in Touch' data, LUMSA University (Palermo) students, March 2020)

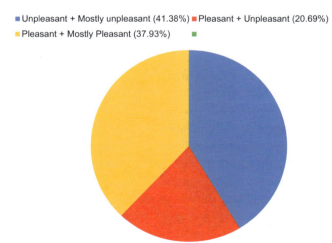

FIGURE 4.2 Pleasant or unpleasant sensation perceived during DL in pandemic (% value) (Source: 'Stay Home & Keep in Touch' data, LUMSA University (Palermo) students, March 2020)

the recurring words are 'colleague' and 'teacher' in the open-ended answers. These lemmas are related to relationship, confrontation, interaction, proximity, share, classroom. These words confirm the importance of face-to-face relations and of university routine. We can say that, in general, university spaces are perceived as a complex scenario of social relations and not only learning opportunities. It is also curious to indicate the lemma 'break', which refers to the informal social moments of having a coffee in the corridors between lectures. These moments are fundamental in a university student's daily routine because of their capacity to stimulate affective and friendly relationships. We could say that the corridor, echoing Goffman's concepts (1959, 1963), is a hybrid space between stage and backstage. It is a place where other students' relationships shape the representation of self-changes. In front of a coffee machine

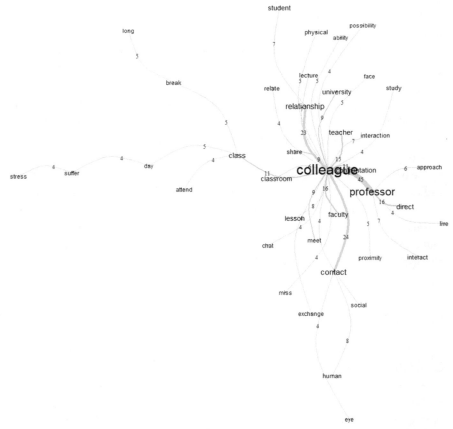

FIGURE 4.3   Question: 'What do you miss from your college life routine before Covid?' Textual analysis with IRaMuTeq software (Source: 'Stay Home & Keep in Touch' data, LUMSA University (Palermo) students, March 2020)

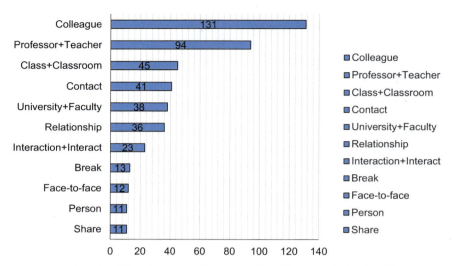

FIGURE 4.4   Question: 'What do you miss from your college life routine before Covid?' Occurrences over 10. Textual analysis of similarities with IRaMuTeq software (Source: 'Stay Home & Keep in Touch' data, LUMSA University (Palermo) students, March 2020)

students are no longer just students; they are multiple subjectivities. While maintaining the student's status, they also become somebody else, and for this reason, in LP, relationships widen in contents and meanings more than in DL.

The prevalence of DL over LP contributes to a specific physical, relational space and prevents the development of a particular dramaturgy. The students indicated along these lines the frustration of losing the 'face-to-face' relationships that took place in classrooms and corridors, where more 'selves' can be represented. Instead, they see the forced implementation of what we might call a 'monitor-to-monitor' relationship, where they are forced to represent a single self, precisely that of a student connected to the platform.

4   Discussion

We now analyse the 'Stay Home & Keep in Touch' research data through the conceptual prism offered by Giddens' theory of space-time deconstruction. This theory emblematically fits for understanding the unprecedented relational dynamics developed during the Covid lockdown in spring 2020. In particular, we refer to the radical change in relational dynamics that many compare to what has happened in other moments of crisis, such as wartime (Battistelli & Galantino, 2020, p. 29). We mainly consider DL as an instrument for both teachers and students to reduce (and often increase) SD. Thus, in our opinion, DL is a tool for understanding the general process of adaptation to a new normality.

4.1 Covid Routinization and De-routinization: A Giddensian Interpretation

Giddens pointed out that time and space are not simply environments where social conduct takes place. The author considered time and space to be active protagonists in relational processes. This underlining is emblematic because it invites us to consider the new spatio-temporal structuring that occurs in pandemics from a new perspective. It is even more so in the light of the necessary new consideration that needs to be given to the concept of SD.

So, have distance teaching platforms brought students closer together or have they distanced them from each other? Has their relationship with teachers changed? Have the Zoom rooms, for example, become new a new reality where virtual and non-virtual, domestic and non-domestic, space has been mixed?

We found the answer by analysing the change in the routine of students. We considered routine, borrowing Giddens, as a rationalization of conduct, to invent a safety system for social actors. Specifically for the author, where routine prevails, the rationalization of conduct readily joins the actor's basic security system and the conventions that exist and are drawn upon in interaction as mutual knowledge. For this reason, in routinized social circumstances actors are rarely able (that is, feel the need in response to the demands they make of each other in the course of social activity) to provide reasons for behaviour that conform to convention. This is what has happened through the use of DL platforms. Faced with the rising contagion curve, there was no other solution than to channel all the lessons online and thus transmigrate people's routines into an online space that more or less reproduced what had always happened with traditional forms of LP.

Routines are also important for understanding everyday life in those circumstances where environments are disturbed by critical situations, as in the coronavirus lockdown. Following Giddens: '[B]y critical situations I mean circumstances of radical disjuncture of an unpredictable kind which affect substantial numbers of individuals, situations that threaten or destroy the certitudes of institutionalized routines' (Giddens, 1984, p. 61). As confirmed by the data we have collected, the direct effect was the production of a high degree of anxiety and 'stripping away' (ibid., p. 63) concerning the management of one's body and the inability to respond as usual to the stimuli that come from social life. So, we can consider DL a prism to understand routinization and the de-routinization directly connected to DL via digital platforms.

4.2 *In the Name of Distance, Is It an Educational Crisis?*

The massive use of digital technologies during the pandemic emergency has broken down and recomposed the interactional space of everyday life. From being mere mediums, communication platforms became the exclusive environment of symbolic interactions. There, it was possible to situate oneself according to circumstances (in addition to DL, chats and video calls with friends and relatives, business meetings, etc.), assuming one's respective roles but still maintaining the same domestic scenic setting.

The consequences regarding relational and learning processes were relevant. These consequences were added to other sociological issues that consider the emergency a state of the norm rather than a mere exception.

The pandemic scenario is certainly not over. This exceptional condition will continue until the vaccine is distributed on a global and universal scale. Thus we need to ask how it is possible to overcome the merely emergency approach. We need to decipher the various facets of the change that the coronavirus has triggered and grasp the actual extent of the shocks caused. Finally, we need to imagine the strategies needed to respond to the crisis on various levels in the new 'Covid society' (Lupton & Willis, 2021).

In this scenario, families, students, and teachers, as we said, have had to reinvent themselves. Digital platforms have become an anchor of salvation. On the other side, it was soon realized that no education could be totally delegated to digital platforms. This was the case because of the many inequalities that existed in access to technological media. Therefore, DL is not a panacea for solving the educational and training aspects caused by the Covid-19 health crisis, just as it cannot be for other crises that will probably (we hope not) come in the future. Therefore, the pandemic introduced us to a social experiment characterized by an emblematic shift in education from the classroom to the web. We have moved from the lesson in a predefined physical 'place' (classroom) to the lesson in another 'place' with another physicality (virtual classroom) and yet real. This place, therefore, cannot be considered 'not real'. The physical place for human beings means defined boundaries within which to feel 'at home'. This 'home' became the platform we accessed, however, while staying at home. For this reason, as other researches show (Ferraro et al., 2020), the transition from LP to DL has often been fraught with difficulties for many students, both from a cognitive point of view and in terms of learning, as well as from an emotional-motivational point of view, with significant repercussions on social relations.

The students emphasized the importance of community ties among themselves and with teachers. This emphasis expresses the adaptability and responsiveness of the educational system to the epidemic emergency and beyond.

This evidence shows how the educational system itself has ample resilient capacities (WEF, 2020) that it developed together with the protagonism of informal education (Merico & Scardigno, 2020). So, is it correct to talk about an educational crisis? Maybe pandemic disruption to learning is an excellent opportunity to redesign educational systems (UN News, 2021) and update the reflection on globalization and internationalization of the ideals of democratic education and the idea of school and university as a common good (Colombo, 2015).

Thus, in-presence learning and DL are two faces of the same interpretative prism and are two key concepts. Using them we can understand how this (post-)Covid-19 society is organizing itself by changing the nature and function of social relations implemented, maybe, in the name of a new idea of 'distance'.

Note

1   The 'mostly pleasant' category consists of 75% pairs of pleasant and 25% unpleasant sensations. The same can be said with pairs of opposite sensations for the unpleasant category.

References

Adnan, M., & Anwar, K. (2020). Online learning amid the COVID-19 pandemic: Students' perspectives. *Journal of Pedagogical Sociology and Psychology*, 2(1), 45–51.

Annisa, R., Nadila, S. M., Salsabila, S. A., Putri, S. A. E., & Nurmajesti, H. (2020). E-learning as an adaptation strategy in facing Covid-19 pandemic: A case study on the 2018 and 2019-generation students of post graduate Sociology Department, University of Indonesia. In Y. Sunesti & A. K. Putri (Eds.), *Proceedings of the 6th international conference on social and political sciences (ICOSAPS 2020)* (pp. 40–44). Atlantis Press.

Battistelli, F., & Galantino, M. G. (2020). *Sociologia e politica del coronavirus. Tra opinioni e paure*. Franco Angeli.

Beck, U. (1992). *Risk society: Towards a new modernity*. Sage.

Bonini, T. (2020). L'immaginazione sociologica e le conseguenze sociali del Covid-19. *Mediascapes Journal*, 15, 13–23.

Colombo, M. (2015). Dinamiche sociali e sistema educativo in Italia dopo la crisi del Welfare State. L'educazione nella crisi del Welfare State. In *L'educazione nella crisi del Welfare State* [Proceedings from the Scholè meeting 2014] (pp. 31–53). La Scuola.

Dhawan, S. (2020). Online learning: A panacea in the time of COVID-19 crisis. *Journal of Educational Technology Systems*, 49(1), 5–22.

Dietrich, N. (2020). Attempts, successes, and failures of distance learning in the time of COVID-19. *Journal of Chemical Education, 97*(9), 2448–2457.

Durkheim, É. (1912). *The elementary forms of the religious life*. George Allen & Unwin.

Durkheim, É. (1952). *The suicide: A study of sociology*. Routledge.

Ferraro, F. V., Ambra, F. I., Aruta, L., & Iavarone, M. L. (2020). Distance learning in the COVID-19 era: Perceptions in southern Italy. *Education Sciences, 10*(12), 355.

Giddens, A. (1979). *Central problems in social theory: Action, structure and contradiction in social analysis*. Palgrave.

Giddens, A. (1984). *The constitution of society: Outline of the theory of structuration*. Polity.

Giddens, A. (1993). *New rules of sociological method: A positive critique of interpretative sociologies*. Polity.

Giddens, A. (1994). *The consequences of modernity*. Polity.

Goffman, E. (1959). *The presentation of self in everyday life*. Doubleday.

Goffman, E. (1963). *Behavior in public places: Notes on the social organization of gatherings*. The Free Press.

Gurajena, C., Mbunge, E., & Fashoto, S. G. (2021). *Teaching and learning in the new normal: Opportunities and challenges of distance learning amid COVID-19 pandemic*. http://dx.doi.org/10.2139/ssrn.3765509

Hanafi, S. (2020, April). *Post-COVID-19 sociology*. ISA Digital Platform. https://www.isa-sociology.org/frontend/web/uploads/files/Post-COVID-19%20Sociology.pdf

Klein, N. (2007). *The shock doctrine: The rise of disaster capitalism*. Picador.

Lassoued, Z., Alhendawi, M., & Bashitialshaaer, R. (2020). An exploratory study of the obstacles for achieving quality in distance learning during the COVID-19 pandemic. *Education Sciences, 10*(9), 232. https://doi.org/10.3390/educsci10090232

Lupton, D. (2015). *Digital sociology*. Routledge.

Lupton, D., & Willis, K. (Eds.). (2021). *The Covid-19 crisis: Social perspectives*. Routledge.

Mascheroni, G., Saeed, M., Valenza, M., Cino, D., Dreesen, T., Zaffaroni, L. G., & Kardefelt-Winther, D. (2021, February). *Learning at a distance: Children's remote learning experiences in Italy during the COVID-19 pandemic*. UNICEF Office of Research – Innocenti. https://www.unicef-irc.org/publications/pdf/learning-at-a-distance-childrens-remote-learning-experiences-in-italy-during-the-covid-19-pandemic.pdf

Matthewman, S., & Huppatz, K. (2020). A sociology of Covid-19. *Journal of Sociology, 56*(4), 675–683.

Merico, M., & Scardigno, F. (2020). Ri-emergenze. Il no schooling ai tempi del COVID-19. *Scuola democratica*. Advance online publication. doi:10.12828/97101

OECD. (2020). *Learning remotely when schools close: How well are students and schools prepared?* Insights from PISA. Organisation for Economic Cooperation and Development. https://www.oecd.org/coronavirus/policy-responses/learning-remotely-when-schools-close-how-well-are-students-and-schools-prepared-insights-from-pisa-3bfda1f7/

Ramella, F., & Rostan, M. (2020, September 21). Universi-DaD. Gli accademici italiani e la didattica a distanza durante l'emergenza Covid-19. *Il Mulino.* https://www.rivistailmulino.it/a/universi-dad

Simmel, G. (2009). *Sociology: Inquiries into the construction of social forms.* Brill.

Simmel, G. (2012). *The metropolis and mental life.* Routledge.

Sokolovskaya, I. E. (2020). Socio-psychological factors of students satisfaction in the context of digitalization of education during the COVID-19 pandemic and self-isolation. *Digital Sociology, 3*(2), 46–54.

Sorokin, P., & Merton R. K. (1937). Social time: A methodological and functional analysis. *American Journal of Sociology, 42*(5), 615–629.

Stebbings, R. A. (2001). *Exploratory research in the social sciences.* Sage.

UNICEF. (2020). *Coronavirus. La disparità di accesso all'istruzione a distanza rischia di aggravare la crisi dell'apprendimento globale.* https://www.unicef.it/doc/9919/coronavirus-la-disparit-di-accesso-allistruzione-a-distanza-rischia-di-aggravare-la-crisi-dellapprendimento-globale.htm

UN News. (2021). Pandemic disruption to learning is an opportunity to reimagine, revitalize education. *UN News.* https://news.un.org/en/story/2021/01/1082792

Vaira, M., & Romito, M. (2020). L'emergenza COVID-19 e la scuola. Una riflessione su alcune contraddizioni emergenti dalla crisi. *Scuola democratica.* Advance online publication. doi:10.12828/97099

Van Dijk, J. (2020). *The digital divide.* John Wiley & Sons.

WEF. (2020). The rise of online learning during the COVID-19 pandemic. World Economic Forum. https://www.weforum.org/agenda/2020/04/coronavirus-education-global-covid19-online-digital-learning/

WHO. (2020). *Pandemic fatigue: Reinvigorating the public to prevent COVID-19.* World Health Organization. http://apps.who.int/bookorders

Zuboff, S. (2019). *The age of surveillance capitalism: The fight for a human future at the new frontier of power.* PublicAffairs.

CHAPTER 5

A New World Is Open?

Distance Teaching in Italian Universities during the Covid-19 Emergency

Francesco Ramella and Michele Rostan

1   Investigating an Unexpected Emergency

On March 4th 2020, a decree by Italy's prime minister suspended classes in all Italian universities, but gave them the '*possibility* of providing remote education'. Less than a week later, almost three-quarters of the country's lecturers had already shifted to virtual classrooms and so-called 'distance teaching' (DT), or in other words, lessons offered via online platforms.[1] For the overwhelming majority of these faculty members, this was the first experience of the kind in their professional careers. For an institution like the university, still regarded as an 'ivory tower' far removed from everyday reality and having little concern for the outside world, this demonstrated an extraordinary ability to respond quickly and efficiently.

But what was distance teaching like for the faculty members on the front lines of education? Did everything in fact go well? And above all, once the emergency ends, what will remain from what this experience has taught us?

To answer these questions, a national survey on distance teaching during the Covid-19 emergency was carried out in June 2020. The survey was based on an extensive sample of 3,398 members of the teaching faculty at Italy's state universities who completed a wide-ranging online questionnaire. The survey was a panel study, as the same 15,000 academics who took part in a 2016 survey on the university's third mission were contacted (Perulli et al., 2018).[2] The survey was conducted immediately after the end of the lockdown in the first stage of the pandemic and was – to the best of our knowledge – the first of its kind in Italy. The analysis in the following pages is descriptive in nature, and will present the conditions under which distance teaching took place, the organizational and individual responses to the situation, university faculty members' perceptions of the situation and their assessment of the distance teaching experience. In addition, this initial report will highlight several issues that merit further thought and discussion.

The chapter centres on two main themes. The first is that of the emergency sparked by the pandemic and its spread. The questionnaires made it possible to collect information about the universities' reaction to the emergency (Section 2), the infrastructures deployed to deal with it, and how they were used (Section 3). Faculty members' assessment of their experience was positive on the whole (Section 4), though its negative and stressful aspects were clearly apparent from the survey (Section 5). The second theme concerns university teaching methods. The survey made it possible to compare pre- and post-emergency teaching methods (Section 6) as well as to tap respondents' opinions about the forms teaching will take in the future (Section 7). The conclusions (Section 8) will discuss several positive and negative features of Italian universities that the pandemic crisis brought to light, emphasizing how the crisis has led universities and faculties to call their teaching and its aims and methods into question, along with the use of digital technologies in higher education.

Two points should be borne in mind while reading this chapter. First, the survey took place at a difficult moment, at the end of the first semester of the emergency, when the first student examinations were being held and there was considerable uncertainty about whether some form of hybrid instruction could be offered during the next semester and what the universities' 'new normal' would be like. Second, the survey provides a snapshot of distance learning based on faculty members' experience and opinions, and does not take students' experience and opinions of the universities' official statements into account. In this connection, it should be pointed out that between May and June 2020, the market research firm IPSOS together with Federica Web Learning – the Università di Napoli Federico II multimedia learning centre – carried out a survey of 1,200 university students throughout Italy, asking them about their relationship with e-learning during the pandemic (IPSOS & Federica Web Learning, 2020). In March 2020, the Conference of Italian University Rectors conducted two surveys of the progress that Italy's universities had made in transitioning to online teaching, monitoring the number of exams, the number of graduates and the percentage of courses held online versus those planned for the semester (CRUI, 2020). When possible, we will refer to some of the findings of these surveys carried out in the same period as our own.

2   An Unexpected Response Capacity

The unforeseen consequences of the Covid-19 health emergency caught Italian universities by surprise. In a very short time – and surrounded by enormous uncertainty – they had to find alternatives to in-person teaching if they were to continue to fulfil their educational mission even during lockdown. The emergency thus put the spotlight on e-learning, as faculty and students found

TABLE 5.1   When did you start distance teaching? (%)

In the week of	ITALY	North-west	North-east	Centre	South
February 24–28	4.2	5.8	8.7	2.8	1.4
March 2–6	21.9	35.2	33.2	18.1	9.4
March 9–13	46.3	39.7	42.1	54.7	46.3
Later	27.6	19.3	16.1	24.4	42.5
Number of respondents	2,838	600	573	741	924

themselves having to experiment (willingly or less so, and with widely varying levels of familiarity) with internet-based remote learning methods accessed via digital platforms.

How did it go? We will start by saying that, in fact, it seems that 'everything turned out fine'. Delays in starting lessons were limited. A full 72% of faculty members were able to start remote teaching by March 13th. Only in the southern Italian universities did the transition to online teaching take place later for over 40% of respondents.

Lecture hours did not depart much from those envisaged for normal years. In the three-year degree programmes, 86% of faculty members held classes for the same number of hours as usual, while 7% even did more. In the five-year degree programmes, 89% of faculty members delivered all of the envisaged number of hours.

The master's degree and doctoral programmes came close to completing the entire number of hours, as the overwhelming majority of respondents were able to cover the entire teaching program. Thus, 80% finished the program and only 11% shortened it, while 9% increased the program by providing students with more online material.

The majority of faculty members adapted their teaching strategies to distance methods: 67% modified both the content and the structure of their courses to some extent. By contrast, 24% made no changes, while 9% took advantage of the opportunity to rethink their teaching.

Streamed lectures predominated, as 66% of respondents broadcast their lessons live. This percentage reached 82% in the universities in the south (Table 5.2). Both live-streamed and pre-recorded classes were held by 15%. In addition, 52% posted educational materials online (lecture notes, slides, etc.), with or without audio commentary. Only 7%, however, provided such material exclusively online or engaged in other activities *without* delivering live-streamed or recorded lectures. This percentage was highest in the north-western universities.

TABLE 5.2   What form did your distance teaching take? (%)

	ITALY	North-west	North-east	Centre	South
I gave live-streamed lectures	66.3	53.0	55.6	65.0	82.4
I gave live-streamed and pre-recorded lectures	14.6	17.7	20.0	14.8	9.2
I gave pre-recorded lectures	12.1	18.5	19.2	13.3	2.5
I posted educational material online WITHOUT giving lectures	7.0	10.8	5.2	6.9	5.9
Total	100	100	100	100	100
Number of respondents	3,397	713	685	878	1,121

The number of students in attendance did not drop. For 53% of respondents, the number of students attending lectures was unchanged. The number even increased for 22%, and dropped for 20%, while differences between the various areas of the country were quite limited.

Examinations proceeded as usual. At the time of the interview, 92% of the faculty members had held at least one online exam session. Oral exams predominated, either on their own or accompanied by a written assignment and/or other form of final assessment (exercises, reports, projects, etc.): 36% of respondents relied entirely on oral exams, while 51% held oral exams plus a written assignment and/or other form of final assessment. By contrast, written exams were scaled back significantly, and were reduced by half nationwide. Before in-person teaching was interrupted because of the health emergency, 62% of respondents had held written exams, while the percentage dropped to 27% after distance teaching was introduced. In any case, 61% of respondents believe that they were able to assess their students' progress even with remote exams.

On the whole, these initial data indicate that:
– Italian universities demonstrated that they were able to respond well to the emergency and maintain their organization;[3]
– Faculty members managed to overcome the challenge of distance teaching quite successfully.

To some extent, these findings are surprising, given that relatively few respondents were familiar with online teaching before the pandemic. Only 9% of the interviewees had had prior experience with distance teaching; 17% had had some experience with e-learning, but it had for the most part been limited to posting educational materials online.

3   Technological Infrastructure and Emergency Governance

Faculty members chiefly taught from home, with enough technological infrastructure to ensure that classes could be held: 68% of respondents delivered lectures at home, and 17% from other places set up as personal offices. In all geographical areas, 88% of respondents reported that their internet connection and IT tools were sufficient to enable them to opt for the teaching approaches they felt were most appropriate (Table 5.3). In addition, the technological solutions available to them at home improved over time. In the passage between the first stage of the emergency (the first two weeks of class) to the second (the remainder of the semester), the percentage of respondents whose infrastructure was adequate rose by approximately four percentage points.

'Technological impediments' vary according to place of residence. The percentage of respondents who report having an unsatisfactory connection rises from 12% for those living in a large city to 23% for residents of towns with fewer than 2,000 inhabitants. The latter percentage reaches 27% in the north-west and 37% in the north-east, where large proportions of the population live in small mountain towns where coverage is problematic.

Though lectures were delivered in private homes, the overwhelming majority of respondents (89%) received support from their universities in order to make the transition to distance teaching. Support was chiefly provided at the university level, and was mostly in the form of emails, written information and video tutorials (Table 5.4). Assistance and information was also provided by

TABLE 5.3   Were the internet connection and IT tools available to you during the emergency good enough to enable you to choose the teaching approaches you felt were most appropriate? (%; stage II)

	ITALY	North-west	North-east	Centre	South
Internet connection					
No, not at all/Quite poor	12.0	11.9	10.4	13.7	11.8
Yes, fairly good/Very good	88.0	88.1	89.6	86.3	88.2
Total	100	100	100	100	100
IT tools					
No, not at all/Quite poor	12.5	12.2	10.6	13.0	13.6
Yes, fairly good/Very good	87.5	87.8	89.4	87.0	86.4
Total	100	100	100	100	100
Number of respondents	2,760	579	559	718	904

TABLE 5.4 What kind of training and support did you receive, and from whom? (%)

	University	Departments[a]
Written information on the website or intranet	55.0	23.9
Information emails	60.8	35.2
Video tutorials on using platforms	48.2	17.3
Training meetings	24.7	14.0
Tech support/help desk	44.6	24.5
Number of respondents	3,398	3,398

a   Departments and degree programmes, schools or faculties.

the decentralized entities (departments, degree programmes, schools, etc.) that acted as proximity networks to amplify the effectiveness of communication and coordinate the general strategies with the many specific disciplines.

The following organizations and support networks were especially important from the technical standpoint.

- The *institutional networks* – in other words, faculty members' relationships with the university, school and department offices and personnel in charge of degree programmes provided technical assistance to 53% of respondents and teaching support to 22%.
- The *professional networks* – relationships with associates and colleagues – provided technical assistance to 33% of respondents and teaching support to 23%.
- The *non-professional networks* – relationships with friends, family, members of other professions – were more marginal, providing technical assistance to 12% of respondents and teaching support to 5%.

All in all, 62% of respondents received technical assistance and 34% received teaching support that they regarded as 'enough or a lot' through at least one of the channels considered in the survey.[4]

Italy's universities reacted to the emergency with a variety of approaches. Consequently, the amount of freedom of choice they left to faculty members also varied (Table 5.5). A minority – 15% – reported that they chose the form of distance teaching they adopted independently, with no restrictions or constraints of any kind. The percentage was higher in the north-western universities and the smaller institutions (21.4%). By contrast, almost one-third of respondents reported that they felt they had entirely lost their independence as teachers during the emergency. This perception was especially strong

TABLE 5.5   Were you able to choose what kind of distance teaching you used? (%)

	ITALY	North-west	North-east	Centre	South
Yes, I was able to choose in complete independence, without restrictions.	15.3	19.2	14.1	16.3	12.7
Yes, I was able to choose from a number of options offered by my university/department.	53.5	66.9	57.5	66.1	32.3
No, I was not able to choose, I had to follow the instructions given by my university/department	31.2	13.9	28.5	17.6	55.0
Total	100	100	100	100	100
Number of respondents	2,818	598	569	731	920

in the southern universities, where over half of all respondents put themselves in this category. Nationwide, however, the majority of respondents stated that they could choose among multiple options made available by their university's teaching facilities.

Thus, Italian universities responded to the emergency with three types of conduct.[5]

– Some had a decidedly *controlling* style: on average, 69% of respondents had no leeway in choosing how to do their distance teaching.
– Others took an opposite and decidedly *liberal* approach, allowing their faculty members to be highly independent. In these universities, the percentage of respondents reporting that they were unable to choose teaching methods dropped drastically, averaging 14%.
– There was then an intermediate class, where the percentage of respondents who were given no choice averaged 43%.

In general, the controlling style was associated with two characteristics: a) more institutional support for transitioning online, and b) greater centralization of support networks (for teaching as well as technical assistance) at the university level (Table 5.6). In other words, the controlling universities issued very precise and binding instructions about how distance teaching was to be done. In addition, they rolled out a consider number of services to support faculty members, especially at the university-level facilities.

TABLE 5.6   Levels of support by institutional response style (support received by faculty members through institutional networks: average scores on a 1–10 scale)

Level of university control	Low	Medium	High
Technical assistance			
University	5.0	5.0	6.0
Departments[a]	4.4	4.7	5.1
Teaching support			
University	2.6	2.5	3.3
Departments[a]	2.8	2.6	3.1
Total support (teaching + technical)			
University	3.7	3.7	4.6
Departments[a]	3.4	3.5	4.0

a   Departments and degree programmes, schools or faculties.

This, however, led to something of a paradox: a trade-off between institutional support and individual learning. On the one hand, it was in the *controlling universities* that academic management garnered the highest scores for how it dealt with the emergency. In the *liberal universities*, on the other hand, a higher number of respondents reported that they increased their professional skills during the emergency, thanks to the experience gained from distance teaching (Figure 5.1).

This 'paradox' suggests that in the universities where faculty members received fewer binding instructions and had to make decisions on their own about how to approach distance teaching, individual learning was more widespread and reached higher levels. In this connection, however, two factors should be borne in mind.

The first is that of *personal proactivity* in activating support networks. Clearly, the more respondents were able to deploy their social capital, or in other words the networks whereby they received resources and support for solving teaching problems, the more they were able to benefit from the remote teaching experience. They thus took advantage of the pandemic emergency to increase their professional skills. Not surprisingly, the mean scores for this question are highest among respondents who were most active in drawing on their institutional, professional and personal networks, and reached a maximum among those who activated all the networks available to them (Table 5.7).

The second factor involved both the amount of support provided by the universities, and the architecture of the institutional support networks. In

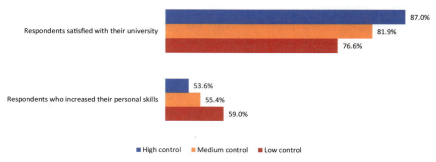

FIGURE 5.1   Respondents' ratings of how the emergency was managed

TABLE 5.7   Perception of the distance learning experience as an opportunity for increasing professional skills, by support from networks (average values; scores from 1 to 10)

Support from institutional networks	
Little	5.4
Enough + A lot	6.4
Support from professional networks	
Little	5.4
Enough + A lot	6.4
Support from personal networks	
Little	5.6
Enough + A lot	6.6
Enough or a lot of support from institutional networks plus:	
a. professional networks	6.8
b. personal networks	6.9
c. professional and personal networks	7.0
Number of respondents	2,948

some universities, the support services and activities are highly centralized in order to achieve 'economies of scale and of scope'. In other universities, the approaches sought to leverage 'network economies' by decentralizing services and activities among individual departments, schools and faculties.

Here, we can distinguish between four different types of emergency governance. The first and least significant relied on faculty member's professional and personal networks, providing little support through institutional networks. In the second, support activities were highly decentralized. The third type, an approach we could call coordinated decentralization, provides considerable

A NEW WORLD IS OPEN? 131

support at both the central and peripheral levels. In the third type, support is highly centralized.

When asked to assess how their university dealt with the emergency and how it affected their personal experience, respondents had the most favourable perceptions of governance based on coordinated decentralization of support (Table 5.8). The highest ratings were assigned when coordinated

TABLE 5.8 Institutional support and respondents' ratings of emergency governance (average values; scores from 1 to 10)

Type of institutional support	Low	Decentralized	Coordinated decentralization	Centralized	Tot
This experience enabled me to increase my professional skills	4.9	5.7	6.3	5.9	5.7
Satisfaction with my distance teaching experience	6.4	6.7	7.2	6.9	6.8
Satisfaction with my university's ability to respond to the emergency and ensure that teaching could continue	6.3	7.1	8.3	7.8	7.5

	Coordinated decentralization		Centralized		
Type of university	Liberal	Controlling	Liberal	Controlling	Tot
This experience enabled me to increase my professional skills	6.7	6.0	6.2	5.7	5.7
Satisfaction with my distance teaching experience	7.2	7.1	6.9	6.9	6.8
Satisfaction with my university's ability to respond to the emergency and ensure that teaching could continue	8.1	8.6	7.5	8.2	7.5

decentralization was accompanied by a liberal approach to choosing teaching methods. In this case, faculty members could make their choices independently knowing that they could rely on strong support from the university network and from the departments, which are more familiar with the specific teaching issues involved in each degree programme.

In conclusion, both the 'quantity' and the 'variety' of the IT and support resources available through institutional and personal resources had a positive impact on the response to the emergency and on respondents' experience during the lockdown. These 'learning networks' – typical of the learning organizations discussed in the organizational literature (Arundel et al., 2007; Dee & Leišyte, 2016) – are an essential part of organizational resilience. We will return to this point in the conclusions.

4 Overall, a Very Positive Judgement

In the light of what we have seen so far, it is not surprising that 80% of the surveyed academics had a positive opinion of how their universities and departments dealt with the emergency, ensuring that teaching could continue.[6] This percentage was quite similar in both small and large universities. The differences between universities in the northern, central and southern parts of the country were also quite limited (Table 5.9).

In addition, 75% of respondents reported that they were satisfied with their own experience of distance teaching, and 57% felt that they had increased their professional skills. Among positive aspects of the experience, 51% of respondents cited a greater awareness of the need for more training in the methods and technique of in-person and distance teaching.

This overall satisfaction explains why many respondents in all parts of the country would like to retain something of this experience after the emergency ends (Table 5.10). 54% would like at least some teaching to take 'hybrid' form, combining face-to-face classes with online activities. However, only 2% believe that distance teaching can *entirely replace* in-person teaching. There are, however, opposite attitudes: 44% of respondents would like to return to the way things were before the emergency, retaining nothing of the experience with remote teaching.[7]

5 The Problematic Sides of Distance Teaching

The reasons for wanting to go back to 'the way things were' are by no means baseless. They spring from a number of negative and stressful aspects of the emergency that our survey brought to light.

TABLE 5.9   Ratings of the experience during the emergency (% Very + Fairly)

How satisfied were you on the whole with the following?	ITALY	North-west	North-east	Centre	South
Your experience with distance teaching	75.2	77.6	74.0	74.5	74.8
Your university's ability to respond to the emergency and ensure that teaching could continue	80.4	78.3	81.1	76.9	84.0
Your department's ability to respond to the emergency and ensure that teaching could continue	76.7	70.8	79.0	73.8	81.4

Thinking of distance teaching, how much do you agree with the following statements?					
This experience enabled me to increase my professional skills	56.8	62.2	62.2	54.6	51.5
This experience made me want to have more training in teaching methods and techniques (in-person and distance)	50.9	52.2	54.8	47.5	50.3
Number of respondents	2,678	571	543	698	866

We will start with the unprecedented workload and organizational stress caused by the emergency. Distance teaching called for enormous effort for universities and individuals alike. From one day to the next, university management and technical and administrative staff found themselves having to try out completely untested approaches to training and providing technical and teaching support to faculty members who for the most part had never even imagined that they would end up lecturing online. As a result, the people in charge of teaching management were under considerable organizational stress. During the Covid semester, 24% of our interviewees had coordinating roles, e.g. as pro-rectors, department heads or degree programme directors. Of these respondents, 70% were heavily involved in meetings for organizing the

TABLE 5.10 What would you like to keep from this distance teaching experience once the Covid-19 emergency is over? (%)

	ITALY	North-west	North-east	Centre	South
Nothing, I would like to go back to in-person teaching	43.7	41.8	46.0	44.3	43.3
I would like teaching to be entirely online	1.7	2.1	0.9	2.2	1.6
I would like at least some teaching to take hybrid form (combining in-person classes with online activities)	54.5	56.1	53.1	53.5	55.1
Total	100	100	100	100	100
Number of respondents	3,172	668	635	822	1,047

response to the emergency, 60% were engaged in coordinating teaching faculty, and 65% were active in communicating with students.

Faculty members were also under significant stress, as distance education proved to be very time-consuming: 70% of respondents reported that the time needed to prepare a class increased, while 73% had to extend the period devoted to holding exams, and 66% stated that remote assessment of students' progress involved a major organizational effort.

It goes almost without saying that a large percentage of respondents complained that they had very little time to adapt their courses for distance teaching (Table 5.11). More surprisingly, three-quarters of respondents stated that one of the critical problems with distance teaching was that there were fewer opportunities to interact with students and/or, for 52%, that practical exercises, workshops, labs and the like were difficult.[8] This was unexpected, given that the international debate often regards the use of new digital technologies in teaching as a chance to increase interaction between students and teachers in a variety of ways. We will return to this point later.

The problems encountered during the emergency can be grouped into four categories.[9]

1. Technological problems associated with the quality of the internet connection or IT tools. *Such problems affected only 14% of respondents.*
2. Technical-logistical problems associated with the lack of suitable spaces at home, the difficulty of reconciling teaching and home or family responsibilities, and the need to help students with technical issues. *Such problems affected 31% of respondents.*

TABLE 5.11 In your experience with distance teaching, how problematic were the following aspects? (Very + Fairly; %)

The little time available for adapting my course to online teaching	43.9
My familiarity with the necessary technologies and apps	26.5
The lack of a suitable space in the place where I held my remote classes	22.2
The difficulty in balancing the time needed for teaching with my family responsibilities	26.5
Having to help students with technical problems	16.5
Fewer opportunities for interacting with students	74.8
The difficulty in accessing educational resources (special-purpose software, library resources, etc.)	28.6
My teaching material is not readily adapted to online delivery	27.1
The difficulty in carrying out practical exercises (workshops, labs, etc.)	52.5
Increased control over my work by the academic authorities	6.7
Privacy and protecting students' and faculty members' data	20.0
The risks associated with improper use and dissemination of material created for teaching purposes	38.1
Number of respondents	3,398

3. Privacy problems associated with the fear that material created for teaching purposes might be improperly used and disseminated, that data protection could be jeopardized, and that the academic authorities can exert more control and reduce faculty members' independence in teaching. *Such problems affected 31% of respondents.*
4. Teaching problems associated with the little available time, lack of familiarity with remote teaching platforms, difficulties in interacting with students, reduced access to teaching resources (libraries, etc.), difficulties in adapting course material to online teaching, and the problems involved with practical exercises. *One or another of these problems was reported by 70% of respondents.*

6   Teaching Methods before and during the Emergency: A Comparison

Up to now, we have discussed the difficulties and problems reported by faculty members themselves. However, the information collected with the questionnaire also enabled us to perform another type of analysis: a comparison

TABLE 5.12 Please indicate your teaching activities prior to the Covid-19 emergency and your distance teaching activities (for your main courses) (%; multiple responses possible)

	In-person	Remote
Classroom lectures	78.9	65.9
Discussions with students	70.6	50.0
Group work (reports, studies, etc.)	42.9	24.6
Exercises and other activities based on collaboration between students	52.5	23.7
Peer-to-peer discussion and/or assessment groups	22.1	11.1
Activities designed specifically to assess and improve student competences	26.8	13.1
Meetings with invited guests	42.3	18.7
Activities designed to stimulate students' creativity and problem-solving abilities	31.6	16.5
Workshops	38.0	12.9
Other (specify)	7.6	5.5
Number of respondents	3,398	3,398

between the teaching methods used before the emergency and those introduced during the Covid-19 semester (Table 5.12).

6.1 *What Was Pre-emergency Teaching Like?*

It is an often-repeated misconception that what educationalist call a *transmissive teaching model* (Bonaiuti, 2014), where the student's role is essentially passive, reigned supreme in university lecture halls. This teaching strategy is exemplified by the traditional professorial lecture, a teacher-centred approach where the student is relegated to being a mere listener.

Today, this stereotype is very far from the kind of teaching that actually takes place in universities. Our survey, in fact, found that three distinct teaching strategies were employed in Italian universities in the period preceding the emergency.[10]

1. A 'transmissive/dialog-based' strategy. This strategy is the closest to the traditional stereotype, but with a significant variation. Though it chiefly features classroom lectures, it is often enriched by discussions between students and the instructor. *Approximately 23% of respondents adopted this strategy.*

2. A 'transmissive-interactive' strategy in which the dialog-based model described above is enhanced through active student involvement in exercises, workshops, group work, etc. *Approximately 33% of respondents adopted this strategy.*
3. A 'collaborative-innovative' strategy where instruction is accompanied by the students' contribution not only in interpreting and processing the information they receive, but also in transforming it into personal competences. This type of teaching is based on interaction between the instructor and the students, and among the students. In addition to group work, this strategy often involves peer discussion and assessment to build transversal competences and work designed to stimulate students' creativity and problem-solving abilities. *Approximately 45% of respondents adopted this strategy.*

As the survey shows, university teaching is less static and traditional than is generally believed. Another noteworthy point is that the collaborative-innovative strategy, though employed in all disciplines, is most frequency used by instructors in the social sciences (59%), an area that includes political science, sociology, education sciences, and psychological sciences, all disciplines that by definition address the normative and relational aspects of social phenomena as well as their socio-cognitive aspects.

What happened to teaching in the Covid-19 semester? The more innovative activities were sharply curtailed. Teaching was simplified, retreating to the traditional transmissive model, albeit with some room for student discussion.
- Use of the first, or transmissive/dialog-based, strategy doubled. *With distance teaching, it was employed by 47% of respondents.*
- Use of the second, or transmissive-interactive, strategy remaining virtually unchanged. *It was employed by 31% of respondents.*
- Use of the third, or collaborative-innovative, strategy was more than halved. *It was employed by 22% of respondents.*

The same process of simplification was seen in examinations. While in-person teaching afforded many more opportunities for assessing learning outcomes, assessment methods were significantly simpler with remote teaching.

With in-person teaching:
- 19% of respondents assessed learning outcomes entirely by means of an oral test;
- 55% of respondents used two distinct forms of assessment (generally a written test and an oral test, or either a written or oral test combined with assessing exercises, reports and projects);

- 26% of respondents used three different assessment methods, viz., a written test, an oral test, and assessment of exercises, reports and projects.

With remote teaching:
- 37% gave only an oral test;
- 50% used two assessment methods;
- 14% used three assessment methods.

In evaluating this 'impoverishment', it should obviously be borne in mind that it resulted from the fact that faculty members were faced with an emergency (often for the first time in their professional careers).

It should also be added that this 'problem' did not have the same negative impact on all respondents. Some, in fact, were able to maintain a 'more complex teaching strategy' even during remote teaching. As is clear from Figure 5.2, these are faculty members who responded proactively to the emergency, leveraging their own social capital. Respondents who continued to use a 'collaborative-innovative' strategy are distinguished from the others, first for their ability to draw on larger amounts of technical assistance and teaching support, and second because they used a wider variety of channels (support networks).

These findings confirm what the network analysis literature tells us about innovation, viz., that relational networks provide social actors with the essential means for achieving their goals (Burt, 1992; Granovetter, 2004; Ramella, 2016). First, because they affect the quantity and quality of available resources (both tangible and intangible), and second, because they produce specific 'information asymmetry advantages' through faster access to reliable information.

These studies suggest that in order to perform well in unconventional activities under extremely uncertain conditions such as those that gave rise to

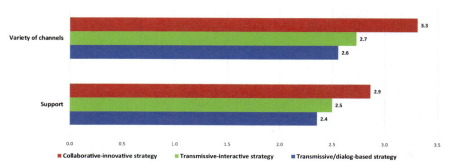

FIGURE 5.2 The teaching strategies employed for online classes, by level of support and variety of channels used by respondents in the transition to distance teaching (1–10 scale for support; 1–7 scale for channels)

remote teaching, it is necessary to leave the usual routines behind and combine previously unconnected resources. This is precisely what academics with 'mixed support networks' (i.e. those who were supported via a plurality of channels) were able to do. These mixed networks create connections between actors belonging to different spheres in academia and elsewhere, thus activating circuits for exchanging information and collaborating that had been separate. This enables the actors to obtain a greater variety of resources, skills and information that improve the overall effectiveness of their actions.

7 Views of the Future

Italian academics' opinions of how the emergency was handled were thus decidedly positive, allowing for the difficulties involved and the uncertainty surrounding the decisions that had to be made. But when they think about the future, what are their views on the use of distance teaching or of hybrid methods combining in-person classes with online activities?

First, let's put one question to rest. As we have seen, almost all respondents believe that distance teaching *cannot and should not* replace face-to-face classes. Only a tiny minority (2%) would like to move permanently to distance teaching. At the opposite extreme, 44% do not want to retain anything of the forms of teaching used during the emergency. At the same time, 54% are well disposed towards hybrid methods.

Thus, over half of the respondents believe that hybrid methods can improve learning performance in individual disciplines by making it possible to post more educational materials of different kinds online, and/or by permitting different ways of interacting with the instructor (Table 5.13). Smaller but still significant percentages believe that these teaching methods would make it possible to experiment with new educational strategies: a) by eliminating the more routine parts of in-person classes and leaving more room for discussion and exploration, b) facilitating activities designed to build competences and integrated interdisciplinary education, and c) encouraging independent learning and greater collaboration between students.

Moreover, many respondents believe that distance teaching would be good for certain categories of student by enlarging the pool of potential beneficiaries of higher education and making it more inclusive (Table 5.14). Around three-fourths think it would help working students and increase lifelong education. Approximately two-thirds believe it would make educational 'mobility' easier and provide more opportunities for people who live in rural areas, other Italian regions or other countries.

TABLE 5.13 How much do you think hybrid teaching, which combines in-person classes with online activities, can contribute positively to the following goals? (A lot + Some; %)

Improving learning performance in individual disciplines (by providing more online material of different kinds, permitting different ways of interacting with the instructor, etc.)	54.5
Employing different forms of teaching (project work, competence building, interdisciplinary education, etc.)	47.3
Experimenting with learning methods based on student collaboration (through dedicated apps, discussion groups, etc.)	44.9
Eliminating the more routine parts of in-person classes to make more room for discussion and exploration	39.6
Developing students' critical thinking skills	27.5
Developing students' creativity	30.5
Increasing the ability to address and solve complex problems	30.1
Stimulate students' independence and active learning	40.4
Number of respondents	3,398

TABLE 5.14 How much do you think distance teaching can help enlarge the pool of potential students in the following categories? (A lot + Some; %)

Working students	76.8
Post-university age adults who want to continue their education	73.3
People living in rural areas	69.1
People living in other regions	69.4
People living in other countries	62.8
Number of respondents	3,398

Over 60% believe distance teaching would help students with specific learning disabilities (Table 5.15). Lastly, almost half of the respondents believe it would help students at a socio-economic disadvantage. That said, it should be noted that there is a certain polarization of views. The percentage of respondents who express concerns about continuing with distance teaching after the health emergency is far from negligible: 40% believe that extending distance teaching would make recruiting new staff more difficult, 57% that it would significantly increase their workload and stress, and 58% that it would increase big tech's interference in university teaching.

TABLE 5.15   How much do you agree with the following statements? (A lot + Some; %)

Distance teaching can help students at a socio-economic disadvantage	47.6
Distance teaching can help students with disabilities	64.0
Continuing with distance teaching after the health emergency will make it more difficult to recruit new staff	39.8
Continuing with distance teaching after the health emergency will increase my workload and stress	56.6
Continuing with distance teaching after the health emergency will gradually increase big tech's (e.g. Google, Facebook, Apple, etc.) interference in university teaching	57.8
Number of respondents	3,398

But who are the academics who take a more favourable view of hybrid teaching methods? How do they differ from the others who would rather return to in-person teaching, just as it was before the emergency? We will start by looking at the 'context factors', or, in other words, the influences exerted by the environment in which the respondents did their distance teaching: size and geographical location of their university, size of the city they live in and how far their home is from the university. No particularly important (or statistically significant) differences were found in this connection. There was only a slight preference for distance teaching on the part of respondents who do not live in the same province as the university, and thus have to do a certain amount of commuting. Socio-demographic factors were also found to make little difference: attitudes do not vary according to age and gender. Passing to the respondents' scientific and academic profile, the highest levels of interest in hybrid teaching were found: among full professors, who have management responsibilities and coordinate teaching, in certain disciplines (health sciences as well as agricultural and veterinary sciences), and among those who work in departments where online activities were already more common.

These variables, which mostly tap individual attributes, show rather small departures from the mean and, with only two exceptions, are not statistically significant. They thus have limited explanatory power.

Several relational and attitudinal variables were found to be more important, including having held higher-level courses or used more innovative teaching methods prior to the emergency (Table 5.16). What makes the real difference, however, is the amount of support received in the transition to working online and the experience gained with distance teaching during the lockdown (Table 5.17). The factors that count are the intensity of the aid that

TABLE 5.16   Preferences regarding post-emergency teaching according to the type of in-person teaching strategy (% per line)

Preferences	In-person teaching	Distance teaching	Hybrid teaching	Total	Respondents
Courses					
Teaches in master's degree programmes**	29.1	3.3	67.6	100	275
Teaches in workshops**	35.5	2.7	61.8	100	602
Had prior experience with distance teaching**	26.7	3.3	70.0	100	303
*In-person teaching strategies***					
Transmissive/dialog-based	51.2	4.3	44.5	100	598
Transmissive-interactive	41.8	1.0	57.2	100	866
Collaborative-innovative	39.9	1.3	58.8	100	1,161
Total	43.7	1.7	54.5	100	3,173

**$p < 0.001$; only teaching types that were found to be statistically significant are shown

respondents received and the variety of relationships through which it was provided, and, above all, having a positive view of distance teaching's effects on professional skills and the level of satisfaction with the experience accrued in the emergency semester.

8   Concluding Remarks

The time has come to summarize some of our survey's main findings. Over and above the costs and negative aspects it has entailed for Italy's universities, the health emergency served an important function in making the crucial importance of teaching – one of the missions that is too often taken for granted and neglected in many Italian universities – clear for all to see. Specifically, the lockdown showed that there is no substitute for in-person teaching. Almost all of our respondents agree that this is true. No technology, no form of platform-mediated teaching can replace the educational interaction that takes place when students and instructor are physically present in the classroom.

TABLE 5.17   Preferences regarding post-emergency teaching according to experience during the emergency (% per line)

Preferences	In-person teaching	Distance teaching	Hybrid teaching	Total	Respondents
*Aid received during the emergency**					
Average or below average	45.9	2.0	52.1	100	1,724
Above average	41.2	1.4	57.3	100	1,449
*Number of support channels used**					
Average or below average	45.7	2.1	52.2	100	2,021
Above average	40.3	1.1	58.5	100	1,153
*Distance teaching enabled me to increase my professional skills*** (Phi = 0.311)					
Somewhat disagree or strongly disagree	60.4	1.4	38.2	100	1,116
Somewhat agree or strongly agree	29.3	2.3	68.3	100	1,459
*Distance teaching made me want to have more training in teaching methods and techniques*** (Phi = 0335)					
Somewhat disagree or strongly disagree	59.6	1.8	38.6	100	1,260
Somewhat agree or strongly agree	26.6	2.1	71.2	100	1,307
*I was satisfied with my distance teaching experience*** (Phi = 0.312)					
Somewhat disagree or strongly disagree	69.9	0.8	29.3	100	648
Somewhat agree or strongly agree	34.1	2.3	63.5	100	1,967
Total	43.7	1.7	54.5	100	3,173

*p < 0.05; **p < 0.001

The crisis also demonstrated an 'unsuspected' ability to respond quickly and efficiently on the part of Italian universities. In the space of a few short weeks, faculty members were able to ensure that teaching activities could be continued online. Classes and programmes were completed in full. Exams and graduate theses proceeded regularly. The number of students attending courses did not drop. Given the context and the conditions, the satisfaction that respondents expressed – not only with their own personal experience, but also with the efforts made by the university and their departments – is thus more than justified.

The crisis highlighted how far the real university is from the imaginary university portrayed in the public debate, often stuck in outdated stereotypes originating decades ago. This is especially true of 'academic teaching'. The teaching that takes place in university classrooms involves much more dialog, interaction and collaboration than is generally believed. Significant percentages of instructors use 'innovative' forms of teaching. Often, however, these are isolated experiments by individuals, attracting little interest and pedagogically ill-grounded. And this brings us to the fragilities and problems that the crisis brought to the surface:

- First, the enormous stress and overwork resulting from the emergency added to the burdens of a short-handed technical-administrative staff and teaching faculty that were already struggling to cope with the innumerable bureaucratic chores introduced in recent years.
- Second, many difficulties arose as a result of faculty members' lack of training in teaching methods in general and in the new digital platforms.
- Third, and as a consequence of the first two points, there was a drastic 'impoverishment' in teaching methods despite faculty members' best intentions and the major efforts made by the universities.

That said, the survey's respondents also offered a more positive view of the new digital platforms' potential for addressing the specific problems of certain categories of student (those from other areas, those with disabilities, working students, etc.). In addition, a majority of respondents (54%) express *a certain willingness to try hybrid forms of teaching once the emergency is over*, combining in-person classes with online activities.

The factor that *had the greatest positive influence on this willingness was the experience with remote teaching*, on both the personal and institutional levels. While the particular academic discipline involved had some influence, much depended on how open the respondent's attitude was during the emergency and, more generally, on whether respondents tended to be proactive. The respondents who had the most positive experience of remote teaching were those who in their in-person classes had already been more oriented toward collaborative and innovative forms of teaching, and who took an exploratory approach to the emergency, drawing on their social capital and turning the crisis into an opportunity for reflecting on their teaching methods. The institutional dimension, however, also made a difference.

Throughout Italy, the support provided by the universities played a crucial role in the transition to online teaching. As regards governance of the emergency, though, the most effective universities where those that:
- employed 'coordinated decentralization' in which the schools and departments were more heavily involved in providing support to faculty members, and
- allowed faculty members greater independence in deciding their approach to distance education.

It was thanks to their stock of social capital that many faculty members were able to turn the 'challenge' of distance teaching into a learning opportunity. In a variety of ways, the universities provided training resources and opportunities, which respondents integrated with their own personal and professional resources to mount an effective response to the crisis.

These 'individual' responses, supported by the institutional networks, enable organizations to learn and innovate, increasing their requisite variety and resilience (Powley, 2009; Dee & Leišyte, 2016). In organizations, resilience is the ability to respond to challenges by demonstrating that they are: (a) *solid*, or in other words able to cope with critical and unexpected events; (b) *cohesive*, i.e. capable of maintaining a high degree of internal integration by motivating their members; and (c) *agile*, or able to face emergencies promptly and arrive at effective answers to the problems (Mousa et al., 2020).

There are, however, two ways of responding to a crisis. The first kind of response is in the short term, when the organization is under stress, to provide an immediate solution through first-order problem solving. The second is a long-term response which puts what was learned from the emergency to good use in modifying the organization's structures and routines to prevent the crisis from reoccurring and/or improve performance. This is referred to as second-order problem solving. The first kind of response is based on single-loop learning, or simple, local and occasional learning dynamics. The second kind calls for double-loop learning, a more complex process which is less contingent and has lasting structural implications (Argyris & Schön, 1978; Tucker & Edmondson, 2003). This brings us to the final point we will address here.

Crises are often opportunities, because they stimulate creative responses and trigger generative mechanisms that enable organizations to change course, moving away from old habits. For the first time in many years, the approaches that had to be used during the Covid-19 semester made Italy's universities and instructors question their teaching and its aims and methods. By contrast with the country's secondary schools, where a technological innovation policy has been implemented for nearly a decade, the universities were caught largely unprepared by this challenge. Few had made significant investments in distance teaching and e-learning.

As is often the case, however, being latecomers can be an advantage. It made it possible to avoid many of the misunderstandings and illusions that beset secondary schools (Gui, 2019), such as the idea that new technologies can by themselves transform teaching and even solve many of the problems encountered in recruiting students. We believe that a number of simple lessons supporting an evidence-based policy for *teaching innovation* can be learned from the experience gained in the Covid-19 semester:

1. In-person teaching is irreplaceable.
2. By themselves, the new digital platforms cannot renew and enrich teaching methods. On the contrary, unless faculty members are appropriately trained in their use, the new platforms created to encourage e-learning tend to impoverish teaching. They are entirely unproductive without mature reflection on educational architectures and teaching strategies that also bears the distinctive features of each learning environment in mind (distance teaching is one thing, hybrid teaching is another, and e-learning is yet another).
3. The universities' responses must be both national and local. In other words, there must be a national plan as well as university-level digital and e-learning projects. This calls on the one hand for an infrastructure investment programme, and on the other for specific attention to supporting faculty members' teaching skills.
4. The new technologies can help build on the 'good practices' for teaching innovation that are already at work in university classrooms. Many of these technologies, rather than replacing in-person teaching, can enrich it by facilitating more interactive and collaborative forms of teaching. Provided they are not used alone, but are supported by personnel measures, they can also help expand the pool of potential students and offer new approaches to lifelong education.

As we have seen, Italian faculty members' views of the post-emergency scene are highly polarized. Apart from that, it seems that the basic attitude that the survey brought to light is not dead set against the new teaching methods and technologies. Many respondents believe that they can help in achieving a

number of goals associated with the four priorities laid down in ET 2020, the strategic framework for European cooperation in education and training:
1. Make lifelong learning and mobility a reality
2. Improve the quality and efficiency of education and training
3. Promote equity, social cohesion, and active citizenship
4. Enhance creativity and innovation, including entrepreneurship, at all levels of education and training (EC, 2020c)

In the last few decades, digital technologies have brought profound changes in our daily lives, and in how we work, do business and interact with others. And they are also changing how we learn and teach. The pandemic and the resulting lockdown have undoubtedly heightened the widespread perception that digital technologies are becoming essential. In this respect, there is a significant gap between Europe and the more technologically advanced countries. A few years ago, the European Investment Bank estimated that the European Union's investments in education, research and infrastructures trailed behind the United States' by 190 billion euros per year (EIB, 2016; EC, 2020b).

Italy is lagging even further behind the rest of Europe in this connection, as can be seen from a glance at the European Commission's Digital Economy and Society Index, which ranks member states by level of digital performance (EC, 2020a). In 2020, Italy ranked 25th overall, 26th in citizens' use of internet services and online transactions, and was *in last place as regards human capital* (number of ICT graduates and ICT specialists, percentage of people with basic and advanced digital skills). These figures speak for themselves. Italian society and the Italian economy risk remaining on the analogue sidelines while the other European partners are seizing the new digital opportunities. The education system can make an essential contribution to narrowing this gap. *The university must not shirk this challenge.*

Notes

1 Our notion of 'distance teaching' largely coincides with what other authors call 'remote teaching', that is, 'a temporary shift of instructional delivery to an alternate delivery mode due to crisis circumstances [which] involves the use of fully remote teaching solutions for instruction or education that would otherwise be delivered face-to-face or as blended or hybrid courses and that will return to that format once the crisis or emergency has abated' (Hodges et al., 2020).
2 Further details are provided in the Appendix.
3 According to the 'dashboard' set up by the Conference of Italian University Rectors, as of March 24th 2020, 88% of the courses offered by the 82 surveyed Italian universities were already being held remotely (CRUI, 2020). As the IPSOS/Federica Web Learning survey

reported, 'while nearly half of the students had had no experience of digital learning at home before the pandemic, 88% now report that they have followed up to 5 online courses in the last three months' (IPSOS & Federica Web Learning, 2020).
4 University offices and personnel, school/department personnel, personnel in charge of degree programmes, associates and assistants (e.g., graduate students, fellowship holders, etc.), colleagues, non-professional networks (friends, family members, etc.), paid consultants and companies.
5 Universities were divided into three classes on the basis of the percentage of faculty members reporting that they were given no choice, as they had to follow instructions from their university or department.
6 According to the IPSOS/Federica Web Learning survey, 'More than three months after the universities closed and it was necessary to shift almost entirely to distance teaching, two out of three students gave the experience passing marks, with some reservations' and the students 'took, on the whole, a positive view of their university: over 70% rated response capacity and the timeliness, clarity and effectiveness of communication as sufficient' (IPSOS & Federica Web Learning, 2020).
7 According to the IPSOS/Federica Web Learning survey, 'Although a majority (four-fifths) of the sample feel that distance teaching can never match the classroom experience, over three-quarters of the students are convinced that teaching's digital transformation is irreversible. For the coming year, only 30% of undergraduates hope for a return to the pre-emergency situation, while the other two-thirds hope for a mixture of in-person and digital lectures, with greater opportunities for hybridizing the curriculum through open teaching' (IPSOS & Federica Web Learning, 2020).
8 According to the IPSOS/Federica Web Learning survey, 'Nine out of ten students reported hitches in following online classes. Connection problems still affected one-third of the interviewees, but most of the reported problems involved streamed lectures. Over half of the interviewed students mentioned difficulties arising from the instructors lack of experience with the particular register used in virtual communication (32%) and managing live-streamed material (26%)' (IPSOS & Federica Web Learning, 2020).
9 The four categories were determined from a factor analysis which is available on request.
10 The typology is the result of a factor analysis of in-person teaching methods prior to the lockdown, which is available on request.

References

Argyris, C., & Schön, D. (1978). *Organizational learning: A theory of action perspective*. Addison Wesley.

Arundel, A., Lorenz, E., Lundvall, B.-Å., & Valeyre, A. (2007). How Europe's economies learn: A comparison of work organization and innovation mode for the EU-15. *Industrial and Corporate Change, 16*(6), 1175–1210.

Bonaiuti, G. (2014). *Le strategie didattiche*. Carocci.

Burt, R. S. (1992). *Structural holes: The social structure of competition*. Harvard University Press.

CRUI. (2020, March 24). *Stato sulla didattica on-line al 24/3*. Conferenza dei Rettori delle Università Italiane, Roma.

Dee, J. R., & Leišyte, L. (2016). Organizational learning in higher education institutions: Theories, frameworks, and a potential research agenda. In M. B. Paulsen (Ed.), *Higher education: Handbook of theory and research* (pp. 275–348). Springer.

EC. (2020a). *Digital Economy and Society Index (DESI) 2020*. European Commission. https://digital-strategy.ec.europa.eu/en/policies/desi

EC. (2020b). *A Europe fit for the digital age: Towards a truly European digital society. Communication from the Commission to the European Parliament, the Council, the European Economic and Social Committee and the Committee of the Regions, Draft*. European Commission. https://www.euractiv.com/wp-content/uploads/sites/2/2020/02/Europe-fit-for-the-digital-age-LEAK.pdf

EC. (2020c). *European policy cooperation (ET 2020 framework)*. European Commission. https://web.archive.org/web/20200809223114/https://ec.europa.eu/education/policies/european-policy-cooperation/et2020-framework_en

EIB. (2016). *Restoring EU competitiveness.* Projects Directorate and the Economics Department of the European Investment Bank. https://www.eib.org/attachments/efs/restoring_eu_competitiveness_en.pdf

Granovetter, M. (2004). The impact of social structure on economic outcomes. *Journal of Economic Perspectives, 19*(3), 33–50.

Gui, M. (2019). *Il digitale a scuola. Rivoluzione o abbaglio?* Il Mulino.

Hodges, C., Moore, S., Lockee, B., Trust, T., & Bond, A. (2020, March 27). The difference between emergency remote teaching and online learning. *Educause Review*. https://er.educause.edu/articles/2020/3/the-difference-between-emergency-remote-teaching-and-online-learning

IPSOS & Federica Web Learning. (2020, June 15). *Indagine Ipsos e Federica Web Learning sugli studenti universitari e l'e-learning.* https://www.federica.eu/media/indagine-ipsos-federica-didattica-universitaria-futuro-ibrido/

Mousa, M., Abdelgaffar, H. A., Chaouali, W., & Aboramadan, M. (2020). Organizational learning, organizational resilience and the mediating role of multi-stakeholder networks: A study of Egyptian academics. *Journal of Workplace Learning, 32*(3), 161–181.

Perulli, A., Ramella, F., Rostan, M., & Semenza, R. (Eds.). (2018). *La terza missione degli accademici italiani.* Il Mulino.

Powley, E. H. (2009). Reclaiming resilience and safety: Resilience activation in the critical period of crisis. *Human Relations, 62*(9), 1289–1326.

Ramella, F. (2016). *Sociology of economic innovation.* Routledge.

Tucker, A. L., & Edmondson, A. C. (2003). Why hospitals don't learn from failures: Organizational and psychological dynamics that inhibit system change. *California Management Review, 45*(2), 55–72.

Appendix: Methodological Note

The nationwide survey of distance teaching during the Covid-19 emergency was carried out in June 2020 by contacting the same 15,000 academics at Italian state universities who had taken part in a 2016 survey on higher education's third mission (Perulli et al., 2018). These academics were asked to complete a questionnaire consisting of seven sections: the Covid-19 emergency and the suspension of in-person classes; distance teaching; preparing for distance teaching; the resources available for distance teaching; comparison with in-person teaching and assessment of the distance teaching experience; risks and opportunities for the future; respondents' personal and professional data.

The survey was coordinated by Francesco Ramella (Università di Torino) and Michele Rostan (Università di Pavia), while participants included Alessandro Caliandro, Flavio Ceravolo, Massimiliano Vaira (Università di Pavia) and Valentina Goglio, together with Anna Padoin and Antonella Rizzello (Università di Torino). Questionnaires were administered by the survey firm QuestLab using computer-assisted web interviewing (CAWI). Three invitations/reminders were sent, one of which was made possible by the cooperation of the heads of department at the 62 participating universities. A total of 3,398 valid questionnaires were collected, with a response rate of 23%. The differences between the theoretical and actual sample were quite limited. To take the different levels of coverage into account, weights ranging from a minimum of 0.67 and a maximum of 2.32 were applied.

CHAPTER 6

Young Europeans, Distance Learning and Trust in Educational Institutions

A Comparative Analysis after Covid-19

Diego Mesa

1   The Challenge of Covid-19 and the Digitization of European Education Systems

The contingent need to ensure didactic continuity even in moments of physical closure or reduction of access flows has led to an acceleration of the digitalization processes of education systems and a wide-ranging diffusion of distance learning practices. It has become more evident how digital inclusion pursued through distance learning is a factor of both social and educational inclusion (Livingstone et al., 2010).

Current literature identifies distance learning as the learning facilitated through the use of digital tools, contents and ICTs, which provides a wide spectrum implementation of online interaction and collaboration between the learners and their instructors or peers outside of a traditional classroom (Gurcan et al., 2020) in both online learning and remote learning mode (Bates, 2019).

From a theoretical point of view, distance learning is a strategic aspect of the broader process of implementing digital education and lifelong learning in the 'knowledge and information society'. (Anderson, 2008; Bell, 1980). Within this framework, digital education represents a powerful device for innovation (Pitzalis, 2016).

This line of development has been followed by most European states for several decades and, more recently, has been placed at the centre of European policy cooperation (EC, 2010; Union, 2014). From a perspective of the integrated development of innovation processes, digital education represents a strategic axis of EU policies in the fields of education and training designed to support action at the level of the Member States who remain responsible for these competence areas.[1] In the context of the pandemic, distance learning represented a way to 'survive in a time of crisis with all available resources, including offline and/or online' (Bozkurt et al., 2020, p. 2; Hodges et al., 2020). The emergency situation thus represented a strong lever for innovation towards distance learning. At the same time, it may also lead in the European context to increased inequalities in educational opportunities in a situation characterized by strong disparities in digitalization levels between countries, within countries, and between population groups (Elena-Bucea et al., 2020). As Colombo recalls, the fundamental challenge concerns the growth of educational opportunities for all: 'does digitalization in education make schools more inclusive, egalitarian and democratic, thus reducing all social gaps?' (2016, p. 7).

In the context of accelerating change imposed by the pandemic, the risk is that ICTs contribute to creating new inequalities rather than reducing existing ones. The term 'digital divide' is defined as differing levels of access to information, knowledge as well as skills, motivation, autonomy, and amount and types of internet usage (Attewell, 2001; Bonfadelli, 2002; Ghobadi et al., 2013). The research in the educational ICT field has highlighted the complexity and multilevel aspects of technology-based school innovations (Pandolfini, 2016; Di Pietro et al., 2020). The factors influencing the innovation processes (and the resulting educational opportunities) are located at different levels of the social systems.

At a macro-social level, the main drivers of change are European and national strategies. All European countries had national strategies in place to encourage the use of digital technology in different areas and 28 countries had adopted a digital strategy devoted specifically to education (EC/EACEA/Eurydice, 2019).

At a meso-social level, it is worth considering, on the one hand, the technological infrastructures that condition the possibility of operating on the network in terms of access to ICTs and speed of the internet connection, while on the other, the level of teachers in terms of their digital competencies, dispositions (habitus) and beliefs about ICTs and pedagogy (Pandolfini, 2013; De Feo et al., 2014).

At a micro-level, the factors contributing to the digital divide are students' different access to computers, the internet at home, family cultural capital (Bourdieu, 1984; Fraillon et al., 2014) and disparities in computer and internet use and digital skills (Wei & Hindman, 2011; Van Deursen & Van Dijk, 2014).

Starting from these considerations, this work intends to investigate, in a comparative perspective, the impact that the pandemic has had on the diffusion of distance learning in the case of Italy, a country in which this teaching practice was scarcely widespread before the health crisis and with a medium-low level of digital skills among the population. The impact on the young population (18–34 years old) was analysed in terms of the diffusion of the practice, the degree of satisfaction and the effects on the level of trust in school and university. Considering the factors linked to the access at distance learning at different levels (macro-meso-micro), this work also tried to understand if in this country the accelerated process of unplanned innovation has amplified or reduced equalities in educational opportunities.

2   The Drastic Shift to Distance Learning in the Italian Context

Italy was the first European country to adopt generalized lockdown measures. Subsequently, there was a continuous succession of measures providing for partial openings and closures, this time differentiated at a territorial level according to the degree of the spread of the infection.

The transition of schools and universities to distance learning is taking place unevenly across the territory and with different speeds of implementation. There are relevant contextual factors that condition the different degrees of use between regions (north, centre, Mezzogiorno), between schools as well as between different classrooms (Pandolfini, 2016).

The Italian case, therefore, represents a privileged observatory of the changes induced by the pandemic on the digitalization processes of education due to both the particularly long duration of the periods of interruption of face-to-face teaching in the upper secondary schools and universities, as well as the extensive nature of the use of distance learning throughout the national territory. The third element of interest is due to the relative backwardness in which Italy was in this area compared to the main European countries before the pandemic at different levels of the education system.

At the macro-social level, although the Italian government has long since launched interventions and investments for the development of ICTs in schools (the first national plan for ICT in education dates back to 1985: the 'National Plan for Informatics'), the digitalization process presents significant shortcomings compared to the European average.

At the meso-social level, in primary and secondary schools, Italy ranks last among the Member States due to the insufficient level and speed of internet connectivity.[2] While virtually all schools have an internet connection (95.4% [MIUR, 2019]), only 26.9% have a high-speed connection, well below the EU average of 47%. Insufficient internet access is reported by 43% of school leaders (OECD, 2019). In addition to the gaps in the country's digital infrastructure policies, one of the causes of the uneven diffusion of ICTs is the particular governance structure of education, which provides for interventions and responsibilities shared between the state, regions and local authorities.[3] Regarding the level of digital skills of the teaching staff, as a recent survey on Italian primary and secondary school teachers notes, only a minority of the teachers are characterized by a 'technology expert' attitude and work assiduously on the development of innovative methodologies and transversal digital skills (Buffardi et al., 2021, p. 129). Universities also suffer a significant delay in the digitization process compared to the international scenario for reasons that are partly common, partly different from schools: (1) the lack of autonomy that has characterized the Italian higher education system; (2) the negative perception of the introduction of technology in education considered more alienating than the traditional didactic relationship; and (3) the habit of associating online courses with private online universities, perceived as providers of lower quality education. Before the pandemic, the application of distance learning was in a preliminary phase, characterized by a bottom-up path and based on the adoption of non-institutionalized good practices that aimed precisely at supporting traditional courses, rarely replacing them (Appolloni et al., 2021). With the lockdown, universities have autonomously organized distance learning by choosing different platforms and technological solutions.

At the micro-level, according to the national statistical office, in 2019 over 12% of children aged between six and seventeen lived in families with no PC or tablet (rising to almost one-fifth in the south), and only 6% lived in families with at least one PC per person. In addition, four out of ten children lived in overcrowded conditions (Istat, 2020).

3   Young People's Views on Education and ICT

The critical issues related to digitalization represent only one of the problematic nodes of the Italian education system, a system in which the rate of young graduates is among the lowest in Europe, and the share of early school leavers, although progressively decreasing, remains among the highest in the EU countries.[4]

The persistence of structural problems despite the numerous reforms, and their impact on the school-to-work transition paths of young Italians, has favoured the development of surveys aimed at gathering not only the perspective of policymakers, managers and teachers but also the experiences and points of view of those who are the main beneficiaries of the education system: young people (Istituto Toniolo, 2013, 2014, 2016, 2017, 2018, 2019, 2020a). What emerged before the pandemic as a transversal feature from a comparative survey carried out with Italian, French, German, Spanish and British young people is not an underestimation of the traditional institutional aims of schools – cultural formation, cognitive development and socialization – but rather the need to combine these objectives with the promotion of more properly enabling skills on the professional and work-related fronts (Mesa & Triani, 2018). This position, which is widely shared, is emphasized more strongly by young people of the Mediterranean area, such as Italians and Spaniards, whose school-to-work transition regimes are more problematic and less supported by active labour policies (Cavalli et al., 1996; Walther, 2006). Young Italians are on average more critical of teachers' skills, in particular regarding their ability to adapt to new situations, problem-solving and actively involving students. They are also those who feel most strongly that their school system needs to change in the direction of a school that is didactically more dynamic, organizationally more flexible and, from the point of view of the curriculum, richer in proposals, with a broad international outlook and a strong push towards digitalization (Mesa & Triani, 2018). Continuing this direction of research, it was decided to return to collect the views of young people by checking what has changed in their representation of school and university in the aftermath of the pandemic.

4 Data and Methods

As mentioned in the introductory part, the research aimed to study in greater detail the following questions:
1. What impact has the pandemic had on the spread of distance learning among young Italians compared to young people from the other countries analysed?
2. How did the young Italians assess this form of alternative education in the emergency phase and how did it change their trust in educational institutions? Are there any differences between young people in other countries?
3. Regarding the different access factors (at the macro-meso-micro levels), has the spread of distance learning led to an increase or decrease in the equality of educational opportunities in the Italian context?

The following hypotheses were made concerning these statements:
1. The more drastic closure of Italian schools and universities has accelerated the digitization processes, reducing the digital divide with other countries.
2. Young Italians who have experimented with distance learning for the first time during the pandemic express more polarized judgements (positive or negative) than young people in other countries.

3. The process of accelerated digitization has increased inequalities in educational opportunities due to territorial areas, technological dotation and human resources of the schools, family background and socio-economic conditions.

The study is based on data from two surveys. The first is an international survey on the state of the new generations in the age of the coronavirus and on post-pandemic expectations, which was funded by the Osservatorio Giovani dell'Istituto Giuseppe Toniolo di Studi Superiori and conducted by Ipsos (a multinational market research and consulting firm) between March 27th and April 7th 2020 (Istituto Toniolo, 2020b). For each country, a stratified and random sample was selected, representative of young people aged 18 to 34, according to gender, age group, educational qualification, employment status and geographical area of residence. The sample number reached was 2,000 cases for Italy and 1,000 cases for each of the other four countries. The interviews were conducted using the CAWI methodology (online interviews).[5]

A comparison was made between the Italian sample and that of the other countries on the following variables:
− Whether or not distance learning has been used (four response modes)
− The degree of satisfaction with distance learning (self-anchoring scale − ten response modes)
− The change in confidence in school and university after the pandemic (three response modes)
− Frequency of use of other digital resources (Likert scales − four response modes)

The second database was created by a national survey promoted by the same institutions between November 9th and 24th 2020 (Istituto Toniolo, 2021). Again the representative sample of young people aged 18 to 34 was stratified by gender, age group, educational qualification, employment status and geographical area of residence. The sample number is 7,012 cases. In this case, the interviews were conducted using the CAWI methodology (online interviews).

A comparison was made of the responses regarding the use of and satisfaction with distance learning of the samples of young Italians of the first and second surveys to verify the deviations over seven months.

Logistical regression was also carried out to assess the effect of contextual factors (territorial areas, conditions of schools and teachers, family conditions) and individual (status ascribed and acquired), the use of distance learning before and after the pandemic and the overall satisfaction related to distance learning.

YOUNG EUROPEANS, DISTANCE LEARNING AND TRUST 157

5 Results

5.1 Use of Distance Learning in the European Scenario

In the current context, distance learning represents an important resource for the expansion of learning opportunities as well as its potential to implement digital skills, considered by the European Commission a key element of inclusive and sustainable economic growth, along with the creation of new jobs and the support of innovation (Council of the European Union, 2018). In this perspective, the degree of diffusion of the use of distance learning among young people was investigated (Table 6.1).

The data collected highlight the significant impact that the pandemic had on the spread of this tool among young people in all the countries analysed. Before Covid-19, less than 50% of young people in all the countries experienced distance learning: just over four out of ten in Spain, three out of ten in the United Kingdom and two out of ten in Germany and France. Italian young people accounted for less than two out of ten (18.4%). If for the latter, the experience of distance learning was therefore rather limited before March 2020, it is precisely in Italy – which was the first European country to have closed schools and universities and one of those in which the closure period

TABLE 6.1   The use of distance learning by country (percentage values)

	April 2020[a]					November 2020[b]
	UK	Germany	France	Spain	Italy	Italy
Yes, even before the coronavirus emergency	14.4	11.2	12.6	22.5	9.0	7.5
Yes, I started because of the coronavirus emergency	20.5	24.1	20.0	24.9	32.6	36.2
No, I've used it/them in the past, but I don't any more	16.1	13.9	10.6	20.1	9.4	11.4
No, neither in the past nor today	49.0	50.8	56.8	32.5	49.0	44.9
Total	100.0	100.0	100.0	100.0	100.0	100.0

a N = 6000
b N = 7012

lasted the longest – that the greatest step forward in the use of this tool was recorded, with an increase of over 30% of young users. In the other countries, there is a significant increase of between 20% and 25%, with a greater incidence in Spain. The overall effect is that of a tendency to realign the quota of young people who have never had any experience of teaching to around 50% of those interviewed, except the Spanish, where this quota is reduced to just over a third of the sample. As far as young Italians are concerned, the data from the September 2020 national survey confirm the trend with a further increase, a few months later, in the number of new users and a significant decrease in the proportion of young people who have never had any experience of distance learning.

The analysis of the profiles of the users allows to highlight common aspects and specificities regarding the opportunities offered by distance learning in the different countries (Table 6.2).

Gender seems to have a significant influence only among young Spaniards and especially among Germans, with males making greater use of distance learning in both cases. In the young people of the other three countries, there are no significant gender differences.

Age, on the other hand, is a discriminating factor for all the sub-samples. The relatively recent nature of the phenomenon means that its prevalence is greater among younger cohorts, penalizing in this respect respondents from older age cohorts. Amongst the 31–34 age group, only the Spanish exceed the 50% threshold of distance learning users, whilst amongst the 27–30 age group, in addition to the Spanish, there are also the Germans. Italians and young people in the UK exceed 50% from the 23–26 age group. In the 18–22 age group, the threshold is also exceeded by young French people, who, together with the Italians, are those in which the gap in use between the age cohorts is greatest. Compared to the Italian case, the October national survey shows a further increase in the difference in the use of distance learning between the age cohorts due to the greater use by the 18–22 age group, i.e. young people attending the last year of upper secondary and the early years of tertiary education.

The educational qualification represents a differentiating factor in the use of distance learning for all the countries, but is more accentuated in Spain and Germany, where the differences in experience between young people with high and low qualifications are greater. In all the cases, young people with tertiary education have more experience of distance learning than young people with lower educational qualifications. Except for young people in the UK, young people with an upper secondary education also have more experience than the respondents with lower educational qualifications. In interpreting this data, two dynamics must be taken into account. Firstly, the use of distance learning is more widespread in higher education institutions. Secondly, a high

TABLE 6.2 The use of distance learning by gender, age, educational attainment and main activity by country (use today or in the past; percentage values)

	April 2020[a]					November 2020[b]
	UK	Germany	France	Spain	Italy	Italy
Gender						
Male	50.8	54.1	44.2	70.0	51.9	55.7
Female	51.2	43.6	42.3	64.9	50.0	54.4
Age						
18–22 years	64.2	61.7	77	74.4	77.3	85.6
23–26 years	54.9	52.4	42.7	76.6	55.4	59.9
27–30 years	46.9	50.4	29.7	66.0	43.5	45.0
31–34 years	42.9	36.9	33.0	57.5	36.7	39.1
Educational attainment						
Primary and low secondary education (ISCED 1–2)	55.2	33.0	33.9	45.6	46.8	48.2
Upper secondary education (ISCED 3)	44.6	50.7	40.5	70.8	49.5	55.9
Tertiary education (ISCED 4–5–6–7)	57.1	58.2	49.5	83.2	59.3	61.4
Main activity						
Only student	71.3	65.6	78.8	80.4	84.2	92.7
Student worker	78.5	71.4	76.1	86.7	72.4	74.3
Only worker	42.7	34.8	30.5	61.5	33	29.4
NEET	42.9	36.5	25.8	49.4	32	25.1

a N = 6,000
b N = 7,012

educational qualification implies a longer stay in the school context with a higher probability of exposure, along the way, to distance learning activities.

Regarding the study/work conditions of the young people surveyed, there is a clear distinction in all the countries in the experience between young people who are still in education and young people who have completed their studies. Between full-time students and student workers, there are slight differences, sometimes in favour of the former, as in the case of France and Italy, sometimes in favour of the latter, as in the case of the UK, France and Germany. In the Italian case, the gap between students and student workers widened between the April and October 2020 surveys. Among the young people who have already left the school circuit, there are insignificant differences between workers and young people not engaged in education, employment or training (NEETs), except in Spain, where more than six out of ten young workers have experience of distance learning, while NEETs do not reach the 50% mark.

5.2 Degree of Satisfaction with Distance Learning

The previous question allowed to explore the structure of opportunities that in each country is associated with this form of learning. The next question considers the outcomes of the use of distance learning from the subjective point of view of the users. The young people who were using distance learning at the time of the survey were asked to express their degree of satisfaction on a range from 1 (not at all satisfied) to 10 (very satisfied). Table 6.3 shows the average levels of satisfaction by country.

In all the countries, the degree of satisfaction expressed by young people is moderately positive, with very similar average values for Italy, Spain and the UK. They are slightly lower in the cases of Germany and France. However, the variance of the answers is rather high. This means that a significant proportion of the respondents expressed a level of satisfaction that was less than sufficient. The dissatisfied ones are 30.7% of the total sample. The highest value of dissatisfaction is expressed by young Germans with 36.9% of the evaluations below 6, while the lowest share of dissatisfaction is recorded among Italians, with 26.2% of the respondents. Comparing the answers of those who used distance learning before the pandemic with those who started after it, a clear deterioration of

TABLE 6.3 Satisfaction of distance learning (DL) by country (mean and st. dev.)

		April 2020[a]					November 2020[b]
		UK	Germany	France	Spain	Italy	Italy
All users of DL	Mean	6.61	6.34	6.24	6.62	6.67	6.60
	St. dev.	2.071	2.287	2.259	2.383	2.124	2.229
Started using DL before Covid-19	Mean	7.23	6.89	6.75	7.21	6.75	7.16
	St. dev.	1.741	2.309	2.291	2.311	2.236	2.403
Started using DL after Covid-19	Mean	6.18	6.09	5.93	6.09	6.65	6.49
	St. dev.	2.177	2.236	2.185	2.326	2.093	2.173

a N = 2,333
b N = 3,064

the level of satisfaction among new users emerges, except for the Italian case in which the differences in evaluation are very small. The national survey of October 2020 shows, a few months after the previous survey, a slight decrease in the overall level of satisfaction due to a worsening of the evaluations of the young people who started to use distance learning after the beginning of the pandemic.

Observing the distribution of the levels of satisfaction in the different profiles (Table 6.4), it is possible to highlight only in two countries – Germany and France – gender differences with slightly more positive judgements from females.

TABLE 6.4 Satisfaction of distance learning (DL) by gender, age and educational attainment by country (mean and st. dev.)

		April 2020[a]					November 2020[b]
		UK	Germany	France	Spain	Italy	Italy
Gender							
Male	Mean	6.55	6.26	6.16	6.61	6.65	6.52
	St. dev.	2.099	2.180	2.411	2.316	2.016	2.306
Female	Mean	6.68	6.45	6.33	6.63	6.70	6.69
	St. dev.	2.047	2.426	2.101	2.454	2.232	2.147
Age							
18–22 years	Mean	6.36	5.81	6.15	6.08	6.58	6.21
	St. dev.	2.171	2.355	2.239	2.428	2.190	2.405
23–26 years	Mean	6.58	6.22	6.52	6.55	6.76	6.85
	St. dev.	2.136	2.208	1.995	2.411	2.110	2.084
27–30 years	Mean	6.80	6.32	6.25	7.20	6.77	6.97
	St. dev.	1.871	2.376	2.502	2.169	1.958	2.048
31–34 years	Mean	6.82	7.05	6.11	6.60	6.59	6.53
	St. dev.	2.062	2.058	2.388	2.425	2.205	2.185
Educational attainment							
Primary and low secondary education (ISCED 1–2)	Mean	4.99	6.10	5.46	6.22	6.56	6.23
	St. dev.	1.462	2.681	2.528	2.353	2.243	2.578
Upper secondary education (ISCED 3)	Mean	6.81	6.28	6.14	6.49	6.67	6.65
	St. dev.	1.902	2.249	2.370	2.484	2.084	2.127
Tertiary education (ISCED 4-5-6-7)	Mean	6.93	6.63	6.57	6.88	6.78	6.81
	St. dev.	2.152	2.204	1.989	2.285	2.093	2.085

a N = 2,333
b N = 3,064

Age has the greatest influence on satisfaction. In all the countries, the most critical opinions are expressed by the respondents in the 18–22 age group, which includes the largest number of young people who began using distance learning after the start of the pandemic. It is in the 27–30 and 31–34 age cohorts that the highest levels of satisfaction are recorded. Amongst Italians in the 18–22 age bracket, the degree of satisfaction, which is on average higher than in the other countries, fell considerably in the October survey, while it increased in the assessments of the intermediate age cohorts (23–26 and 27–30).

A higher educational qualification, as well as offering greater opportunities to access the experience of distance learning, also leads to a higher level of satisfaction. The biggest gap between young people with a low qualification and young people with tertiary education is in the UK and France, to a lesser extent in Germany and Spain. In the Italian case, the gap, which was very small in the international survey, increases in the subsequent survey due to a twofold effect of a reduction in the degree of satisfaction among young people with low qualifications and an increase among those with high qualifications.

5.3 *Distance Learning and Other Ways of Using Digital Resources*

The differences in the profiles of users and non-users of distance learning about certain ways of consulting and finding information on the internet were considered (Table 6.5) to obtain an indication of how the experience of distance learning can be associated with actual disparities in the use of computers and the internet (Wei & Hindman, 2011; Van Deursen & Van Dijk, 2014).

In all the sub-samples, albeit with different intensities, the frequency of online behaviour outlines a common hierarchy ranging from the frequent use of social networks, which represents the mainstream activity, to the consultation of apps and websites of official newspapers and institutions, up to the consultation of discussion forums and blogs, which represents a niche behaviour. The greater recourse of young Italians to the use of social and various digital information channels can be partly explained by the fact that during the survey phase Italy was the country most affected by the impact of the pandemic and the restrictions imposed by the government. Comparing the profiles of those who have had an experience of distance learning and those who have not, there are small differences in the use of social networks, while the gap increases in the other modes of consultation, especially in the case of young Spaniards, Germans and French. Having experienced structured forms of distance learning, therefore, seems to exert a positive influence on the ability to make a more sophisticated and extensive use of the digital resources available.

TABLE 6.5   Frequency of consulting apps/websites/social networks/forums and blogs by use of distance learning and country (very or fairly frequent use; percentage values)

	UK	Germany	France	Spain	Italy
Frequent use of social networks					
Users of distance learning	74.5	70.3	76.2	86.8	86.0
Not users of distance learning	78.6	67.2	78.0	82.8	87.6
Frequent consultation of official media apps and websites					
Users of distance learning	49.6	55.6	55.8	57.9	72.8
Not users of distance learning	43.1	43.4	44.4	34.8	66.2
Frequent consultation of apps and institutional websites					
Users of distance learning	41.6	45.2	40.7	40.2	67.2
Not users of distance learning	31.2	28.9	28.7	21.2	59.8
Frequent consultation of forums/blogs and other discussion spaces					
Users of distance learning	29.4	33.2	34.7	35.9	49.2
Not users of distance learning	18.0	15.3	20.1	23.1	36.2

Note: N = 6,000

5.4   *Trust in School and University in the Time of Covid-19*

The emergence of the Covid-19 crisis does not seem to produce, at least in the short term, any drastic changes in trust in school and university that young people in the various countries have (Table 6.6).

In all the countries, especially France, the UK and Germany, the absolute majority of the respondents declare that their trust in the education system remains unchanged. However, considering the differences between those who have lost trust and those for who it has increased, the balance is significantly negative in the cases of Germany, Spain and France, while in the UK and Italy the young people who have increased their level of trust prevail. Distinguishing the answers according to the profiles of the users/not users of distance learning, a greater polarization of the answers both in a positive and negative sense is evident in the profiles of the users. The differences between increase and decrease in the trust are relatively similar to the trend of the overall sample both for users and not users. In the Italian case, there is the highest level of increase of trust among the users of distance learning, while among the not-users the level of trust remains substantially unchanged.

TABLE 6.6 Trust in school and university by use of distance learning and country (percentage values)

	April 2020				
	UK	Germany	France	Spain	Italy
Changes in trust in school and university (overall sample)					
Increased	18.9	14.9	12.3	19.2	21.2
Remained the same	66.6	65.9	70.1	59.3	61.9
Decreased	14.5	19.2	17.6	21.5	16.9
Trust in school and university (users of DL)					
Increased	20.6	20.3	16.4	22.0	28.0
Remained the same	61.9	56.1	59.5	54.4	53.2
Decreased	17.5	23.6	24.1	23.5	18.8
Trust in school and university (not users of DL)					
Increased	17.1	9.6	9.1	13.5	14.2
Remained the same	71.5	75.4	78.0	69.5	70.9
Decreased	11.4	14.9	12.8	16.9	14.9

Note: N = 6,000

5.5 Use of and Satisfaction with Distance Learning (DL) in the Italian Case

After describing the different degrees of diffusion of and satisfaction with distance learning among young people in the five European countries most affected in the first phase of the pandemic, the chapter is concluded by commenting on the data of a logistic regression carried out on the Italian sample of the November 2020 survey.

The logistic regression was carried out to estimate the effects of the use of distance learning (1) before Covid-19 and (2) after Covid-19 and (3) the satisfaction with distance learning of a set of variables. In the order in which they are reported in Table 6.7, the independent variables considered are indicative of the following dimensions: individual ascribed (age, gender) and acquired characteristics (study/work status, educational attainment), characteristics of the family context (parents' educational qualification, material deprivation index), characteristics of the school context attended (technological

TABLE 6.7   Independent variables included in logistic regression

Independent variables	%
Age	
18–22 years (reference)	19.4
23–26 years	25.4
27–30 years	27.9
31–34 years	27.3
Gender	
Male (reference)	51.3
Female	48.7
Main activity	
Only student (reference)	34.3
Student & worker	10.6
Only worker	37.2
NEET	18.0
Educational attainment	
Tertiary education (ISCED 4–5–6–7) (reference)	22.2
Upper secondary education (ISCED 3)	50.6
Primary and low secondary education (ISCED 1–2)	27.2
Educational attainment of parents	
Both have a tertiary degree (ISCED 4–5–6–7) (reference)	10.5
One of them has a tertiary degree (ISCED 4–5–6–7)	13.5
At least one of them has a secondary school diploma (ISCED 3)	50.4
Neither of them have secondary school diploma (ISCED 3)	25.6
Material deprivation	
Absence of material deprivation (reference)	55.5
Presence of one or more situations of material deprivation	44.5
Technological equipment of the secondary school attended	
Positive assessment 1–5 (reference)	38.8
Negative assessment 6–10	61.2
Technological skills secondary school teachers	
Little or not at all widespread (reference)	53.5
Very or fairly widespread	46.5
Territorial areas	
South and islands (reference)	38.1
Centre	19.2
North-west	24.7
North-east	17.8

Note: N = 7,012

equipment and technological skills of secondary school teachers) and territorial context (macro-areas).

Table 6.8 shows the results of three logistic regressions. In the first regression, the dependent variable considered is represented by those who have only used distance learning in the past before Covid-19. In the second regression, young people who currently use distance learning are considered. In the third regression, the dependent variable is given by the young people who use distance learning currently and declared a good level of satisfaction (ratings between 6 and 10).

As highlighted above, only one out of ten young Italians (11.4%) had resorted to distance learning before the pandemic without continuing it in the following period. On the other hand, 43.7% of the young people at the time of the interview were doing distance learning activities (7.5% had started before the pandemic; 36.2% after). Age does not affect past users but does affect current users. Young people aged 18–22 are more likely to be among current users than other age cohorts. Women are less likely to be among past users and more likely to be among current users, in contrast to student-workers, workers and NEETs who are more likely than students to be among past users. The low cultural background of parents negatively affects both the probability of having experienced distance learning in the past and the probability of doing so in the present. The situation of material deprivation significantly increases the probability that distance learning, if experienced in the past, has not been carried on in the present. As far as the support offered by the high school is concerned, the good technological equipment of the school is a highly predictive factor for the use of distance learning in the past, but it is not very significant in the present, since most of the students are engaged in university studies. Having had teachers with good technological skills, on the other hand, influences both the probability of having used distance learning in the past and the probability of having used it in the present. At a territorial level, those who live in the north-west area are less likely to have used distance learning in the past, while those who live in the north-east are less likely to have experienced it in the present. Finally, considering the data of the third regression, it emerges that age is the only individual variable that affects satisfaction. Satisfaction is at its lowest in the 18–22 age group and reaches its peak among the respondents aged 27–30. The situation of material deprivation negatively affects satisfaction, while good equipment and technological skills in secondary school increase the level of satisfaction. Among the territorial areas, young people in the centre and the north-west are less appreciated, while young people in the south and the islands are more satisfied with distance learning.

TABLE 6.8 Results of logistic regression models of use of distance learning in the past, use in the current phase and satisfaction with distance learning

Independent variables	Past use of distance learning	Actual use of distance learning	Satisfied with distance learning
Age			
18–22 years (reference)			
23–26 years	−.083	−.562***	.572***
27–30 years	.053	−.643***	.830***
31–34 years	.044	−.522***	.417**
Gender			
Male (reference)			
Female	−.225***	.139**	.080
Main activity			
Only student (reference)			
Student & worker	.660***	−1.381***	−.002
Only worker	.555***	−3.229***	−.252
NEET	.332**	−3.218***	−.276
Educational attainment			
Tertiary education (ISCED 4-5-6-7) (reference)			
Upper secondary education (ISCED 3)	−.133	−.351***	−.057
Primary and Low secondary education (ISCED 1-2)	.173	−.486***	.118
Educational attainment of parents			
Both have a tertiary degree (ISCED 4-5-6-7) (reference)			
One of them has a tertiary degree (ISCED 4-5-6-7)	−.171	−.131	.049
At least one of them has a secondary school diploma (ISCED 3)	−.580***	−.147	.158
Neither of them have secondary school diploma (ISCED 3)	−.427***	−.275**	−.045
Material deprivation			
Absence of material deprivation (reference)			
Presence of one or more situations of material deprivation	.795***	−.006	−.324***

(cont.)

TABLE 6.8 Results of logistic regression models of use of distance learning in the past, use in the current phase and satisfaction with distance learning (*cont.*)

Independent variables	Past use of distance learning	Actual use of distance learning	Satisfied with distance learning
Technological equipment of the secondary school attended			
Positive assessment 1–5 (reference)			
Negative assessment 6–10	.507***	.019	.806***
Technological skills secondary school teachers			
Little or not at all widespread (reference)			
Very or fairly widespread	.183**	.173**	.262**
Territorial areas			
South and islands (reference)			
Centre	−.152	.040	−.251**
North-west	−.259**	.018	−.202*
North-east	.068	−.330***	−.179
Constant	−2.768	2.439	.380
N	7,012	7,012	3,504

***$p < 0.01$, **$p < 0.05$, *$p < 0.1$

6 Conclusions

The results highlight some aspects of the processes of change taking place in European education systems and, in particular, in Italy.

Compared to the first question concerning the impact of the pandemic, the data confirm that the use of forms of distance learning has increased greatly in all the countries considered, with an overall effect of reducing the gap between the various systems. The greatest effort in terms of activation has been made by the Italian education system, in which before Covid-19 young people had fewer opportunities to experience formal education of this kind than their peers in other countries. The process of technological development and the forced 'reconversion' of the teaching staff towards a teaching method more open to the use of new technologies, which has been underway for decades, have undergone a traumatic acceleration in the emergency of a prolonged lockdown, configuring a sort of de facto reform of education methods and practices. An emblematic sign of the resilience and, at the same time, of the fragility of the Italian education system, distance learning became the chosen ground for an experiment that continued in the following academic year, further expanding the number of young people who took part in it.

For the second question, concerning the assessment of distance learning and trust in educational institutions by the respondents, the majority of young people in all the countries showed a generally positive approach, in line with the previous surveys that highlighted openness to change, the desire for more dynamic education systems open to innovations also in a work perspective (Mesa & Triani, 2018). However, there is no shortage of critical points. More than a third of the overall sample gave less than adequate marks for distance learning, particularly the Germans and the French. In all the countries, the most critical are the young people in the 18–22 age group who attend upper secondary school, most of whom began experimenting with distance learning during the pandemic. Compared to other countries, the response of young Italians to the start of the pandemic tended to be more positive in terms of satisfaction with distance learning. The recourse to this didactic mode was probably interpreted by many of them as a sign of reactivity of the educational system, also confirmed by the average higher level of trust in the school and university expressed at the very moment when access to the classrooms was banned. However, in the space of a few months, the level of satisfaction among the youngest fell considerably, approaching that expressed by their peers in other countries, a sign of growing difficulty in coping with the continuation of the emergency condition. The disorientation and adjustment difficulties experienced by education systems did not lead to a drastic change in confidence attitudes in the short term. However, among young people who have experienced distance learning, there is a greater polarization – especially in Italy – between those who are confident and those who are distrustful, between those who have experienced at first hand the fibrillations of the system, have intensely felt all its limits and iniquities, and those who, on the other hand, have recognized its practical and symbolic value despite everything: a sign of resilience and resistance of the educational system.

The third question concerns the effect of these changes in terms of the increase or reduction in the equality of educational opportunities. The analysis of the Italian case shows that not all the categories of young people, were involved in the same way in this growth of the digital learning ecosystem (Uden et al., 2007). The vast spread of distance learning has mainly affected younger cohorts (18–22 years), progressively reducing the gender gap in favour of women. Worker-students, who could have benefited more from access to more flexible forms of education, were less involved than full-time students. In other countries, the gap between the two categories is much smaller. Workers and especially the NEETs, young people not engaged in education, employment or training, a large segment of the population in Italy whose risk of social exclusion has been amplified during the pandemic, had even fewer opportunities.

Taking into account the educational profiles, the increase in opportunities has mainly concerned young people with the highest levels of education, who also show greater skills in the use of the internet and social media in an extra-curricular context. What can represent in a sense a virtuous circle of development and maturation of digital competencies, if observed from the perspective of young people with less education and low family cultural capital, represents a further factor of digital exclusion if adequate compensatory measures are not adopted.

The data also highlighted in the Italian context the persistent influence of the cultural capital of the family of origin. In particular, the low level of education of the parents acts as a brake. On the other hand, the influence of material deprivation on participation in distance learning has been reduced, although it remains one of the factors that most affects the level of satisfaction.

The technological equipment of upper secondary schools can make a difference in terms of approach to the experience of distance learning, while learning guided by teachers with good digital skills is a predictor of the possibility of satisfactory experiences even in higher orders of education. In light of this evidence, the significant digital gap in Italy among different schools in different territorial areas and the digital competence gap among teachers represent an even more critical factor in terms of equality of learning opportunities on which it is urgent to intervene.

In conclusion, the results show how the process of digital education in the Italian context is entering a new phase with a growing impact on the functioning of teaching, on the processes of innovation in education systems and on the learning dynamics of the youth population. Despite the emergent nature of these changes, the young Italians welcomed the challenge with confidence and positively. However, to avoid the risk of the emergency becoming chronic and to reduce the impact of digital innovation on the most disadvantaged groups, it is necessary to work on an integrated planning of the education system capable of consolidating the innovation process by orienting it towards an increase in educational opportunities for all.

Notes

1 The first digital education action plan, developed by the European Commission in 2018, reflects the dual need for the pedagogical use of technologies and development of digital competence through its two main priorities: (1) making better use of digital technology for teaching and learning and (2) developing relevant digital competence and skills for the digital transformation. In addition, the latest digital education action plan (2021–2027) establishes a further fundamental goal which at the same time constitutes a prerequisite for the realization of the two previous objectives: the development of a high-performing digital education ecosystem for changing society and the transition to a green and digital economy.
2 https://op.europa.eu/webpub/eac/education-and-training-monitor-2020/en/index.html
3 As the OECD notes in an in-depth study on this issue, 'in Italy, school buildings are built and maintained under the responsibility of local governments (provinces for upper secondary schools, and municipalities for primary and lower secondary schools): some communes and provinces made broadband access and cabling a priority in the context of school renovation or building projects. Moreover, schools are granted significant administrative autonomy, and can raise funds from private non-profit organizations or from local authorities to improve their infrastructure' (Avvisati et al., 2013, p. 15).
4 The share of young people aged 30–34 with a university or tertiary degree is 27.9%, compared to 42.1% of the European average, second to last in the ranking before Romania (25.2%) and 14 points behind Europe. In the second quarter of 2020, 13.5% of 18–24 year-olds left education at a very early age (early school leavers), a figure that is stable compared to the second quarter of 2019. The share of those not in education or employment (NEETs) among 15–29 year-olds remains high and is increasing again after several years of decline to 23.9% of young people in the second quarter of 2020 (21.2% in the second quarter of 2019) (Istat, 2021).
5 The use of a web-based survey methodology may have caused problems in covering the share of respondents who do not have adequate digital skills. The percentage of those who have never experienced distance learning may be underestimated.

References

Anderson, R. E. (2008). Implications of the information and knowledge society for education. In J. Voogt & G. Knezek (Eds.), *International handbook of information technology in primary and secondary education* (pp. 5–22). Springer.

Appolloni, A., Colasanti, N., Fantauzzi, C., Fiorani, G., & Frondizi, R. (2021). Distance learning as a resilience strategy during Covid-19: An analysis of the Italian context. *Sustainability, 13*(3), 1388.

Attewell, P. (2001). The first and second digital divides. *Sociology of Education, 74*(3), 252–259.

Avvisati, F., Hennessy, S., Kozma, R. B., & Vincent-Lancrin, S. (2013). *Review of the Italian strategy for digital schools*. OECD Education Working Papers, No. 90. OECD Publishing. https://www.oecd.org/education/ceri/Innovation%20Strategy%20Working%20Paper%2090.pdf

Bates, A. W. (Tony). (2019). *Teaching in a digital age: Guidelines for designing teaching and learning for a digital age* (2nd ed.). Tony Bates Associates, Ltd. https://pressbooks.bccampus.ca/teachinginadigitalagev2/

Bell, D. (1980). The social framework of the information society. In T. Forester (Ed.), *The microelectronics revolution: The complete guide to the new technology and its impact on society* (pp. 533–545). Basil Blackwell.

Bonfadelli, H. (2002). The internet and knowledge gaps: A theoretical and empirical investigation. *European Journal of Communication, 17*(1), 65–84.

Bourdieu, P. (1984). *Distinction: A social critique of the judgment of taste.* Routledge.

Bozkurt, A., Xiao, F., Jung, I., & Vladimirshi, V. A. (2020). Global outlook to the interruption of education due to COVID-19 pandemic: Navigating in a time of uncertainty and crisis. *Asian Journal of Distance Education, 15*, 1–126.

Buffardi, A., Calzone, S., Mazza, C., & Taddeo, G. (2021). What do Italian students and teachers ask about digital? Data and reflections from schools participating in national operational programs. *Italian Journal of Sociology of Education, 13*(1).

Cavalli, A., & Galland, O. (Eds.). (1996). *Senza fretta di crescere. L'ingresso difficile nella vita adulta.* Liguori.

Colombo, M. (2016). Introduction to the special section: The digitalization of educational practices: How much and what kind? *Italian Journal of Sociology of Education, 8*(2).

Council of the European Union. (2018). *Council recommendation on key competences for lifelong learning.*

De Feo, A., & Pitzalis, M. (2014). Arrivano le LIM! Rappresentazioni e pratiche degli insegnanti all'avvio della scuola digitale. *Scuola democratica, 1*, 97–115.

Di Pietro, G., Biagi, F., Costa, P., Karpiński, Z., & Mazza, J. (2020). *The likely impact of COVID-19 on education: Reflections based on the existing literature and recent international datasets.* Publications Office of the European Union. doi:10.2760/126686

Elena-Bucea, A., Cruz-Jesus, F., Oliveira, T., & Coelho, P. S. (2020). Assessing the role of age, education, gender and income on the digital divide: Evidence for the European Union. *Information Systems Frontiers, 23*, 1007–1021. https://doi.org/10.1007/s10796-020-10012-9

EC. (2010). *A digital agenda for Europe.* European Commission. Publications Office of the European Union.

EC. (2018). *Communication from the Commission to the European Parliament, the Council, the European Economic and Social Committee and the Committee of the Regions. On the digital education action plan.* European Commission. Publications Office of the European Union.

EC. (2020). *Digital education action plan 2021–2027.* European Commission. Publications Office of the European Union.

EC/EACEA/Eurydice. (2019). *Digital education at school in Europe: Eurydice report.* European Commission. Publications Office of the European Union.

Fraillon, J., Ainley, J., Schulz, W., Friedman, T., & Gebhardt, E. (2014). *Preparing for life in a digital age: The IEA international computer and information literacy study: International report.* Springer.

Ghobadi, S., & Ghobadi, Z. (2013). How access gaps interact and shape digital divide: A cognitive investigation. *Behaviour & Information Technology, 34*(4), 330–340.

Gurcan, F., & Cagiltay, N. E. (2020). Research trends on distance learning: A text mining-based literature review from 2008 to 2018. *Interactive Learning Environments.* doi:10.1080/10494820.2020.1815795

Hodges, C., Moore, S., Lockee, B., Trust, T., & Bond, A. (2020, March 27). The difference between emergency remote teaching and online learning. *Educause Review.* https://er.educause.edu/articles/2020/3/the-difference-between-emergency-remote-teaching-and-online-learning

Istat. (2020). *Spazi in casa e disponibilità di computer per bambini e ragazzi.* https://www.istat.it/it/files//2020/04/Spazi-casa-disponibilita-computer-ragazzi.pdf

Istat. (2021). *Rapporto BES 2020: il benessere equo e sostenibile in Italia.* https://www.istat.it/it/files//2021/03/BES_2020.pdf

Istituto Toniolo. (2013). *La condizione giovanile in Italia. Rapporto giovani 2013.* Il Mulino.

Istituto Toniolo. (2014). *La condizione giovanile in Italia. Rapporto giovani 2014.* Il Mulino.

Istituto Toniolo. (2016). *La condizione giovanile in Italia. Rapporto giovani 2016.* Il Mulino.

Istituto Toniolo. (2017). *La condizione giovanile in Italia. Rapporto giovani 2017.* Il Mulino.

Istituto Toniolo. (2018). *La condizione giovanile in Italia. Rapporto giovani 2018.* Il Mulino.

Istituto Toniolo. (2019). *La condizione giovanile in Italia. Rapporto giovani 2019.* Il Mulino.

Istituto Toniolo. (2020a). *La condizione giovanile in Italia. Rapporto giovani 2020.* Il Mulino.

Istituto Toniolo. (2020b). *Young people in the age of coronavirus: A generation in lockdown dreaming in a different future.* Vita e Pensiero.

Istituto Toniolo. (2021). *La condizione giovanile in Italia. Rapporto giovani 2021.* Il Mulino.

Livingstone, S., & Helsper, E. (2010). Balancing opportunities and risks in teenagers' use of the internet: The role of online skills and internet self-efficacy. *New Media & Society, 12*(2), 309–329.

Mesa, D., & Triani, P. (2018). Sistemi formativi e di orientamento. Le istanze di cambiamento dei giovani europei. In Istituto Toniolo (Ed.), *La condizione giovanile in Italia. Rapporto giovani 2018* (pp. 49–78). Il Mulino.

MIUR. (2019). *Focus: La dispersione scolastica nell'anno scolastico 2016/2017 e nel passaggio all'anno scolastico 2017/2018.* Ministry of Education, University and Research.

OECD. (2019). *TALIS 2018 results (volume I): Teachers and school leaders as lifelong learners*. OECD Publishing. https://doi.org/10.1787/1d0bc92a-en

Ottestad, G., & Gudmundsdottir, G. B. (2018). Information and communication technology policy in primary and secondary education in Europe. In J. Voogt et al. (Eds.), *Second handbook of information technology in primary and secondary education* (pp. 1343–1362). Springer.

Pandolfini, V. (2013). Innovation and education systems: Teachers experiencing interactive whiteboards. *International Journal of Scientific and Research Publications (IJSRP), 3*(10).

Pandolfini, V. (2016). Exploring the impact of ICTs in education: Controversies and challenges. *Italian Journal of Sociology of Education, 8*(2), 28–53.

Pitzalis, M. (2016). The technological turn: Policies of innovation, politics and mobilisation. *Italian Journal of Sociology of Education, 8*(2), 11–27.

Uden, L., Wangsa, I. T., & Damiani, E. (2007, February). The future of e-learning: E-learning ecosystem. In *2007 inaugural IEEE-IES digital ecosystems and technologies conference* (pp. 113–117). Institute of Electrical and Electronics Engineers.

Union, I. (2014). *Communication from the Commission to the European Parliament, the Council, the European Economic and Social Committee and the Committee of the Regions. A new skills agenda for Europe*.

Van Deursen, A. J., & Van Dijk, J. A. (2014). *Digital skills: Unlocking the information society*. Springer.

Walther, A. (2006), Regimes of youth transitions. Choice, flexibility and security in young people's experiences across different European contexts. *Young, Nordic Journal of Youth Research, 14*(2), 119–141.

Wei, L., & Hindman, D. B. (2011). Does the digital divides matter more? Comparing the effects of new media and old media use on the education based knowledge gap. *Mass Communication and Society, 14*(2), 216–235. https://doi.org/10.1080/15205431003642707

CHAPTER 7

Inside the Emergency

Digital Teaching from the Point of View of Teachers

Eduardo Barberis, Nico Bazzoli, Domenico Carbone and Joselle Dagnes

1   Introduction

This chapter aims to discuss how primary and secondary teachers in Italian schools interpreted their professional role in the emergency reorganization of education via online remote teaching tools during the first lockdown in early 2020. In particular, we aim to explore teachers' (a) representations about distance education in general, and about its accessibility in particular – in reference to associated risks of educational inequalities; (b) difficulties experienced during the lockdown; and (c) use and adaptation of teaching methods during the digital transition.

We adopt here a specific lens to analyse representations, perceived problems and teaching choices – i.e. that of professional cultures and values. We maintain that representations on the professional role of teachers, professional satisfaction and the individual paths that led our respondents to embark on a career in education – including their socio-demographic characteristics (age, gender, education, seniority, etc.) influence adaptations and coping strategies in an emergency. As a side implication, this means that structural features in the construction of teaching professions, and in the recruiting of teaching staff, affect how unexpected conditions – like the emergency digital transition in early 2020 – are experienced.

We are aware that this is just part of the story, and that there are factors with as much relevant influence. We can mention as an example previous digital skills (that influence professional fatigue in transiting to online education [Argentin, 2018; Gui, 2019]) and structural factors related to institutional resources and organizational features that we explored in other research output from this research campaign (see Dagnes et al., 2021) and that have been mentioned here by Colombo et al. (this volume). Anyway, we maintain that spelling out how professional cultures, values and paths affect emergencies, irrespective of contexts where teachers are inserted, may prove useful both from an analytical point of view (i.e. personal determinants of collective action) and from a practical point of view (to suggest which kind of resources school management can activate in emergency situations).

This argument will be based on a web survey administered between April and May 2020, concerning practices of distance teaching during school closures in the aftermath of the Covid-19 outbreak. Our survey focused on teachers' management of teaching (methods and tools used) and on their representations, opinions, expectations and worries in a time of exceptional educational practices. It consisted of four areas: background information; individual and organizational practices enacted to implement emergency distance education; change in professional routines during the first lockdown; and representations by the teaching profession.

The questionnaire was completed by more than 2,000 teachers throughout Italy, working at different levels. The sample is not representative, as it was administered via a web survey, in which self-selection of respondents may be an issue. However, gender, age and the territorial distribution of our sample do mirror quite well the general distribution of Italian teachers. In reference to the analyses made in this chapter, we shall also mention a limitation of our survey, related to reported behaviours. We cannot assess actual actions (e.g. teaching methods used in practice) and behaviours, or their real effects on educational outcomes: we deal just with opinions, representations and reported behaviours. While they can be subject to misrepresentations related to socially desirable answers, we deem these fundamental as a frame of action.

The chapter is organized as follows: the next section (Section 2) will define our theoretical background, discussing relevant themes in the sociology of (teaching) profession, and in the sociology of emergency, used to make sense of our research questions. Section 3 will present the analysis of survey data, and Section 4 will discuss its implications.

2 Being a Teacher: Professional Paths and Identity

As accounted by Argentin (2018), the sociology of education has explored – among the various dimensions of the teaching profession – the social characteristics of those choosing this career and, more extensively, their role in the (re)production of inequalities. These two dimensions may be related, suggesting a correlation between teachers' personal and social backgrounds and the way they perform their role. Career choices, opportunities and motivations are also related to gender, social class, age, education and training – and the intersection of these characteristics may affect their understanding and practice of the teaching profession (Argentin, 2013, 2018). What is more, such characteristics act in relation with institutional constraints to affect the recruitment and career path of teachers (e.g. the difference between permanent and temporary staff), with a further effect on motivations and professional identities. Finally, the level and type of school also plays a role, with further relevance assigned to subject and pedagogical expertise (Beijard et al., 2000).

One the one hand, we can debate if the teaching profession has all the conditions to be sociologically defined as a profession, and thus having a solid, collective (and enforced) ethical practice and collective identity. On the other hand, we may explore the ethics teachers actually display. The teaching profession is often considered to be in a permanent state of crisis, to be at the crossroads of societal transformations that challenge their role in socialization and stratification processes, and there is a consistent perception by teachers that they are unfairly in the eye of the storm and unrecognized in their role. As a consequence, it seems to be a profession characterized by some stressors, even though not necessarily by high dissatisfaction (OECD, 2020), and torn between different dilemmas and professional orientations (Besozzi, 1981) concerning their external and internal professional goals, and how to achieve them. In particular, dealing with social change is identified as a key element of the profession, with different profiles of teachers responding in different ways (Romano, 2012; Argentin, 2010), according to their professional identity.

2.1 *Emergency: A Challenge or a Litmus Test for Teaching Professions?*

Representations of teachers' professional identity may be even more relevant when business does not go as usual – as in the emergency transition to distance teaching observed here: institutional and individual answers cannot be based on solid assets and skill sets, and individual teachers have to go back to basics of their expertise, motivation and professional identity, and to resort to their own personal resources (Kim & Asbury, 2020; Colombo et al., 2020).

Unfortunately, the literature on (teaching) professions and emergencies/disasters is not so helpful in framing Covid-19-related challenges. On the one hand, teaching professions are not highlighted in such literature; on the other hand, educators and educational institutions are more often referred to when other aspects are addressed, such as prevention of/communication about disaster, post-disaster recovery or trauma management. Actions taken during emergencies themselves are poorly explored. In this respect, the challenges presented by Covid-19 are unprecedented, not so much in their early effects (school closures during epidemic crises are documented as is delivering education during an epidemic [Howard & Howard, 2012]) as much as in their management (i.e. in the ICT-based solutions adopted during the emergency itself). Not by chance, literature in this strand developed in reference to Covid-19 lockdowns only (Koenig et al., 2020) with few and limited antecedents related to the H1N1/09 pandemic (Allen & Seaman, 2010).

In this respect, the literature on teachers' resilience and well-being may be more useful in predicting emergency-related challenges, as it focuses on coping strategies that teachers may resort to in stressful events, and on the effect of stressors on practice (Day, 2018). Even though the focus is usually on stressors and risks poorly related to health emergencies, this strand of literature looks at individual and environmental stressors and protective factors: for example, gender, education and experience are relevant to cope with stress (Nasser Abu-Alhija, 2015; Gu & Day, 2007). Professional, emotional, social and motivational factors can influence identity, resilience and coping (Canrinus et al., 2011; Daniilidou & Platsidou, 2018). We will focus here mainly on professional and motivational dimensions, as most consistent with our disciplinary interest and research question.

2.2 *Emergency Digital Transitions*

One of the recent transformations that entailed a re-elaboration on how to be a teacher is the pervasive societal role of ICT and its increasing role in education (Gui, 2019). Such a challenge found a sudden acceleration in the wake of the Covid-19 emergency. This may be particularly demanding in Italy, since Italian teachers (as mentioned by Colombo et al. in the introduction to this volume) are not particularly supportive of or confident with ICT innovations (Wastiau et al., 2013; OECD, 2019). On the other hand, we can call into question whether such a crisis can be seen as something radically new in the teaching experience – producing path-breaking consequences – or whether it is just the last challenge within the normality of dealing with unexpected, novel social phenomena (Colombo, 2007).

At first, most likely, the transition to distance teaching as an exceptional, temporary emergency stopgap solution was not perceived as the new normal. (Now, after further pandemic waves and selective lockdowns involving school operations, this is a debatable point.) This may be mirrored in the solutions chosen and in the personal and professional consequences for teachers. Even though perceived as temporary, nevertheless, emergency online remote teaching may have challenged expectations and practices teachers perceive as normal and viable. Thus, some of the challenges ICT transitions pose to teachers' professional identity that the literature stressed in the pre-Covid-19 era are still there (Gui, 2019; Avidov-Ungar & Forkosh-Baruch, 2018) and will likely have enduring ripple effects (see Colombo et al., this volume).

For example, the urgency to implement distance teaching leaves an open question about the reception of digital innovations, as most of the literature underlines the time needed for digital adaptations (Capogna, 2020). Such time pressure may have affected the way in which technological innovation has been practiced – leaving limited room for pedagogical innovation: pre-Covid research already questioned the awareness and reflexivity present in technology-driven changes in education (Capogna et al., 2018), a problem that may be magnified here.

In practical terms, the de-standardization and de-routinization of teaching and non-teaching activities may have influenced teachers' workload: from a quantitative point of view, while some time may be spared (e.g. commuting), the redesign of teaching, but also of the whole personal life (e.g. balancing family and personal commitments) may have implied heavier burdens. On the qualitative side, developing skills and expertise in using ICT tools and in adapting educational methods to available means may have been a serious challenge, increasing work-related stress (Koenig et al., 2020).

As we mentioned above, teachers' satisfaction may be related to a number of dimensions – workload and labour conditions, wages and careers, social recognition and professional well-being. We may expect that this sudden transition had

1. put critical perceptions of online education and conflicts into brackets, as readiness to online transition becomes an emergency duty that may have favoured willingness to be part of the game and to commit to moral and professional obligations (Gudmundsdottir & Hathaway, 2020);
2. where this trend is not so decisive, more of the same effect, increasing stress and dissatisfaction among those already dissatisfied. In particular, those with non-standard careers (temporary staff), and those with instrumental or accidental professional identities may be more at risk of work-related stress;
3. finally, an ironing out effect on different ways of being teachers: in consideration of unplanned online transition and low ICT skills, the emergency online transition may have turned into a 'race to the bottom' in teaching methods (something discussed for the tertiary level also by Ramella and Rostan in this volume). In other words, online remote teaching may have been more a constraint than an opportunity, as teachers may have felt that they were stripped of their professional tools, identity and efficacy (Kim & Aubury, 2020; Reich et al., 2020).

3   Results

In this section, we present analyses based on survey data. We will try to answer three related research questions:

1. What perceptions do teachers have of inequality and accessibility problems in the online transition of their teaching activities?
2. What kind of personal difficulties, satisfaction and discomfort with the online transition do they report?

3. What kind of teaching tools and methods did they use during the emergency transition to online education, compared to 'business as usual' periods?

We maintain that these dimensions are focal in understanding how teachers coped with the new pandemic situation. We will analyse these dimensions as dependent on (a) socio-demographic characteristics (age, gender, education); (b) career paths (school type and level they work in, seniority, contract); and (c) motivation and satisfaction to be a teacher.

Consistent with the frame outlined in Section 2, we maintain that (a), (b) and (c) are factors influencing teachers' coping strategies and self-efficacy, as they are deeply rooted background characteristics affecting their professional identity and agency.

As for (c), we run a principal component analysis extracting four dimension of motivation to be a teacher (see Table 7.1): instrumental (1); vocational (2); accidental (3); and status-related (4). In the following analyses, we will classify cases using the component score (fourth quartile).

3.1 Perceptions of Inequality in Accessibility of Online Education

An important question in the transition to emergency online education is its effect on students' performance and careers. At the moment, the evidence is limited and prone to see a 'more of the same' effect for underperforming and vulnerable students (see also Colombo et al., this volume). Here we aim to discuss another point: teachers themselves do not have such evidence. They have representations based on their personal experience, sometimes on (online) discussions with colleagues and principals, but with limited chance to compare dropout and underachievement across schools and classes, and to follow up vulnerable students at a distance.

We aim to inquire here if and how accessibility problems and underachievement in distance teaching settings is perceived by teachers. Our survey inquired about (1) what share of students did not attend, (2) did attend irregularly and (3) did attend regularly but with poor results. Also, we inquired the reasons of such problems according to the teachers. We do not treat the answers as real data (as actual % of dropouts), but – in relation to main influencing factors – as a proxy for the concerns of teachers (especially as of the third question and the reasons of problems they ascribe).

Seniority and age produce a visible gap in the concerns for learning outcomes, with younger and junior teachers reporting higher underachievement than older and senior teachers (see Table 7.2). Is it because they perceive a lower self-efficacy due to limited experience? Does this intersect with their under-representation in the permanent staff, so that their more negative

TABLE 7.1   Teachers' motivation to start their job; matrix of rotated components

	Components			
	1	2	3	4
I was interested in a job in the public sector because it is guaranteed	.780	.063	−.038	.144
I could not find better job opportunities	.762	−.180	.171	.019
The field I majored in didn't offer any other interesting job opportunity	.685	−.096	.117	−.053
I was interested in a job in a public body	.680	.018	−.042	.453
I could make a living with this job	.674	.064	.158	.092
Teaching was a good way to make the most out of my degree	.571	.102	.379	−.048
I was interested in a job with a good work schedule	.565	.077	.178	.379
I liked to work with youth	−.105	.773	−.061	.027
I thought that teaching was a way to improve society	−.016	.687	−.016	.053
I was interested to transmit knowledge of the field I studied	.162	.641	.020	−.011
I aspired to become a teacher	−.147	.563	−.559	.165
I started this job by chance	.182	−.365	.713	−.061
I started as a substitute teacher and I got on well	.175	.205	.706	.218
My family had a tradition in teaching and education	.070	−.105	.049	.728
I thought it was a high-status job	.122	.223	−.014	.716

Note: Extraction method: principal component analysis; rotation method: Varimax with Kaiser normalization; rotation converged in six iterations

perceptions may be related to limited resources (e.g. less acquaintance with students and the school environment) and a less solid professional identity (as junior teachers are over-represented among those expressing accidental motivations)? Or are their concerns greater because younger and junior teachers pay more attention to educational inequalities?

To put such questions in context, we analyse opinions on the reasons why students struggled to participate and achieve. We surveyed nine reasons (lack of devices; limited connectivity; limited digital skills; social and cultural

TABLE 7.2 According to your direct experience, on average what share of students… (Mean values, % for selected groupings in the sample)

Groupings	…could not get into online education	…could not take part regularly into online education	…took part regularly into online education, but struggled to learn
Total	7.3	10.1	21.5
Male	10.0	11.9	25.9
Female	6.7	9.8	20.7
Permanent staff	6.6	9.3	20.5
Fixed-term staff	10.9	14.3	25.2
Under 40	8.3	13.3	27.6
Over 60	9.3	8.5	19.0
Junior (less than ten years' experience)	8.9	12.4	24.2
Senior (more than thirty years' experience)	7.6	8.4	19.2
Degree in education	8.4	11.2	21.5
Degree in science and technology	8.7	9.7	22.4
Primary-lower secondary	7.1	9.8	21.7
Upper secondary	7.4	10.6	21.3
Instrumental motivation, 4th quartile	8.7	11.2	21.9
Vocational motivation, 4th quartile	7.0	10.0	21.2
Accidental motivation, 4th quartile	8.9	12.3	24.1
Status-related motivation, 4th quartile	8.0	11.6	21.3
Dissatisfied[a]	9.4	11.3	23.1
Satisfied	7.1	10.2	21.2

a   This indicator of satisfaction and dissatisfaction has been computed summing up answers to the following battery with six questions, and dividing the sample in quartiles according to general satisfaction levels: 'Regardless of specific conditions under the Covid-19 emergency, how much are you satisfied with the following elements of your profession? Wage; school climate; career opportunities; working hours; contract; activities.' The answers could be ranked from 1 (very dissatisfied) to 5 (very satisfied).

background; health issues and impairments; learning disabilities; unsupportive families; careless students; and family problems). Just two indicated variation among our respondents and reached statistical significance – attributing problems to a range of context and structural issues, and blaming individual students. For example, teachers in primary and lower secondary education attribute problems to students' lack of ICT skills and family background, but also to the lack of support from their family and learning disabilities, while teachers in upper secondary schools refer slightly more to individual responsibilities, i.e. students' carelessness.

As shown in Table 7.3, again, age and seniority are particularly relevant, also within school levels. Younger and junior teacher usually identify more causal factors than older and senior ones, but this gap is magnified in upper secondary

TABLE 7.3 In your view, how relevant were the following reasons why students struggled to participate? (Selected items, mean value, range 1–4)

Group	Disadvantaged cultural and social background	Students' carelessness
Total	2.95	2.61
Male	2.84	2.76
Female	2.96	2.58
Permanent staff	2.93	2.57
Fixed-term staff	3.03	2.76
Under 40	3.13	2.70
Over 60	2.74	2.56
Junior (less than ten years' experience)	3.06	2.74
Senior (more than thirty years' experience)	2.85	2.54
Degree in education	3.22	2.30
Degree in science and technology	2.81	2.87
Primary-lower secondary	3.17	2.46
Upper secondary	2.67	2.79
Instrumental motivation, 4th quartile	3.00	2.72
Vocational motivation, 4th quartile	2.99	2.60
Accidental motivation, 4th quartile	3.00	2.73
Status-related motivation, 4th quartile	2.93	2.67
Dissatisfied	3.03	2.64
Satisfied	2.89	2.55

schools. Students' carelessness is a primary motivation for upper secondary teachers aged more than 40, while younger colleagues focus more on the lack of proper internet connection and on family backgrounds. This may be also related to intervening factors, i.e. the type of contract and the related professional identity, as younger (and obviously enough junior) teachers are over-represented among those with short-term contracts, and junior teachers are among those with accidental motivations to be a teacher: those with open-ended contracts and vocational motivations to be a teacher report fewer 'dropouts' and problems. This may be related to the acquaintance with the class, the chance to reach out to students, but also self-efficacy, motivation and professional attachment, as temporary staff is much less satisfied than permanent staff.

To summarize, cross-tabulating reasons by age and contract, we can see that gaps are more related to age than contract. For example, older teachers with fixed-term contracts report more troubles in involving students than younger ones – maybe as an effect of ICT skill gap, but also as an effect of limited professional attachment that may be related to an accidental motivation into the profession, and to lower levels of satisfaction. Also, within those with long-term contracts, the age gap looks wide, with younger teacher reporting more access and accessibility problems, and less 'individual' and more plural causes.

In the same vein, teachers with an education in psychology and pedagogy are more keen to problematize structural problems of accessibility (in particular, related to personal and family background) and less keen to blame individual students. For example, at upper secondary level, where we already observed a trend in blaming students' 'indolence', teachers graduated in psycho-pedagogical disciplines rank this item third, behind socio-economic background and the quality of the internet connection.

All in all, we can see that the perception of accessibility and achievement problems is at least partly related to career and background characteristics, and to professional motivation and satisfaction. In this respect, we can cross-tabulate with other items concerning satisfaction and perception of the profession, showing that 'pessimistic' views hold. Those more concerned with students access and success are over-represented among those perceiving that the social appreciation of the teaching profession has worsened (a large majority of our sample, by the way). The reported share of students with learning problems in online education range from 14.8% among those thinking that teachers are improving their prestige, to 21.9% among those thinking the opposite. Such a share is also higher among those perceiving themselves as rank-and-file civil servants more than professionals or persons with a social function. A low level of satisfaction with the school climate is associated with a perception of higher barriers for students' participation into online education. All in all, we see relations that call into question motivations, satisfaction and self-efficacy.

3.2 Navigating a Pandemic: How Teachers Coped

This calls for further attention on teachers' well-being during the pandemic emergency. Anxiety about the emergency situation has been widely discussed in the public arena, and we inquire how such problems were deployed in working environments in education, as teachers had to cope with unprecedented educational challenges, at the same time balancing their work and life, and managing – as everyone else – personal concerns for health and uncertainty. Again, we maintain that the connection between socio-demographic characteristics, career paths, motivation and satisfaction on the job are related to the coping of stressors during the emergency, and with the perception of self-efficacy that may curb anxiety in dealing with such an unexpected situation. In this respect we included in our survey a battery on work-related stress perception during the pandemic emergency.[1]

As shown in Table 7.4, women feel usually worse than men. (This also means that – due to female over-representation in such categories – primary teachers and teachers with a background in psychology and education feel more

TABLE 7.4 During the pandemic, how often did you feel… (mean value, range 1–4)

	Work-related stress
Total	2.57
Male	2.26
Female	2.62
Permanent staff	2.59
Fixed-term staff	2.46
Under 40	2.54
Over 60	2.56
Junior (less than ten years' experience)	2.46
Senior (more than thirty years' experience)	2.64
Degree in education	2.67
Degree in science and technology	2.45
Primary-lower secondary	2.68
Upper secondary	2.43
Instrumental motivation, 4th quartile	2.64
Vocational motivation, 4th quartile	2.55
Accidental motivation, 4th quartile	2.59
Status-related motivation, 4th quartile	2.60
Dissatisfied	2.85
Satisfied	2.32

anxious.) While there is no significant effect due to age, senior teachers were more anxious than junior ones and – relatedly and counterintuitively enough – those with a permanent contract feel a bit more unease than those with fixed-term contracts. The latter can be explained again as female teachers are over-represented among permanent staff.[2]

We may suspect that such feelings are related to professional attachment, motivation and satisfaction: actually, those who are more satisfied and have vocational motivations are less stressed in the Covid-19 emergency, showing again that well-being is protecting from stressors. More anxiety is associated with those who accidentally or instrumentally chose the teaching profession.

3.3 From Perceptions to Actions: How Was Distance Teaching Conducted?

Our survey included two batteries of questions on the frequency of use of some teaching methods, and of digital resources. Both batteries required respondents to report their use before and after the Covid-19 outbreak. We are aware that such ex-post reconstructions can be biased. As a result, we do not treat answers as facts, aiming to measure the exact difference in the use of methods and tools before and after. Instead, we analyse these items as self-reported perceptions of change that teachers experienced under Covid-19 in the reorganization of their teaching activities.

We aim to compare respondents' perceptions of the viability of teaching methods to see who basically thinks that distance teaching can be done in the same ways as before and who maintains that things have changed. We analyse these data by socio-demographic characteristics, and according to motivations and satisfaction. Frequencies show a clear ironing out effect, with a strong reduction of most interactive methods – even the ones that may not be considered particularly challenging in 'business as usual' moments (e.g. adding debate and Q&A sessions at the end of taught lessons). A result strikingly consistent with those in tertiary education, as discussed by Ramella and Rostan in this volume.

Cross-tabulating with the main socio-demographic, career, motivation and satisfaction dimensions, such ironing out may be represented as a convergence towards more 'traditional' taught classes, as the gap among teachers' subgroups seems reduced. On the one hand, before the emergency female, younger, primary and lower secondary teachers, teachers with vocational motivations and those whore were more satisfied with their jobs were less used to delivering 'chalk-and-talk' lessons. Nevertheless, it seems they were not in position to funnel their experience into online platforms. On the other hand, there is a 'more of the same' effect: teachers using a reduced number of teaching methods and those with fixed-term contracts started to use even less.

TABLE 7.5 How often did you use the following teaching methods before and during the Covid-19 emergency? (Only comparable items; columns A and B: sum of answers 'Often + Always'; column C and D: difference in the frequency of use)

Method	(a) % of use before	(b) % of use during	(c) % of teachers that used more often	(d) % of teachers that used less often
Taught class	59.5	56.5	22.9	32.9
Taught class plus debate/Q&A	83.1	62.8	10.8	43.2
Dialogic teaching	87.2	55.8	7.8	48.3
Classroom discussion	71.6	41.8	9.3	48.1
Reinforcement learning	79.9	57.7	8.5	37.6
Active learning (cooperative learning, flipped classroom, peer education, etc.)	54.8	35.4	13.8	45.0

This issue is patent when we do not just check the use of a specific method, but we sum up the methods we surveyed, to check who frequently utilized a wider set of educational approaches, and what consequences pandemic education had. The percentage of teachers who used a limited set of methods passed from one in five to three in five (see Table 7.6). Four in five teachers who used to utilize a few teaching methods continued to do so, while only one in six teachers who used a large variety of methods continued to do so during the pandemic. In fact, just 2% of respondents increased the number of teaching methods during the pandemic.

Those who continued to use chalk-and-talk methods to teach are usually male, in upper secondary education and had a background in areas other than pedagogy. The more interactive methods have been strongly curbed among those who have experience of using them, i.e. female and younger teachers in primary and lower secondary schools with a background in psycho-pedagogic disciplines – but also teachers with a more vocational view of their role.

In this respect, the emergency online remote teaching has flattened and impoverished the variety of teaching methods used by teachers overall, resulting in a shift towards mainstream, 'chalk-and-talk' classes. Discouragingly

TABLE 7.6 Share of respondents who often used a few methods among the above

	Before	During
Total	20.7	58.0
Female	18.9	57.2
Male	34.5	65.2
Under 40	21.9	63.6
Over 60	21.2	50.0
Junior (less than 10 years experience)	25.4	62.3
Senior (more than 30 years experience)	18.7	59.2
Degree in education	15.9	60.7
Degree in science and technology	25.4	57.4
Primary-lower secondary	13.1	61.8
Upper secondary	29.6	53.1
Permanent staff	19.7	57.7
Fixed-term staff	26.1	60.2
Instrumental motivation, 4th quartile	22.6	61.9
Vocational motivation, 4th quartile	18.8	54.0
Accidental motivation, 4th quartile	22.5	60.7
Status-related motivation, 4th quartile	19.0	57.7
Dissatisfied	18.2	56.5
Satisfied	20.7	55.4

enough, teachers perceived themselves to be constrained (rather than enabled) in their ability to use or experiment with ICT-based educational tools and strategies. Such ironing out is also visible, considering both motivation and satisfaction, and do not produce many significant variations – except in a few specific areas: for example, those with a vocational motivation to become teachers are a bit more resilient than other teachers.

4   Conclusions

Our research confirms existing research conducted before the Covid-19 emergency on work-related stress among teachers: seniority, motivation and satisfaction do protect from stressors and increase self-efficacy. We should not take this for granted, but this tendency also applies to radical or sudden shocks – such as the pandemic lockdowns and the subsequent transition to online education.

Our results highlight two important dimensions, relevant for both future research and for policy and practice.

First, there are some groups of teachers who have found it hard to do their job under pandemic conditions, who feel less equipped to manage and cope. Temporary staff – especially older teachers with fixed-term contracts – more frequently exhibit accidental motivation to do the job and higher dissatisfaction with the job. Teachers who have followed a professional educational career, including those who had long, varied, non-standard careers as well as returnees into the teaching profession, experienced a lack of opportunities, resulting in limited self-efficacy – a problem particularly evident in the fragmented Italian recruiting system (Mincu, 2018). We cannot state if their teaching activity is also negative for students, but it very likely has a negative impact on their work-related stress, commitment and identity.

Second, while education, seniority, motivation and satisfaction tend to protect teachers from stress, they do not protect their teaching practice. As shown in Section 3.3, there was a strong ironing out of teaching methods towards traditional 'chalk-and-talk' approaches. This is evident based on a comparison of reported previous experience with participatory and interactive methods, and the potentiality of ICT-based educational resources. This shows that there were limits in the extent to which schools and teachers were prepared for the emergency. In a way, this outcome was expected, but we have to analyse it in prospective terms, too. On the one hand, it is likely – as shown in other case studies (Bergdahl & Nouri, 2021) – that teacher preparedness focused more on organizational and technical issues rather than on pedagogical strategies. This is consistent with the concerns expressed in much of the Italian literature in the field (Capogna et al., 2018; Gui, 2019; Volpi, 2021). This is a shortcoming that could possibly have severe long-term effects, both during the lockdowns and emergency distance teaching that have been rolled out in the school over the 2020–2021 and 2021–2022 academic years, and in the future, when blended and mixed forms of education – also under the impulse of emergency ICT developments – may become a 'new normal'. Again, while we cannot assess and predict the consequences on students' achievement and learning processes, we see the evidence of the ironing out of teaching methods as one of the biggest challenges for the efficacy of teachers and schools.

Notes

1 The battery included five statements, each to be rated in terms of frequency (on a four-step scale): feeling cannot cope; feeling that work is burdensome; feeling anxious due to work; feeling frustrated at work; feeling emotionally drained. For the sake of simplicity, here we will just report analyses based on mean levels of the five statements above.
2 Same 85% of female respondents are permanent staff, versus some 70% of males.

References

Allen, I. E., & Seaman, J. (2010). *Learning on demand*. Babson Survey Research Group.

Argentin, G. (2010). 'Scegliere' di insegnare: vocazione, vantaggi e caso. In A. Cavalli & G. Argentin (Eds.), *Gli insegnanti italiani: come cambia il modo di fare scuola* (pp. 51–74). Il Mulino.

Argentin, G. (2013). Male routes to a teaching career: Motivations, market constraints and gender inequalities. *International Review of Sociology, 23*(2), 271–289.

Argentin, G. (2018). *Gli insegnanti nella scuola italiana*. Il Mulino.

Avidov-Ungar, O., & Forkosh-Baruch, A. (2018). Professional identity of teacher educators in the digital era in light of demands of pedagogical innovation. *Teaching and Teacher Education, 73*(1), 183–191.

Beijard, D., Verloop, N., & Vermunt, J. D. (2000). Teachers' perceptions of professional identity. *Teaching and Teacher Education, 16*, 749–764.

Bergdahl, N., & Nouri, J. (2021). Covid-19 and crisis-prompted distance education in Sweden. *Technology, Knowledge and Learning, 26*, 443–459.

Besozzi, E. (1981). Professione insegnante: le ricerche sociologiche sugli insegnanti in Italia dal 1960 ad oggi. *Studi di Sociologia, 19*(1), 77–92.

Canrinus, E. T., Helms-Lorenz, M., Beijard, D., Buitink, J., & Hofman, A. (2011). Profiling teachers' sense of professional identity. *Educational Studies, 37*(5), 593–608.

Capogna, S. (2020). The profession of educating amid contexts, digital innovation and professional habitus. *Italian Journal of Sociology of Education, 12*(1), 249–269.

Capogna, S., De Angelis, M. C., & Musella, F. (2018). Exploratory Investigation about the use of ICT in the school. *Italian Journal of Sociology of Education, 10*(2), 24–40.

Colombo, M. (2007). Conseguenze non previste e apprendimento professionale. *Studi di Sociologia, 49*(3), 263–283.

Colombo, M., Poliandri, D., & Rinaldi, E. E. (2020). Gli impatti dell'emergenza COVID-19 sul sistema scolastico-formativo in Italia. *Scuola Democratica*. Advance online publication. doi:10.12828/97098

Dagnes, J., Carbone, D., Barberis, E., & Bazzoli, N. (2021). Decision-making processes, conflict and coordination in Italian schools in the era of distance education. *Studi Organizzativi, 1*, 51–78.

Daniilidou, A., & Platsidou, M. (2018). Teachers' resilience scale. *Hellenic Journal of Psychology, 15*, 15–39.

Day, C. (2018). Professional identity matters. In P. A. Schultz, J. Y. Hong, & D. Cross Francis (Eds.), *Research on teacher identity* (pp. 61–70). Springer.

Gu, Q., & Day, C. (2007). Teachers resilience: A necessary condition for effectiveness. *Teaching and Teacher Education, 23*(8), 1302–1316. https://doi.org/10.1016/j.tate.2006.06.006

Gudmundsdottir, G. B., & Hathaway, D. M. (2020). 'We always make it work': Teachers' agency in the time of crisis. *Journal of Technology and Teacher Education, 28*(2), 239–250.

Gui, M. (2019). *Il digitale a scuola*. Il Mulino.

Howard, P., & Howard, J. (2012). Pandemic and pedagogy. *Phenomenology & Practice, 6*(1), 18–35.

Kim, L. E., & Asbury, K. (2020). 'Like a rug had been pulled from under you': The impact of COVID-19 on teachers in England during the first six weeks of the UK lockdown. *British Journal of Educational Psychology, 90*, 1062–1083.

Koenig, J., Jaeger-Biela, D. J., & Glutsch, N. (2020). Adapting to online teaching during COVID-19 school closure. *European Journal of Teacher Education, 43*(4), 608–622.

Mincu, M. E. (2018). Overcoming fragmented professionalism? In R. Normand, M. Liu, L. M. Carvalho, D. A. Oliveira, & L. LeVasseur (Eds.), *Education policies and the restructuring of the educational profession* (pp. 235–244). Springer.

Nasser-Abu Alhija, F. (2015). Teacher stress and coping. *Procedia – Social and Behavioral Sciences, 185*, 374–380.

OECD. (2019). *Results from Talis 2018 – Country Note Italy*. Organisation for Economic Cooperation and Development.

OECD. (2020). *TALIS 2018 results (Volume II): Teachers and school leaders as valued professionals*. OECD Publishing. https://doi.org/10.1787/19cf08df-en

Reich, J., Buttimer, C. J., Coleman, D., Colwell, R., Faruqi, F., & Larke, L. R. (2020). *What's lost, what's left, what's next: Lessons learned from the lived experiences of teachers during the pandemic*. MIT Teaching Systems Lab.

Romano, T. (2012). *Le riflessioni dei docenti*. Liguori.

Volpi, B. (2021). *Docenti digitali*. Il Mulino.

Wastiau, P., Blamire, R., Kearney, C., Quittre, V., Van de Gaer, E., & Monseur, C. (2013). The use of ICT in education: A survey of schools in Europe. *European Journal of Education, 48*(1), 11–27.

CHAPTER 8

Distance Learning/Teaching during the Covid-19 Emergency

The Perspective of School Principals

Stefania Capogna, Maria Chiara De Angelis and Flaminia Musella

1   Introduction

The pandemic which affected not only Italy and its education system, but the entire world, caused an unprecedented crisis by imposing distance teaching/learning (DTL), in hopes of bestowing continuity on the educational function. Although attempts to incorporate digital technologies were widespread here in Italy (Capogna et al., 2017, 2020), the turning point imposed by the forced closure of schools caused an organizational, personal and professional shock to all the system's stakeholders.

Within this critical scenario, the figure of the school principal (SP) appeared more central than ever with its mandatory task of connecting and constructing the 'techno-social' scholastic spaces within which to enable technologies to operate in order to overcome the emergency.

The survey discussed here was conducted using a multidimensional perspective and a design geared to investigate a number of different targets such as SP s, students, teachers and parents. Its focal tool was a multifaceted questionnaire divided into five common sections featuring parallel and target-specific items. The first section outlined the respondents' profiles and provided professional information about them. The second investigated the organizational (Barnard, 1968; Cocozza, 2020; Mintzberg, 1983) and methodological aspects activated to provide remote teaching/learning solutions designed to meet the challenges caused by the emergency. The third section explored the digital divide (Hargittai, 2010; Jackson, 2008; Light, 2001; Lopez, 2010; Mossberger et al., 2003; Norris, 2000; Stansbury et al., 2003) – considered a focal topic – which foregrounds the profound cultural and social state of inequality existing in Italy. The fourth section examined the overall satisfaction of the various actors involved in the process, paying particular attention to internal organizational processes, following SWOT analysis-based self-evaluation principles. The final section of the questionnaire collected the answers to open questions in order to go more deeply into the transformation taking place, in particular, that regarding the

© STEFANIA CAPOGNA, MARIA CHIARA DE ANGELIS AND FLAMINIA MUSELLA, 2022
DOI:10.1163/9789004523234_009

SPs, repercussions on their role and the managerial responsibilities assigned to them by DTL.

The main research questions we shall discuss here are:
– What are the main critical factors identified and the relevant strategies adopted by the schools during the emergency?
– What are the key issues that were experienced daily by the school's main actors during the pandemic?

In other words, what factors ensured that schools rediscovered their role as 'resilient organizations'?

By listening to the protagonists of this epochal crisis, we sought to become acquainted with the strategies adopted by the SPs to tackle the organizational problems that arose in their schools. Schools were plunged into a series of changes which radically redesigned all their previous internal and external organizational processes. This chapter, of an empirical nature, reconstructs and analyses a new set of primary data collected using a web survey. It was carried out between May and July 2020 and, with the help of the social media, involved 474 SPs, 3,444 teachers, 787 students and 2,116 parents, for a total of 6,821 interviewees. This chapter focuses on the experiences of the SPs consulted, with specific emphasis on the impact of distance learning/teaching upon the organization and implementation of school e-leadership. Although the sample was auto selected and not probabilistic,[1] it was ample enough to trigger a reflection regarding the lockdown setback, through the lens of the concept of organizational resilience applied to schools, in particular, to the role of the SL.

Because brevity is essential here, this report focuses on the factorial analysis carried out regarding three of the dimensions observed in relation to the profile of the SPs. Hence, starting from the framework of the organizational perspective assumed (Section 1), we shall illustrate, in brief, the methodology and sample (Section 2), discuss the solutions adopted (Section 3), provide an analysis of some latent dimensions (Section 4), in order, ultimately, to reflect upon the school as a *resilient organization* (Section 5).

2   The Organizational Perspective

Organizational resilience means the 'capability of a system to maintain its function and structure in the face of internal and external changes and to degrade gracefully when it must [...]. Resilience occurs when the system continues to operate despite failures in some of its parts' (Weick & Sutcliffe, 2007, p. 69).

Earlier studies of organizations carried out using the lens of resilience focused on the issue of organizational reaction to external threats (Staw et al., 1981). In view of its explanatory power, the concept of resilience was adopted in several areas and applied in depth to different aspects of a question. These might be summed up as adaptation (McKinnon, 2013); adjustment (Sanna & Salvati, 2014); renewal (Chapman et al., 2004); substitution (Martin, 2012); learning (Sutcliffe & Vogus, 2003), up to the point of understanding the concept of risk (Olivos, 2014). Organizational resilience can be connoted negatively, but also positively, as the ability to seize opportunities (Hubbard, 2009) emerging at times of crisis. The concept of risk management, intended as the management of uncertainty, is only slightly removed from that of the culture of security (McManus et al., 2008). It allows one to shift one's attention more and more towards the interconnections occurring within the relationships between the different components of organization while highlighting the centrality of collaboration (Keong & Mei, 2010), which is useful and necessary when fostering adaptation, growth and development (Braes & Brooks, 2010). Even though scholars have not reached a consensual univocal definition of organizational resilience, due to the multidimensionality of the concept, many of them hold that interaction, communication, trust in relationships and role systems are potential constituents of the phenomenon (Weick, 1993; Sutcliffe & Vogus, 2003; Chuna et al., 2013).

Because this theoretical framework can be applied in numerous ways and to vast areas, we shall carry out an in-depth analysis of the three points which appeared most fruitful in order to understand the organizational shock experienced by SLs when faced with the sudden closure of schools and the need to adopt distance teaching/learning.

Weick (1969) introduced the theory of *retrospective sense-making* and *organizing*, explaining that '[o]rganizing consists of the resolving of equivocality in an enacted environment by means of interlocked behaviours embedded in conditionally related processes' (Weick, 1969, p. 91). The concept of retrospective sense-making helps us to describe how members of an organization – consciously or unconsciously – choose different apt cues from the surroundings where they act in a given situation. Based on the outcomes of their action, and thanks to the negotiation of meaning which develops thanks to intersubjective relationships, existing structures of meaning are maintained or changed. Using this continuous process of negotiating signification, organizations construct their reality socially. By becoming aware of the power of retrospective sense-making, organizations can prevent crises before they actually become such or they can act mindfully during crises (Weick, 1988). In specific situations of crisis, according to Weick, a cosmology episode occurs 'when people suddenly and deeply feel that the universe is no longer a rational, orderly system. What makes such an episode so shattering is that both the sense of what is occurring and the means to rebuild that sense collapse together' (Weick, 1993, p. 633). In similar situations, communication is essential to safeguard organizational resources and prevent an organization from dissolving in the face of a complex and ambiguous situation (Weick et al., 2005). Without going more deeply into the debate on organizational communication, which is extremely fertile, it is important to mention that an organization comprises different flows of communication (McPhee & Zaug, 2000; McPhee & Iverson, 2009) which are *text, conversation* and *text dialects* (Taylor et al., 1996; Robichaud & Cooren, 2013). For this reason, both SLs and scholars need to analyse the phenomenon of resilience in order to understand the effort required to overcome ambiguous situations and crises of meaning. Within a school, to build shared meaning, team members need to be able to collaborate in order to share, communicate and coordinate information (Klein et al., 2010; Wolbers & Boersma, 2013).

Schraagen and Van de Ven (2011, p. 179) state that efficient information management, sharing and communication are essential to collective sense-making processes; in their opinion, when team members share the same information, a 'common frame of reference' is created.

For Sutcliffe and Vogus, resilience 'refers to the maintenance of positive adjustment under challenging conditions' (2003, p. 95). According to Keck and Sakdapolrak (2013), resilience is a social process existing between members of an organization who face events characterized by ambiguity and complexity. In these instances of uncertainty, individuals can no longer count and act on the basis of their repertoires of knowledge and experience which are no longer able to guide them in a world that has lost all rational order and points of reference.

One can imagine the uncertainty that invested SLs faced with the sudden closure of their schools in a context of widespread confusion. As a matter of fact, when addressing the recent emergency, SPs had to tackle multiple problems such as the lack of local internet connectivity;[2] the absence of broadband connections in their schools; the availability and security of spaces which would not normally belong to their sphere of action. Another element outside the SP's decision-making remit regards incoming resources (teaching and technical-administrative staff, student access). On the other hand, internal organizational processes concern the sphere of action and the decision-making strategies by means of which 'institutional micropolicies' (Benadusi & Serpieri, 2000) are expressed. During the lockdown, all internal and external processes collapsed and the entire educational system – comprising SLs, teachers, students and families, who lost all those points of reference capable of providing them with an interpretative framework and useful guidelines – threw the entire system into an unprecedented state of ambiguity, tension and concern. In this situation, the figure of the SL emerged in all its strategic importance because it was charged with the onus of acting consciously in critical situations and fostering the organization of adaptation, adjustment, renewal and learning in conditions of deep-seated uncertainty. In this complicated picture the maturity of the SP's e-leadership appears relevant, in order to its serve 'as a social influence within organizations incorporating advanced information technology to produce a change in attitudes, feelings, thinking, behavior, and/or performance with individuals, groups, and/or organizations' (Avolio et al., 2000).

Beginning from the systemic complexity described briefly above, this essay focuses on the responses of the SPs interviewed, to explore both the most important critical organizational issues they identified during the emergency and the strategies they adopted to deal with them.

3 The Methodology Adopted

The empirical study carried out here was based on what is called the *survey-research* explanatory framework (Lazarfield, 1972). It aimed at obtaining specific, empirically grounded social information (Merton, 1966), with specific reference to the ways in which the role of school SPs was geared to face and capable of dealing with the pandemic, starting from the attitudes and behaviour of the protagonists. The starting point was the individual actors (in this case the SPs) which the study sought to understand and appraise on the basis of how they interacted with the system. The survey aimed at grasping how these two factors influenced each other mutually and generated reciprocal feedback (Rovati, 1986). For this reason, we analysed the SPs' *retrospective sense-making* expressed with regard to their organizational responses; the strategic processes adopted and the degrees of satisfaction perceived.

3.1 A Description of the Sample

Of the sample, 474 were school principals. For purposes of data analysis, only the questionnaires completed by 355 SPs were taken into consideration. These SPs, mainly women (74%), were aged between 51 and 60 (51%) and represented 4.38% of the 8,094 SPs in active service during the 2019–2020 school year, according to the information provided by the Open Data system of MIUR (Italian Ministry of Education, University and Research). The majority of the SPs consulted worked in state schools, mostly comprehensive institutions

(57%). Most of them declared having activated a distance teaching method (DTM) in less than one week (41%) or in a week (42%) following the onset of the lockdown; 93% of them declared having activated a DTM for all the subjects taught in their schools.

The region represented most frequently was Lombardy, followed by Lazio, a datum which caused a certain over-representation of these compared to other regions like Campania, Sicily and Puglia, characterized by a significant presence of comprehensive institutions.

Although schools, especially in Italy, denote a considerable delay when it comes to processes of digitalization and the inclusion of digital resources within teaching/learning practices (OECD, 2019), in recent years several interventions have led to an enhancement of this aspect of education (Palmeri, 2021). One datum emerging from the survey was that about 37.75% of the SPs interviewed claimed they had not had the chance of dealing with the issue of the integration of ICT before the emergency. However, these results need to be read in the light of the prevalence of comprehensive institutions (57.18%) where, one can imagine, investments aim at fostering the gaming, experiential and manual dimensions, designed to favour motor and cognitive development during early childhood.

4   Critical Issues and the Solutions Adopted

The pandemic dramatically highlighted the issue of inequality. By inequality is meant 'different possibilities of access to economic, social and natural resources' (Strangio et al., 2018, p. 61). The matter of the digital divide appears to be the primary criticality SPs encountered when dealing with teachers, students and families (Figure 8.1), a situation where they had little or no scope to intervene to ensure the resolution of the problems.

For many families, the infrastructural and socio-economic gap represented the first stumbling block against didactic continuity and true membership of the educational community (Figure 8.2). This factor represented the first crisis of meaning the entire school community had to face. Suddenly, the usual educational 'stage' with its reassuring spaces, times and rituals disappeared while school space-time was transferred online and many did not know how and/or were unable to access it. Figure 8.2 illustrates the impact this dramatic experience had on family life, increasing emotional stress, workload and tensions, due to the need to reorganize living spaces because of the coercive cohabitation measures imposed by the authorities. These mandatory restrictions caused the sense and the ordinary, orderly flow of everyday life to break down

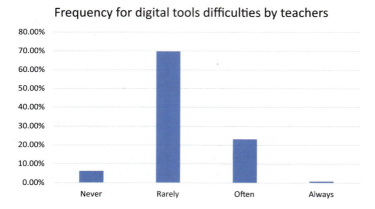

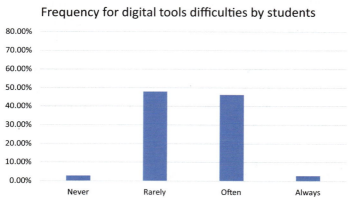

FIGURE 8.1   Difficulties experienced by teachers and students in terms of access to digital tools

along with the means by which to rebuild them, as the closure of schools, changes in the roles, schedules, borders and responsibilities of school-family relationships crumbled.

The percentage of absences, levels of distraction, learning difficulties, especially of young people with learning disabilities or impairments, increased dramatically. In this situation, the school failed in its primary mission, that is, inclusion, as the entire system of certainty governing the educational alliance between school and families disintegrated overnight.

With this in mind, it is easy to appreciate the calls for help and collaboration launched by the SLs during the lockdown. At best, it took some of them a week to get their schools up and running again by working on the main aspects of strategic reprogramming: the setting up of learning/teaching platforms; the reorganization of teaching calendars and schedules; the overhaul of general management; didactic continuity. All the pillars of organizational action

DISTANCE LEARNING/TEACHING DURING THE COVID-19 EMERGENCY

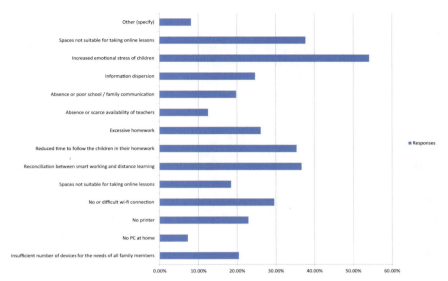

FIGURE 8.2   Difficulties encountered by families during the emergency

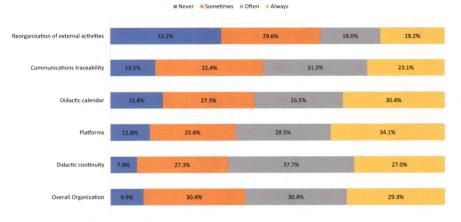

FIGURE 8.3   The frequency of updating activities

entered into a state of crisis, requiring continuous updating. In compliance with Weick's perspective, this effort may be interpreted as a process of continuous negotiation aimed at bestowing new meaning on unexpected courses of action (Figure 8.3).

In some cases, the reorganization of the activities was associated with the drawing up and sharing of standards and guidelines vital to the preparation of digital material. However, 62% of respondents stated that they failed to provide this kind of material. This fact seems to be in keeping with the sense of loneliness many members of the teaching community experienced. Yet, the impossibility of devising standards and guidelines is perfectly plausible considering a stage where cognitive and organizational prerequisites were wanting. This emerged especially in situations lacking previous use of online learning environments, fruition of a common modus operandi, sharing of a certain professional habitus and embedded practices (Bourdieu, 1980).

These features usually underscore the methodological, relational and technical skills required to systemize the processes as well as the socializing and explicative traits of the didactic practices required to set up online environments. They are recollective of spirals of knowledge based on procedures and stages which virtuous circles of organizational learning (Nonaka & Takeuchi, 1995) needs to pursue: socialization, outsourcing, combination and internalization. A process of this kind is often fluid and liquid and considers the flow of communication as its principal strategic element, one capable of generating shared learning through the 'cultivation of community practice' (Lave & Wenger, 1991). It is no coincidence, therefore, that the tools adopted by most of the SPs – and emerging from this survey – were video conferences (91.2%). As communicative media capable of providing, despite all the specific limitations of the case, the dynamics proper of face-to-face interaction were availed of by teachers to guide them and ensure the continuity and uniformity of their didactic practice. As we know, communication plays an essential role in the coordination, negotiation and accompaniment of processes of attribution of meaning when it comes to unexpected and/or incomprehensible situations arising to upset established routines. As the sedimented, formalized and explicit aspect of the texts defining organization disappears, this experience confirms the fact that in situations of crisis people need to make a greater effort than ever to foster conversation and continuous interaction. It was within this relational effort that the organizations run by the SLs resumed their form and adopted courses of action around which it was possible for stakeholders to see themselves as members of a community that was conceptual and cultural rather than physical and structural.

Almost half of the SPs (47%) claimed that they activated 'online e-learning environments', a description that includes a variety of solutions implemented in many different kinds of schools. All of the strategies activated, however, sought to integrate their schools' organizational and educational processes with digital resources. Without claiming generalization, the analysis carried out here revealed that an alarming 16% of SLs had not organized any activities to ensure didactic continuity, while a further 18% said they counted only on chat rooms and communication platforms like WhatsApp to provide some kind of service. In many cases, the latter solution was the only form of contact between the schools, pupils and families because of the depth of the digital divide due to a grave socio-cultural gap. We noticed that different situations corresponded to diverse SL strategies aimed at compensating for the closure of the schools and guaranteeing some degree of continuity. There is no evidence that gender affected the choice of whether or not to activate a given solution; on the other hand, it was noted that age played a significant role; as it was the younger SPs who failed to activate tools aimed at ensuring didactic continuity. This may have been due to the fact that the exercise of a form of e-leadership capable of restructuring, rethinking, re-inventing, re-designing and re-aligning the entire process required in-depth knowledge of the system within which the SPs were called upon to act. While acknowledging the ability of the school system to react to ensure continuity by reorganizing activities in a mere handful of weeks, it is necessary to reflect on the fact that during the first stage of the lockdown it was possible to provide emergency solutions only. This meant that the most widely used methodological tools consisted in the transmission of didactic materials through the digital platforms available to the schools and teachers as well as the organization of videoconferences (Figure 8.4). Generally speaking, the SLs tried to replace the traditional face-to-face lesson with screens without rethinking or adjusting them in any significant manner. In any case, the functions favoured by most seem to have privileged traceability rather than the creation of didactically effective learning environments. Additionally, other widely used tools were the independent transmission of pre-recorded material by teachers availing themselves of the electronic roll

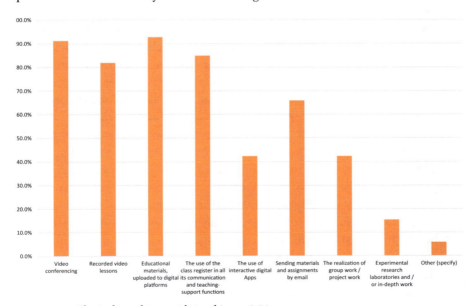

FIGURE 8.4   The tools used to provide teaching activities

book. Many principals, when defining the 'other' category provided in the questionnaire, indicated the social media, blogs and streaming as the means their schools chose as teaching/learning solutions. Only 16% used the class's electronic roll book to communicate and provide teaching support to students and families. One explanation for this may be the fact that the majority of the SPs who completed the questionnaire were managers of comprehensive institutions where the impact of DTMs proved particularly tiring, as emerges also from the comparisons made between the data provided by the different categories of interviewees.

In the SP sample considered by the survey, the most frequently used digital platforms were Google Meet (25.2% of all the cases) and Classroom (20.8% of all the cases) because of their ease of use as well as their ability to penetrate and thanks to the cost-effectiveness of Google Suite. If one needs to talk about the valorization of digital technologies in the school system, one cannot do so at the expense of the voluntary goodwill shown by individual teachers within the 'jungle' of the digital-educational solutions and resources made available by the market. It would prove necessary to reflect upon the possibility of offering a minimum range of resources (internet connections at school, video conferencing platforms, resources for digital teaching and support for students with disabilities or special needs, access to OER contents, digital libraries, etc.) to which schools, principals and teachers might gain charge-free access permitting them to carry out their activities for the benefit of the scholastic (and entire) community.

Decades of studies on the culture of quality in organizations have shown that amongst the most relevant problems encountered, technical dysfunctions or the tools used should not be listed but, rather, the lack of interrelations between the different parts comprising the organization as a whole: processes, people, information, etc. (Oakland et al., 2000; Catalin et al., 2014; Talib & Rahman, 2015).

Furthermore, considering the central role that communication plays in developing organizational resilience, the research discussed here aimed at detecting the time dedicated by the SPs to the collective communicative dimension used to rebuild the modi operandi and processes abruptly interrupted at the beginning of the pandemic. Analysing the time spent weekly by SPs on activities of interaction with teachers and school coordinators, it appears that the majority of the principals interviewed felt that their work time had increased dramatically and that they had devoted much more time to interaction with school coordinators than to the teaching staff.

This latter information should not appear surprising, especially if we consider the role of middle management that the staff assumes in the ordinary and extraordinary running of the organizational and didactic complexity that characterizes the independent schools system, regardless of the pandemic. In fact, one of the essential elements that studies on organizational resilience highlight is the functional ability of the chain of command to provide clear and consistent indications capable of handling crises.

5 The Analysis of Latent Dimensions

The variables pinpointed by the survey need to be considered as indicators of latent constructs extracted by means of multivariate statistical techniques like exploratory factor analysis.[3] This statistical methodology makes it possible to simplify the amount of information collected when extracting factors regarding latent structures emerging from within the data gathered, with a minimum loss of information or variability. However, before proceeding to a reduction of the data, an evaluation of the internal coherence of the scale (the batteries of questionnaire items) using the Cronbach's alpha method was deemed useful (Cronbach, 1951). This is a simple but widely used measure, applied in social studies to indicate degrees of agreement, that is, consistency, existing between several measures of the same theoretical concept obtained during the same administration and using the same detection method.[4] This analysis was applied to three aspects directly linked to the determination of organizational resilience in Italian schools during the pandemic.

To understand the perspective of the SPs regarding how their school communities faced the emergency, they were invited to express their level of agreement/disagreement (on a Likert scale of 1 to 5 to which was added the option 'I don't know') related to a series of points considered strategic while managing the emergency, and regarding, above all, the immaterial dimension of organizational action. In particular, the dimensions investigated using this statistical technique were:
– the organizational response to the DTM experience;
– the exploration of the assessment of the SPs regarding certain strategic organizational processes;
– the SLs' overall degree of satisfaction with their management of the emergency.

5.1 *The Organizational Response*
The analysis of the internal coherence of the scale, with reference to the organizational response, shows that the scale, 0.7990, was fairly consistent, a datum which increased to 0.8495 when the first item (*Distance learning can replace*

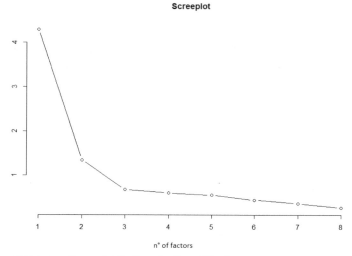

FIGURE 8.5　Scree plot for the selection of the factors

on-site learning) was eliminated. From this it was deduced that the consistency of the questions belonging to the first dimension (scale) was satisfied for the majority of the items considered for ulterior reduction. Based on the variability replicated by the factors as well as by the scree plot (Figure 8.5), three factors were extracted; factors which cumulatively accounted for over 70% of all the information, beyond which the eigenvalues were significantly lower than one while the curve tended to change its gradient.

From the output provided before the rotation of the axis, we found that the first factor accounted for 51% of all variability. Together with the second factor, it accounted for 66% of the above-mentioned variability. When accumulated with the third factor, the threshold of 70% was exceeded.[5] Therefore, it may be argued that the organizational response was characterized by the factors shown in Table 8.1.

As regards the organizational response, when examining how the organizational collapse determined by the pandemic was dealt with, the analysis of the latent factors revealed both the centrality of the role of communication as a means of creating and negotiating meanings between SPs, teachers, structures and coordinators, as well as the relevance of an extended form of participation, capable of engaging all the members of the group in the effective and timely reorganization of activities availing themselves of the digital mode. Distance teaching acted within a framework of meaning as well as organizational relationships rather than personal and professional ones; the effort made to foster coordination between management, school personnel and teachers proved strategic to the management of this exceptional situation.

TABLE 8.1   Organizational response factors

Factors	Variance	Items
Organizational and collaborative effectiveness	51%	Positively correlated with: – The interaction amongst colleagues was facilitated and implemented either by single class coordinators or by departments; – There was a goodly degree of coordination between management, school personnel and teachers; – The pacing of the lessons increased the stress levels of teachers; – During the emergency, experimentation with DTMs permitted teachers to appreciate digital technologies applied to teaching/learning.
The response of the teachers	15%	Positively correlated with: – Teachers having been able to adapt their teaching programmes to distance learning; – The entire school board having engaged in the reorganization of its activities through DTMs; the teachers were trained/rendered competent when dealing with distance teaching.
Communicative effectiveness	8.3%	Negatively correlated with: – Following the introduction of distance teaching, the interviewees' organization of internal communications was satisfactory.

By means of the conversational effort between all the members of the school community, processes of action and rituals were re-established and were gradually able to assume the concrete form of texts, regulations, guidelines and reprogramming that bestowed new form and structure on the organization by helping its members to overcome the organizational collapse.

The second aspect analysed concerned the assessment of some of the organizational processes considered strategic by the SPs who were asked to express their degree of agreement and disagreement regarding a set of thirteen items.

5.2 Evaluation of the Strategic Organizational Processes

The second aspect analysed concerned the assessment of some of the organizational processes considered strategic by the SPs who were asked to express their degree of agreement and disagreement regarding a set of thirteen items.

From an examination of the distribution of the responses it emerged that the aspects upon which the SPs agreed most were:
- the emergency brought to light the formative needs of teachers;
- the organization and effectiveness of distance teaching might act as items useful to self-assessment reports;
- schools found themselves left very much to their own devices when facing the emergency.

On the other hand, the aspects upon which the SPs disagreed most were:
- the emergency led to significant problems regarding the management of absences, turnovers and substitute teachers;
- local government bodies intervened in support of the school system to help plan the new academic year;
- the school networks proved very supportive when seeking sustainable solutions and solving problems.

In this case too, the information was summed up using factor analysis and carried out following the evaluation of the internal coherence of the scale using the Cronbach's alpha system. Additionally, the scale was calculated using both the indicators taken together as well by means of an iterative exclusion of each indicator.

Figure 8.6 – which represents the scree plot of the eigenvalues – suggested extracting three factors, which made it cumulatively possible to account for about 70% of all the information provided. Beyond the three factors mentioned, the eigenvalues were significantly lower than one and produced a curve which tended to change its gradient.

According to the results obtained before rotating the axis, the first factor accounted for 42.5% of all the variability. Taken together with the second factor, it accounted for about 62% of this variability; while, when the third factor was added, the threshold of 70% was exceeded (Table 8.2).[6]

The analysis of the latent dimensions relating to strategic organizational processes revealed that the school is not a closed environment, but that a lot depends on its ability to acknowledge and muster the external context (both nearby and remote), to activate virtuous relationships and to attract resources, skills and experiences. In this case, this includes the ability of the SPs to envision and know how to read internal and external clues capable of guiding decision-making processes. The definition of priorities and the development strategies by means of active internal and external communication skills

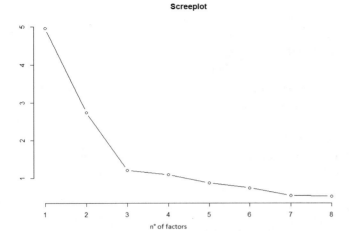

FIGURE 8.6 Scree plot of the selection of the factors

TABLE 8.2 Evaluation of strategic organizational-process factors

Factors	Variance	Items
Territorial networks	42.5%	Positively correlated with: – The emergency permitted new virtuous relationships with subjects external to schools as well as with other educational institutions to commence; – The emergency permitted the maintenance of relationships with subjects external to the schools and with school networks; – School networks proved very supportive when seeking sustainable solutions to the problem.
Strategic effectiveness	19.1%	Positively correlated with: – The emergency permitted the school system to redefine its decision-making processes; – The emergency permitted the school system to redefine its strategic priorities for the following year; – The emergency improved internal communications between SP s, school personnel and teaching staff; – The emergency brought to light the educational needs of teachers.
School-family relationship	9.6%	Negatively correlated with: – The emergency permitted effective communication and better collaboration with the students' families.

appear to be the keystone of success when seeking to construct broader meanings, aimed at bringing together an ever-increasing number of allies bent on implementing shared objectives capable of addressing the emergency. Trust and clarity are elements essential to the construction of this virtuous communications process if one wishes to eliminate, or at least contrast, the ambiguity caused by the crisis and by organizational collapse.

5.3 Overall Satisfaction

Finally, the overall satisfaction expressed by the SPs regarding the way the school succeeded in reacting to the crisis was investigated by comparing a series of internal organizational factors, strongly influenced by the DTM emergency. The ten items relating to this point proved consistent when subjected to Cronbach Alpha analysis. The distribution analysis showed that few school principals belonging to the sample were profoundly dissatisfied (score 1); the elements that generated the greatest satisfaction were the collaboration and availability of teachers and the platforms used for distance teaching/learning.

In this case too, exploratory factor analysis proved useful when seeking to grasp the latent factors.

Considering the information illustrated in Table 8.3 before axis rotation and in Figure 8.7, it emerges that more than 70% of the variability of the entire set of questions was replicated by four factors, as shown in Table 8.3.

Furthermore, when examining the latent dimensions underlying the evaluation by the SPs of strategic organizational processes, with a view to ex-post reflection regarding the elements that contributed most to defining the organizational

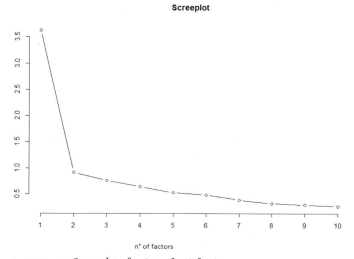

FIGURE 8.7 Scree plot of points of satisfaction

TABLE 8.3   Overall factors of satisfaction

Factors	Variance	Items
Collaboration and sharing	44.6%	Positively correlated with: – Teachers' sense of collaboration and openness; – Teaching staff's participation in the quest for shared solutions; – Families' sense of collaboration and openness; – The overall degree of competence and mastery of distance teaching techniques shown by the teaching staff.
Organizational resilience	10.5%	Positively correlated with: – Time management while organizing the activities that needed to be carried out; – The management of technical issues arising from the urgent organization of distance learning/teaching.
Enabling technologies	8.7%	Positively correlated with: – The distance learning platforms used; variable; – The overall redesign of distance learning activities and variable; – The technological resources available to the teaching staff.
Learning performances	7.7%	Negatively correlated with – Students' overall learning outcomes.

response, the centrality of collaboration and the sharing of information, meanings, experiences and anxieties alone represented 45% of the variable. This is a dimension, therefore, that brings to the fore once more communication as a strategic asset vital to management of the organizational collapse caused by the pandemic. This kind of communication goes well beyond the mere informative dimension of transmission to embrace the much more complex and multifaceted one of the relational paradigm functional to the creation of a community of meaning and membership which the mandatory closure of schools and the imposition of smart teaching and smart working interrupted so brutally.

The dimension of time management also assumed a certain significance as it represented the pace of the resolution of problems, through coordination,

TABLE 8.4   Factorial weights and communality of extracted and rotated factors[a] (sorted rotated factor loadings and communalities)

Variable	Factor 1	Factor 2	Factor 3	Communality
The interaction amongst colleagues is facilitated and implemented either by single class coordinators or by departments	0.690	0.434	−0.224	0.715
There is good coordination between management, school personnel and teachers	0.639	0.313	−0.441	0.700
The pace of lessons increased teachers' stress levels	0.580	0.083	−0.119	0.358
During the emergency, experimentation with distance teaching methods has permitted teachers to appreciate digital technologies while teaching	0.522	0.253	−0.404	0.500
Teachers have been able to adapt their teaching programmes to distance learning	0.307	0.619	−0.302	0.569
The entire faculty board has engaged in the reorganization of its activities through distance teaching methods	0.449	0.603	−0.228	0.618
Teachers are trained/competent when dealing with distance teaching	−0.055	0.537	−0.068	0.297
Distance learning can replace on-site learning	0.307	0.245	−0.916	0.993
Variance	1.8868	1.4536	1.4093	4.7497
% Var	0.236	0.182	0.176	0.594

a   The output shows several cross loadings, i.e. variables explaining several factors at the same time. In this case, variables were attributed to factors in relation to the absolute weight of factor loadings. As far as the commonalities are concerned, these proved good enough (greater than 0.25).

TABLE 8.5 Factorial weights and communality of extracted and rotated factors[a] (sorted rotated factor loadings and communalities)

Variable	Factor 1	Factor 2	Factor 3	Communality
The emergency permitted new virtuous relationships with subjects external to schools as well as other educational institutions to commence	0.885	0.189	−0.099	0.830
The emergency permitted the maintenance of relationships with subjects external to schools and school networks	0.796	0.227	−0.133	0.703
School networks have proven to be very supportive in the quest for sustainable solutions and the solution of the problem	0.549	0.014	−0.105	0.312
The emergency has allowed the school system to redefine its decision-making processes	0.173	0.900	−0.079	0.846
The emergency permitted the school system to redefine its strategic priorities for the following year	0.074	0.599	−0.213	0.409
The emergency has improved internal communications between the SPs, school personnel and teachers	0.153	0.574	−0.403	0.515
The emergency has brought to light the formative needs of teachers	0.127	0.387	−0.347	0.287
The emergency has permitted the construction of more effective communication and greater collaboration with the students' families	0.189	0.270	−0.815	0.773
Variance	1.8296	1.8072	1.0377	4.6745
% Var	0.229	0.226	0.130	0.584

a The scale is fairly consistent (0.7427) but coherence increases to 0.7695 when eliminating the item: *Schools have found themselves alone when facing the emergency*. Iteratively, the measure of coherence tends to increase further (0.8011) when eliminating the following items: *The emergency has led to significant problems in managing absences, turnovers and substitute teachers* and *the emergency has forced a reallocation of economic and professional resources in order to guarantee the continuity of distance teaching activities*. From this it follows that the coherence of the scale is satisfied when considering the eight items from which the latent factors were extracted.

TABLE 8.6 Factorial weights and communality of extracted and rotated factors (sorted rotated factor loadings and communalities)

Variable	Factor 1	Factor 2	Factor 3	Factor 4	Communality
Teachers' sense of collaboration and openness	0.809	0.000	0.250	0.000	0.733
Teaching staff's participation in the quest for shared solutions	0.563	0.470	0.000	0.000	0.573
Families' sense of collaboration and openness	0.495	0.000	0.217	−0.239	0.367
The overall degree of competence and mastery of distance teaching techniques shown by the teaching staff	0.404	0.260	0.380	−0.260	0.443
Time management while organizing the activities to be carried out	0.000	0.838	0.000	0.000	0.760
The management of technical issues arising from the urgent organization of distance learning	0.000	0.593	0.303	0.000	0.488
The distance learning platforms used	0.215	0.000	0.790	0.000	0.694
The overall redesign of distance learning activities	0.295	0.382	0.462	−0.277	0.523
The technological resources available to the teaching staff	0.288	0.258	0.425	0.000	0.341
Students' overall learning outcomes	0.203	0.219	0.000	−0.883	0.896
Variance	1.6829	1.6454	1.4239	1.0654	5.8176
% Var	0.168	0.165	0.142	0.107	0.582

timeliness and a collective response to the pursuit of these very same strategies. The enablement of technologies, unquestionably indispensable when endeavouring to guarantee continuity of schooling 'at a distance', expressed only 8.7% of the variance, confirming the fact that the revolution the school system needs to bring about is cultural rather than technological if it wishes to meet the digital challenge. In this context, it does not seem strange that students' learning outcomes appeared problematic. A school that is still engaged in redefining itself and how to cope with the digital society does not seem to have understood, as yet, what learning/teaching really means and how it should be implemented if schools are to fulfil their mission.

6 Conclusions

Having scrutinized this analysis, a number of brief considerations emerge in relation to the questions that informed the investigation. Concerning the first point investigated – the main kinds of criticisms addressed and the strategies adopted by SPs during the emergency – we can say that the foremost and gravest problem emerging concerned the social inequalities dramatically brought to light by the closure of the schools, an issue also confirmed by a cross-reading of the responses provided by the different interviewees and by other reports regarding this issue (INVALSI, 2021).

Faced with the loss of the primary educational function aimed at guaranteeing human and social development by means of a close network of formal, informal, affective and friendly social relationships that unfold within the school community, SPs and teachers tried to cope with the trauma of the unexpected lockdown recurring to all the means they could, although they were often obliged to act in solitude and without any particular order, due to the absence of coordination and general guidelines (including national ones).

As regards the second point, i.e. the key issues that – during the pandemic – were experienced daily by the main actors of the school, in view of the exceptional nature of the total closure of schools, the need for strategic reprogramming seems to have been the issue that absorbed most of the efforts of SPs during the initial phase of the pandemic. When the sense of the unimaginable event and the means by which to reconstruct a semblance of ordinariness both collapsed (Weick, 1993), the strategy chosen to address the crisis was that of making a conversational-dialogic effort designed to rebuild a system of shared meaning within which to act in a situation of unforeseen emergency. For this reason, the collective efforts of the school community, driven by the SLs, were directed towards a reorganization of the internal processes aimed at drawing up/managing internal and external information and communications; towards a reorganization of the environments/modalities of delivery of educational action; towards redesigning the system and its internal interactive factors; towards re-scheduling school activities, etc. The school discovered that it was a resilient organization where the strategic role of the SP and the middle-management staff emerged to recompose and harmonize a system that needed to be reinvented overnight.

In conclusion, we can say that the organizational collapse determined by the pandemic highlighted the relevance of styles of school leadership. It also showed that there is an urgent need for an adequate form of initial training to prepare SPs for their role and the provision of in-service retraining, capable of guaranteeing a proper understanding of processes of leadership that emphasizes importance and effectiveness of collaborative work, clear communication and the use of structured territorial networks.

Acknowledgements

This chapter is the result of extensive research carried out previously by the DiTES (Digital Technologies, Education and Society) research centre of Rome's Link Campus University, acting as the coordinator of a multi-stakeholder partnership. This collaborative effort involved the Department of Business Administration of Rome's Roma Tre University, the ANP (the national Italian association of public administrators and top school professionals), the Forum of Family Associations (FAF) and the Italian Digital Revolution Association (AIDR). We thank the referees for the valuable advice provided during the submission/evaluation phase.

Notes

1 For a detailed description of the frequencies and the sample, see Capogna et al. (2022).
2 Compared to levels of territorial coverage that potentially allow 88.9% of Italian households to access internet services with speeds greater than or equal to 30 Mbps, only 37.2% of all schools enjoy a similar connection. Coverage differs considerably from place to place in Italy. In the southern regions, in fact, the gap between coverage (infrastructure) and dissemination (penetration) of broadband and ultra-broadband services appears to be much greater. In the regions where the state invested most in infrastructures (such as Sicily and Calabria) there was no subsequent takeoff of the services (AGCOM, 2020).
3 For further methodological information on the technique and application of the technique, see De Lillo (2007).

4 According to the literature (Nunnally & Bernstein, 1994), statistical values of between 0.8 and 0.9 are considered adequate (the scale does not need to be reviewed); values lower than 0.8 suggest that the scale is incomplete (the item battery needs to be integrated); values above 0.9 indicate redundancy (the number of questions in the questionnaire needs to be reduced). This analysis, conducted using Minitab, also permits one to verify how to adapt the consistency of the scale to the exclusion of one of the indicators deemed inconsistent.
5 The values for the three factors extracted, rotated orthogonally, are shown in Table 8.4, which illustrates the weight brought to bear upon the rotated factor by each variable of the dataset, in relation to the absolute weight of factor loadings (Varimax).
6 For interpretation purposes, the three factors were extracted and rotated orthogonally using the Varimax procedure. The results are visible in Table 8.5, showing that all the items are well represented by the factors since the medium-high level of commonality. The output shows several cross loadings, yet the factor loadings have been attributed in relation to their significance. As far as commonalities are concerned, these are all good enough (above 0.25) and the following statements can be expressed.

References

AGCOM. (2020, June). *Le comunicazioni nel 2020. L'impatto del Coronavirus nei settori regolati. Allegato alla relazione annuale.* Autorità per le garanzie nelle comunicazioni.

Avolio, B. J., Kahai, S., & Dodge, G. E. (2000). E-leadership: Implications for theory, research, and practice. *Leadership Quarterly, 11*(4), 615–668. doi:10.1016/S1048-9843(00)00062-X

Barnard, C. (1968). *The function of the executive.* Harvard University Press.

Benadusi, L., & Serpieri, R. (2000). *Organizzare la scuola dell'autonomia.* Carocci.

Bourdieu, P. (1980). *Le Sens pratique. Structures, habitus, pratiques.* Éditions de Minuit (Italian translation: *Il senso pratico.* Armando Editore, 2005)

Braes, B., & Brooks, D. (2010, November 30). Organisational resilience: A propositional study to understand and identify the essential concepts. In *Proceedings of the 3rd Australian security and intelligence conference.* Edith Cowan University, Perth, Western Australia. https://ro.ecu.edu.au/asi/2/

Capogna, S. (2014). *Scuola, Università, e-learning: un'analisi sociologica.* Armando.

Capogna, S., Cocozza, A., & Cianfriglia, L. (2017). *Le sfide della scuola nell'era digitale. Una ricerca sociologica sulle competenze digitali dei docenti.* Eurilink University Press.

Capogna, S., Cocozza, A., & Cianfriglia, L. (2020). *Digital culture for educational organizations: Guidelines for teachers and education agencies.* Eurilink University Press.

Capogna, S., Musella, F., & Cianfriglia L. (2022). *Analisi della didattica a distanza durante l'emergenza Covid-19.* Eurilink University Press.

Catalin, S. H., Bogdan, B., & Dimitrie, G. R. (2014). The existing barriers in implementing total quality management. *Annals of the University of Oradea, Economic Science Series, 23*(1).

Chapman, K., MacKinnon, D., & Cumbers, A. (2004). Adjustment or renewal in regional clusters? A study of diversification amongst SMEs in the Aberdeen oil complex. *Transactions of the Institute of British Geographers, 29*(3), 382–396.

Chuna, M. P., Canstanheira, F., Neves, P., Story, J., Rego, A., & Clegg, S. (2013). *Resilience in Organizations.* Working paper. Faculdade de Economia, Nova School of Business and Economics.

Cocozza, A. (2020). *L'agire organizzativo.* Franco Angeli.

Cronbach, L. J. (1951). Coefficient alpha and the internal structure of tests. *Psychometrika, 16*(3), 297–334.

De Lillo, A. (2007). *Analisi multivariata per le scienze sociali.* Pearson Italia Spa.

Giancola, O. (2010). *Performance e disuguaglianze nei sistemi educativi europei. Un tentativo di spiegazione del 'caso' italiano.* Quaderno di Ricerca no. 31, Dipartimento Innovazione e Società, 'Sapienza' Università di Roma.

Hargittai, E. (2010). Digital na(t)ives? Variation in internet skills and uses among members of the 'Net generation'. *Sociological Inquiry, 80*(1), 92–113.

Hubbard, D. W. (2009). *The failure of risk management: Why it's broken and how to fix it.* John Wiley & Sons.

INVALSI. *Rilevazioni nazionali degli apprendimenti, 2020–21. I risultati in breve delle prove INVALSI.* https://invalsi-areaprove.cineca.it/docs/2021/Rilevazioni_Nazionali/Rapporto/14_07_2021/Sintesi_Primi_Risultati_Prove_INVALSI_2021.pdf

Jackson, L. A., et al. (2008). Race, gender, and information technology use: The new digital divide. *CyberPsychology & Behavior, 11*(4), 437–442. https://doi.org/10.1089/cpb.2007.0157

Keck, M., & Sakdapolrak, P. (2013). What is social resilience? lessons learned and ways forward. *Erdkunde, 67*(1), 5–19. doi:10.3112/erdkunde.20

Keong, F. W. F., & Mei, L. Y. (2010, March 15–16). *Sustainable development: The effect of adopting green technology on Small and Medium Enterprises' (SMEs) business resilience and competitiveness* [Paper]. International conference on business and economic research (ICBER 2010), Malaysia. Global Research Agency.

Klein, G., Wiggins, S., & Dominguez, C. O. (2010). Team sensemaking. *Theoretical Issues in Ergonomics Science, 11*(4), 304–320. doi:10.1080/14639221003729177

Lave, J., & Wenger, E. (1991). *Situated learning: Legitimate peripheral participation.* Cambridge University Press.

Lazarsfeld, P. F. (1972). Foreword. In A. Oberschall (Ed.), *The establishment of empirical sociology: Studies in continuity, discontinuity, and institutionalization.* Harper & Row.

Light, J. S. (2001, Winter), Rethinking the digital divide. *Harvard Educational Review,* 710–734. http://www.hepg.org/her/abstract/101

Lopez, P. (2010). From laptops to competences: Bridging the digital divide in higher education. *RUSC: Universities and Knowledge Society Journal, 7*(1). http://rusc.uoc.edu/ojs/index.php/rusc/article/viewFile/v7n1_pena/v7n1_pena

Martin, R. L. (2012). Regional economic resilience, hysteresis and recessionary shocks. *Journal of Economic Geography, 12*(1), 1–32.

McKinnon, J. (2013). The pedagogy of adaptation: Using specialised disciplinary knowledge to develop creative skills. *Journal of Perspectives in Applied Academic Practice, 1*(2).

McManus, S., Seville, E., Vargo, J., & Brunsdon, D. (2008). Facilitated process for improving organizational resilience. *Natural Hazards Review, 9,* 81–90.

McPhee, R. D., & Iverson, J. O. (2009). The communicative constitution of organizations: A framework for explanation. In L. L. Putnam & A. M. Nicotera (Eds.), *Building theories of organization: The constitutive role of communication* (pp. 129–140). Routledge.

McPhee, R. D., & Zaug, P. (2000). The communicative constitution of organizations: A framework for explanation. *Electronic Journal of Communication, 1*(1).

Merton, R. K. (1966). *Teoria e struttura sociale*. Il Mulino.

Mintzberg, H. (1983). *La progettazione dell'organizzazione aziendale*. Il Mulino.

Mossberger, K., Tolbert, C. J., & Stansbury, M. (2003). *Virtual inequality: Beyond digital*. Georgetown University Press.

Nonaka, I., & Takeuchi H. (1995). *The knowledge creating company: How Japanese companies create the dynamics of innovation*. Oxford University Press.

Norris, P. (2000, April 10–13). *The worldwide digital divide: Information poverty, the internet and development* [Paper]. Annual meeting of the Political Studies Association of the UK, London School of Economics and Political Science. http://www.hks.harvard.edu/fs/pnorris/Acrobat/psa2000dig.pdf

Nunnally, J. C., & Bernstein, I. H. (1994). The assessment of reliability. *Psychometric Theory, 3,* 248–292.

Oakland, J., et al. (2000). *From quality to excellence*. Department of Trade and Industry. https://webarchive.nationalarchives.gov.uk/ukgwa/20050302172152/ http://www2.dti.gov.uk/quality/

OECD. (2019). *Skills outlook 2019: Thriving in a digital world*. OECD Publishing. https://doi.org/10.1787/df80bc12-en

OECD. (2020). *Education at a glance 2020: OECD indicators*. OECD Publishing. https://doi.org/10.1787/69096873-en

Olivos, A. M. (2014). *From individual to organizational resilience: A case study review* [MS thesis]. University of Pennsylvania. https://repository.upenn.edu/cgi/viewcontent.cgi?article=1073&context=od_theses_msod

Palmeri, E. (2021). Le politiche adottate per fronteggiare l'emergenza: inquadramento culturale-normativo. In S. Capogna, F. Musella, & L. Cianfriglia (Eds.), *La didattica a distanza durante l'emergenza COVID 19*. Eurilink University Press.

Robichaud, D., & Cooren, F. (2013). *Organization and organizing: Materiality, agency, and discourse*. Routledge.

Rovati, G. (1986). La 'survey': un possibile passaggio dal micro al macro. *Studi di sociologia, 24*(3/4), 416–441.

Sanna, V. S., & Salvati, L. (2014). Resilienza economia: dibattito teorico e metodi di valutazione. *Memorie Geografiche, n.s., 12*, 85–88.

Schraagen, J. M., & Van de Ven, J. (2011). Human factors aspects of ICT for crisis management. *Cognition, Technology & Work, 13*(3), 175–187. http://dx.doi.org/10.1007/s10111-011-0175-6

Stansbury, M., et al. (2003). *Virtual inequality: Beyond the digital divide*. Georgetown University Press.

Staw, B. M., Sandelands, L. E., & Dutton, J. E. (1981). Threat rigidity effects in organizational behavior: A multilevel analysis. *Administrative Science Quarterly, 26*(4), 501–524. https://doi.org/10.2307/2392337

Strangio, D., & Ambrosetti, E. (2018). *Public policies towards the family in Italy. An analysis of the evolution of the Italian welfare state and its impact on gender and generations*. Routledge.

Sutcliffe, K. M., & Vogus, T. J. (2003). Organizing for resilience. In K. S. Cameron, J. E. Dutton, & R. E. Quinn (Eds.), *Positive organizational scholarship: Foundations of a new discipline* (pp. 94–110). Berrett-Koehler.

Talib, F., & Rahman, Z. (2015). Identification and prioritization of barriers to total quality management implementation in service industry. *TQM Journal, 27*(5), 591–615.

Taylor, J. R., Cooren, F., Giroux, N., & Robichaud, D. (1996). The communicational basis of organization: Between the conversation and the text. *Communication Theory, 6*(1), 1–39.

Vogus, T. J., & Sutcliffe, K. M. (2007, October 7–10). Organizational resilience: Towards a theory and research agenda. In *Proceedings of the IEEE international conference on systems, man and cybernetics*, Montréal, Canada. doi:10.1109/ICSMC.2007.4414160

Weick, K. E. (1969). *The social psychology of organizing*. Addison-Wesley.

Weick, K. E. (1988). Enacted sensemaking in crisis situations. *Journal of Management Studies, 25*(4), 305–317.

Weick, K. E. (1993). The collapse of sensemaking in organizations: The Mann Gulch disaster. *Administrative Sciences Quarterly, 38*, 628–652.

Weick, K. E., & Sutcliffe, K. M. (2007). *Managing the unexpected: Resilient performance in an age of uncertainty* John Wiley & Sons.

Weick, K. E., Sutcliffe, K. M., & Obstfeld, D. (2005). Organizing and the process of sensemaking. *Organization Science, 16*(4), 409–421.

Wolbers, J., & Boersma, K. (2013). The common operational picture as collective sensemaking. *Journal of Contingencies and Crisis Management, 21*(4), 186–199. doi:10.1111/1468-5973.12027

Zani, S., & Cerioli, A. (2007). *Analisi dei dati e data mining per le decisioni aziendali*. Giuffrè editore.

CHAPTER 9

The Platformization and Commodification of Italian Schools during the Covid-19 Crisis
Implications for Policy and Future Research

Gianna Cappello

Washington, DC
In 2011 Sarah Wysocki finished her sophomore year as a teacher at a Washington, DC, middle school. Everyone (students, parents, principals) appreciated her, yet she found herself inexplicably fired. The decision followed from the results of a teacher evaluation software introduced by local authorities to reform the school system. The software assigned each teacher a score calculated half based on the observation of experts during class lessons and half by an algorithm that – combining several factors – established how much of students' academic progress was due to the teacher. This software was not without problems, however. For example, the marks in the previous year's profit tests weighed heavily while the impact of personal and family events on school performance was highly simplified. Wanting to know how her score had been calculated, Wysocki discovered that the algorithm's code was impenetrable. Furthermore, her suspicion that students in her class had got above-average grades in the previous year was confirmed by the *Washington Post* and *USA Today*. Their investigations revealed a significant number of erasures on the standardized tests run by many schools in the district, including Wysocki's, hence raising questions of cheating. Indeed, the algorithm seemed to generate a perverse effect whereby teachers modified their behaviour to conform to what was rewarded (O'Neil, 2016).

Italy
In 2016 almost 10,000 Italian teachers, newly recruited through a public competition, were to be assigned positions across the nation according to their scores and geographical preferences. To optimize and speed up the process, the ministry adopted an algorithm developed by Hewlett Packard Enterprise, as an investigation from a public television programme revealed.[1] However, something in the algorithmic calculations went wrong, and almost 7,000 teachers were assigned positions that did

not take account of their scores or geographical preferences. Through the legal experts of a trade union, some of them asked the ministry to access the algorithm's code in compliance with Law 241/1990 concerning the right to access documents and acts of public administration procedures. The ministry denied it, arguing that the code was incomprehensible to non-experts and that access could not be given because the algorithm was not 'a public administrative act' and was protected by copyright law. As a consequence of the teachers' appeal, the administrative court issued a historic sentence establishing three groundbreaking principles: (1) the expertise required to understand the subject (the algorithm's code) cannot be considered a reason for not giving access to non-expert citizens since they can rely on party consultants; (2) the algorithm is a 'digital' administrative act; (3) neither copyright nor intellectual property may prevent access provided that it is not motivated by commercial reasons.[2]

1 Introduction

These two examples reveal the crucial role Big Data and algorithms play as they increasingly inform public policymaking and institutional practices, producing an impact on people's everyday lives. An emerging body of scholarly research – Critical Data Studies – has been working on this role, shedding light on how society's current platformization is linked to a much longer privatization and reorganization of the public sector.

This chapter intends to reflect on how the Covid-19 pandemic has dramatically accelerated these processes, focusing on school education in particular. Health Big Data and apps have been crucial in the effort to take concrete measures to fight the pandemic, while platforms have helped organize vaccination rounds. Nevertheless, they have also been politicized, if not ignored, manipulated or used to control. Digital services and solutions have been crucial for schools, too. At the beginning of April 2020, one month after the World Health Organization declaration of the global pandemic, schools and universities in 173 countries were closed, affecting almost 1.5 billion learners (84.8% of total).[3] The adoption of technology to support remote teaching – in most cases praiseworthily offered for free by big tech companies – was the only solution, making it difficult to untangle the link between philanthropy and capitalism and discern between profit goals and charitable efforts. In a way, schools have become 'experimental laboratories', producing data and insights at an unprecedented scale, allowing educational technology businesses to make better plans for the future (Williamson et al., 2020).

In this chapter I present a brief review of the growing body of critical research interested in opening up the 'black-box society' (Pasquale, 2015) to understand the 'materiality' of Big Data, algorithms and platforms and how they affect policymaking. I will then argue that the pandemic has given big tech companies new territories to colonize and ultimately lock into self-perpetuating cycles of expansion. Finally, focusing on Italian public schools, I intend to show how during the pandemic remote teaching was mainly provided through corporate platforms, raising concerns on how the industry-led digitalization and platformization of Italian schools – underway well before the outbreak of the pandemic – is going to change the notion of education and public policymaking in this field.

2   The Politics of Big Data and Algorithms

On an average day, people worldwide produce massive amounts of Big Data, nurturing the algorithms that govern the ubiquitous digital devices they interface with for work and leisure. Only recently, the functioning of Big Data and algorithms has drawn attention from scholars of social sciences and the humanities, contrasting an approach that usually looks at their technical features, as with Laney's (2001) popular 'three Vs': Big Data as an increase in volume, velocity and variety. They question their presumed neutrality, arguing that they are 'framed technically, economically, ethically, temporally, spatially and philosophically' and 'do not exist independently of the ideas, instruments, practices, contexts and knowledges used to generate, process and analyse them'. They are collected from a 'total sum of all possible data available' and hence are 'inherently partial, selective and representative, and the distinguishing criteria used in their capture has consequences' (Kitchin, 2014, pp. 2–3). By searching, analysing, profiling and visualizing data in a certain way, algorithms regulate and discipline people, processes, places and events. As such, they are profoundly *performative* as they *make things happen* (Beer, 2019). Although their creators might argue that they reduce or even remove biased human intermediation and subjectivity from decision-making, they deepen and exacerbate traditional problems rather than reforming them. In other words, Big Data and algorithms have an intrinsic political nature and contribute to developing specific 'ideological and political ontologies and epistemologies' (Prinsloo, 2019, p. 3), being cause and effect altogether of neoliberal forms of governance, policymaking and capital accumulation (Zuboff, 2019).

Policymakers across many fields of public provision – healthcare, welfare, education, law enforcement – are sharing 'the widespread belief that large data sets offer a higher form of intelligence and knowledge that can generate insights that were previously impossible, with the aura of truth, objectivity and accuracy' (Boyd & Crawford, 2012, p. 663). Adopting the ideology of 'dataism' (Van Dijck, 2014), they endorse the emancipatory promises of Big Data as 'the holy grail of behavioural knowledge. Data and metadata culled from Google, Facebook, and Twitter are generally considered *imprints* or *symptoms* of people's actual behaviour or moods, while the platforms themselves are presented merely as neutral facilitators' (p. 199, emphasis in original). This 'technological solutionism' (Morozov, 2013) legitimates a much longer transition from centralized to decentralized forms of rule- and decision-making where both state and non-state actors are supposed to interact *on equal terms* for the common good. In reality, this transition is creating an asymmetrical situation where the market's biggest actors have taken a predominant role, at the detriment of less powerful actors such as citizens, communities, civil society organizations, smaller companies, bringing to an oligopolistic privatization of the internet governance (De Nardis, 2019). Familiar binaries upon which the institutional and legal frameworks of social order have traditionally been predicated – private vs public, market vs state, consumer vs citizen – are increasingly blurred, supporting the view that private actors are more efficient than the public ones for provision in key fields such as healthcare or education. This situation is nourished by a rhetoric of technological 'disruption' that, while celebrating the role of the private sector as the driver of progress and innovation, fosters a 'de-governmentalization of the state' (Van Dijck et al., 2018, p. 46), creating a powerful and perverse self-fulfilling prophecy. The space left vacant by inefficient states is occupied by big tech corporations whose services and evidence-based expertise solve problems better than any government could ever possibly do.

3   'Participatory Culture' and Educational Policies in the Platform Society

In 2009 Jenkins et al., in a seminal and quite controversial book, described the emerging wave of online social networks – Web 2.0 – as an expression of 'participatory culture', i.e. a

> culture with relatively low barriers to artistic expression and civic engagement, strong support for creating and sharing creations, and some type of informal mentorship whereby experienced participants pass along knowledge to novices. In a participatory culture, members also believe their contributions matter and feel some degree of social connection with one another (at the least, members care about others' opinions of what they have created). (Jenkins et al., 2009, pp. 5–6)

THE PLATFORMIZATION AND COMMODIFICATION OF ITALIAN SCHOOLS 223

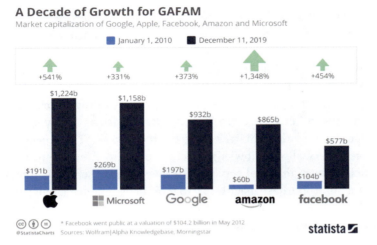

FIGURE 9.1   GAFAM growth (2010–2020) (from statista.com/chart/20285/market-capitalization-of-google-apple-facebook-amazon-and-microsoft/, CC BY-ND)

In today's 'platform society' (Van Dijck et al., 2018), the benefits of 'participatory' culture are more and more reconfigured and exploited within into the platform logic and corporate interests of high-tech companies, the GAFAM (Google, Apple, Facebook, Amazon and Microsoft). In the last decade, collecting and processing massive amounts of data about their users, they have managed to make huge profits, as Figure 9.1 shows.

GAFAM make their profits by *steering* social interaction (by producing new data) and also by *shaping* it through a constant adaptation/renovation of their interfaces and functionalities as they are being tested daily by users. This produces effects both at an economic and social level, like when Facebook, having been criticized for its biased approach when soliciting personal information about gender and sexual orientation, introduced a more comprehensive range of 'other' identity options in the drop-down menu. 'Not only did this change make economic sense, eliciting more refined customer information, but it also actively influenced social norms by expanding the conventional binary options' (Van Dijck et al., 2018, p. 11). Indeed, through a simple technical change in the interface, Facebook succeeded in appearing politically correct and getting more specific data from users, hence more profit. Increasingly, users let platforms and their algorithms be the mute and invisible 'experts' who select information and shape interactions for them while still thinking that it is their choice.

As said, one key field where these processes are increasingly apparent is education. For decades, public funding has gone to educational-technology devices and infrastructures and more recently to platform-based teaching and school management forms. Embracing a rhetoric of 'disruption', educational policymakers have aligned themselves with transnational bodies such as the OECD in celebrating the revolutionary potential of the 'tool industry' that is

> a population of specialised firms that invent, design and commercialise educational tools [...] [which] involves a process of relocation of knowledge at least in part away from the point of delivery of the educational service. A shift in knowledge 'holding' is taking place as a new site of knowledge accumulation emerges: the tool producer. [...] The process of relocation of specialised knowledge about tools away from the institution which delivers the final service – in this case the school – allows generic and multi-purpose machines and tools to be produced, replacing the specialised tools which would formerly have been developed within each organisation delivering the service. (OECD, 2016, p. 134)

An example of this process of 'relocation' occurs when AI statistical modelling and classification are used to grade essays by turning large bodies of text into numbers (Selwyn, 2016). Of course, machine-graded testing is not entirely new, especially in higher education. What is new, however, is the introduction of automated scoring systems into mainstream school education, on the one hand, and their use to grade qualitative assignments such as essays (and not simply multiple-choice or true/false tests), on the other. What usually happens is that the system first 'learns' how to grade by analysing a sample of human-graded essays in terms of word use, semantics, text structure, organization and so on. It then uses this learning to develop complex mathematical models for future grading. These systems are increasingly regarded as valid, reliable and fair as their human counterpart (the teacher), indeed even better as they can work 24/7, provide instant feedback and, above all, deal with large amounts of grading. Another important aspect worth mentioning is that the algorithm also learns from the data flows produced by the users (teachers, students, principals, administration staff, parents), allowing the platform to improve its productivity by constantly adapting itself to their needs and preferences and predicting future developments.

As this example makes clear, data-driven education aspires to be *'speedy, accessible, revealing, panoramic, prophetic and smart'*: *speedy* because data analytics delivers and analyses information in real time and continuously, closing the 'gap between data capture and analysis'; *accessible* because its final product (but not the process that led to it) is available in one button touch to everybody; *revealing* and *panoramic* because, by bracketing out the subjectivity of human judgement, it can process vast and complex amounts of information otherwise impenetrable to the human 'naked eye'; in revealing the unseen, data analytics emerges as *prophetic* because, by constantly learning from its operations (machine learning), it can predict the future and enable *smart* measures and outcomes (Beer, 2019, pp. 22–23; emphasis in original).

Neil Selwyn (2016) questions this 'allure of data for educators and educationalists', arguing that 'algorithms, analytics and data mining all carry the promise of bringing technical precision to what is otherwise an imprecise and unpredictable area of society' (p. 96). How precise and predictable can you be by quantifying aspects of education such as attention, satisfaction, motivation? Indeed, there is an implicit reductionism in the idea that education can be measured through artificial intelligence, a reductionism that decontextualizes educational processes from the subjective, social, cultural and political realities of what data are supposed to measure. As Selwyn puts it, '[t]he danger exists of educational data systems only measuring what can be easily measured, rather what cannot be easily measured but is nevertheless important' (2016, p. 98). There is also a problem of 'dataveillance', i.e. the constant monitoring and tracking of educational actors as they engage in online learning environments. This raises important ethical questions with regards to four interrelated aspects: (a) how these actors alter and self-regulate their behaviours (consciously or not) to conform to the 'norms' established by the algorithms; (b) the power and control asymmetry existing between users and platforms' proprietors; (c) the need to safeguard data privacy and transparency on how data are used; (d) how data 'portray' people's identities and performance and how this impacts on their career and public life, as the examples opening this chapter show.

To sum up, the digitalization and platformization of education touch important issues regarding privacy, autonomy and how education is conceived, delivered, practised and governed (Williamson, 2017; Landri, 2018; Selwyn, 2019). 'Platformization is likely to redefine education as a common good as it gets caught between two ideological sets of values: *Bildung* vis-à-vis skills, education versus learnification, teachers' autonomy versus automated data analytics, and public institutions versus corporate platforms' (Van Dijck et al., 2018, pp. 118–119). As we shall see with the Italian case, schools are becoming data-production centres where every aspect of the schooling performance (from teaching and learning to management and governance) is being recorded, processed and turned into complex indicator metrics and institutional data dashboards to facilitate decision-making and planning. Undoubtedly, educational technologies, including recent developments in online teaching, learning analytics and AI, can promote positive developments towards academic improvement, personalized and evidence-based learning, school efficiency and innovation. However, they can also exacerbate existing forms of discrimination and promote excessive standardization and privatization. Platforms' constraints and affordances may also cause a de-professionalization of teaching as they require teachers to coordinate with (and subordinate themselves to) their functionalities, and ultimately 'outsource' part of their work to automated machines, such as 'teacher bots' that interact with students and give real-time assessment. As Perrotta et al. (2021) argue:

> The introduction of automation in the pedagogic environment does not eliminate teachers' labour, but reconfigures it by generating new tasks that require teachers to synchronize effectively with the platform, and by slowly but perceptibly shifting their efforts from actual teaching to the 24/7 coordination, moderation and facilitation of student engagement. In this sense, the pedagogy of teachers and students, understood as a form of educational and developmental agency, is becoming equated with pedagogy in the use of platforms, e.g. signing on, assigning tasks, looking for tasks, submitting items, moderating interactions in the classroom 'stream' (Google Classroom's equivalent of Facebook's Timeline) and so forth. (p. 108)

4 The Platformization of Italian Schools before and during the Covid-19 Pandemic

4.1 *Governing the Pandemic between Philanthropy, Corporate Profit and Public Interest*

As said, the outburst of the pandemic in 2020 gave high-tech companies, after years of investment in developing efficient and profitable models of distance education, the occasion to exercise philanthropy but also to escalate and experiment with those models in view of further uses in the post-pandemic world. National ministries of education were obliged to collaborate with them to facilitate the continuity of schooling through remote learning. The immediate philanthropic response of these companies brought many policymakers across the globe to share the enthusiastic words pronounced in March 2020 by the governor of California after Google announced its free support of remote education in rural households: 'We need more Googles' (Elias, 2020).

However, several commentators have raised concerns about this philanthropic involvement during the pandemic (De Angelis, 2020; Pievatolo, 2020; Klein, 2020; Magalhaes & Couldry, 2020). In her 2015 study of the Bill and Melinda Gates Foundation, sociologist Lindsey McGoey reminds us that, while philanthropists may certainly be well-intentioned in directing resources to important and often neglected causes, their charitable donations are subsidized by taxpayers, either because they receive tax privileges for donations or because their unpaid taxes could have gone to social programmes chosen by citizen-elected policymakers. She also reminds us that wealthy donors can withdraw their charity whenever and for whatever reason. No law enforcement may compel them to redistribute their wealth for charity. Besides expressing their gratitude, citizens and public policymakers have little say in philanthropists' charitable practices; and that is precisely the problem. As Saint Augustine professed in earlier times, charity is no substitute for justice withheld.

For sure, the pandemic has produced sound profit for GAFAM. According to company filings reported by Statista,[4] if we look at their total revenues in the first nine months of 2020 vs 2019, we see an increase for all of them: Google-Alphabet +9%, Amazon +35%, Facebook +17%, Apple +4%, Microsoft +13%. Of course, investments in education are presumably only part of this increase, but a part that will escalate soon. As Holon IQ experts have recently predicted,[5] investments in digital education will increase from $227B in 2020 to $404B by 2025. Much of this spending will be invested in integrating into core education delivery and learning processes augmented/virtual reality (from $1.8B in 2020 to $12.6B in 2025) and artificial intelligence (from $0.8B in 2020 to $6.1B in 2025). Finally, they calculate that venture capital investments in digital education have doubled from $7.08B in 2019 to $16B in 2020.

In Italy, the Covid-19 pandemic has accelerated the platformization process of the school system and its increasing subordination to big tech industries' expertise and services. This process dates back to 2011 when the Ministry of Education launched Scuola in Chiaro (SiC),[6] a web platform to collect, standardize, reorganize and visualize transparently (*in chiaro*) all the statistical data that were previously scattered in different sources. Following Landri's reconstruction (2018), we can see that, over the years, Scuola in Chiaro has widened its scope and scale so that today it includes:

1. all available data about the single school collected by the ministry;
2. SIDI (Sistema Informativo dell'Istruzione), a web application for the uploading of information about the school drawn from centralized datasets such as self-evaluation reports (RAV, *rapporto di auto-valutazione*), the school plan for improvement, students' standardized scores collected by INVALSI (Istituto nazionale per la valutazione del sistema educativo di istruzione e di formazione);
3. additional data provided by the school at local level;
4. a geolocalizing application to locate the school and its surroundings;
5. the online school application procedure (the idea being that by consulting all data provided by SiC students and parents can make more informed choices for enrolment).

The development of SiC is part of a contract with Hewlett Packard Enterprise Services Italia, meaning that the entire information system of Italian schools is the result of a public-private partnership where the technical partner 'translates political aims and bureaucratic lines into an apparatus composed of an infrastructure of data and a set of interlocking software applications' (Landri, 2018, p. 72).

Another important application developed within this partnership is the Dashboard, an algorithmic function that generates a meta-content analysis of the RAVs, checking if and how the school's objectives and priorities have been achieved. Using particular formulas, the Dashboard makes (its own) sense of RAV's Big Data and offer solutions which are then passed to school principals soliciting them to take responsibility and be accountable for their RAV. Indeed, the Dashboard perfectly exemplifies how algorithms do not simply collect and analyse data but also inform policymaking decisions and act as *performative agents* (Prinsloo, 2019). The whole self-evaluation procedure promoted by the ministry through the Dashboard is not simply a bureaucratic matter as it 'affect[s] the way headteachers will be nominated and evaluated' and counts as a policy tool 'for discipline and control' (Landri, 2018, p. 93). Undeniably, the Dashboard is valuable in finding contradictions, inconsistencies, superficialities in the RAVs, but how this is done are 'opaque and imbued with politics. [...] The lines of code of the algorithms searching for inconsistencies are not public' (p. 101).

The pandemic rushed Italian schools to strengthen their digital infrastructures and online services. After the national lockdown declaration on March 8th 2020, the government issued a series of legislative acts, among which the activation of *didattica a distanza* (DAD, distance learning) and online meetings for all school collegial bodies. A couple of weeks later, a fund of €85M was designated to enhance infrastructures, platforms, connectivity and devices for students and support teacher training. In June, DAD was established as mandatory and not 'recommended', as in the first emergency period. Finally, at the end of August, in the School Plan for 2020–2021, the Ministry of Education announced the replacement of DAD with DID (*didattica integrata digitale*, integrated digital education), a combination of in-presence and distance education, depending on the evolution of the pandemic.

Along with these acts, the Ministry of Education created a portal – Didattica a Distanza[7] – listing a series of free resources and services for teachers and students (e-learning platforms, multimedia materials, tools for cooperation and exchange of best practices, online communities). As for e-learning platforms, in the absence of an institutional one, the Italian ministry (unlike the French one[8]) suggests three private platforms: Google Suite for Education, Microsoft and WeSchool.[9] The sub-section called Solidarietà Digitale[10] offers other services, again mainly private. There is also a space for a 'Community'[11] developed in cooperation with Cisco, Google and IBM and hosted on the WeSchool platform. Undeniably, the ministry made the choice to give little mention to free and/or open-source solutions such as Open didattica,[12] or FARE (Free Architecture for Remote Education),[13] developed within public institutions such as the Polytechnic of Turin or the GARR network[14] promoted by the ministry itself in the late 1980s.[15]

Admittedly, this choice was forced by the urgent need to reorganize teaching across the country relying on what teachers and principals were already familiar with (as findings below show). But questions arise: Why and how did we get to the point that corporate solutions were the only choice left with all the concerns about copyright and privacy issues that come with it?[16] How is it possible that out of all the massive investment done over the years to digitalize Italian schools, none has ever gone to create (as in France) an institutional platform and to promote free and open-source solutions? Doesn't this ultimately prove that *lock-in* and *network effects*[17] are well in place, forcing us to recognize the conflict of interest between philanthropic efforts and the search for profit carried out by raising brand awareness and fidelity at the earliest schooling age?

4.2 *Corporate Platforms in Italian Schools during the Pandemic: Some Empirical Findings*

Empirical findings on the platformization of Italian schools during the pandemic can be drawn from research done to study the pedagogical, psychological and socio-economic effects of lockdown measures.[18] For example, findings from a survey[19] of almost 4,000 teachers from all school levels carried out by INDIRE (2020a, 2020b) in June 2020 show that Google Suite for Education and WhatsApp were used by over 60% of teachers (specifically, Google Meet 66.5%, WhatsApp 61.7%, Google Classroom 51.3%). Other platforms are far below this percentage (Zoom 20.5%, WeSchool 11.2%, Microsoft Teams 7.2%, Webex 6.4% and Moodle at just 4.6%). Indeed, a jungle of corporate solutions derived from decisions taken mostly locally, either at school management level (77.6%) or personally. Personal choices were made 'after confronting different solutions' (66.5%), 'because I already knew them' (65.6%), 'because I followed the digital education coordinator's suggestion' (61.7%), 'taking into account technological equipment and students' competence' (51.3%). Even parents played a role, as 20.5% of respondents declare they followed the suggestion of 'expert parents'. Unsurprisingly, the topics on which 84% of teachers had some training during the pandemic included platforms and online tools (66%), teaching methodologies (53%) and evaluation (34%). Barely 6% chose the open-ended option 'other'. It is within this tiny percentage that the word 'privacy' appears, suggesting that, for the time being, certain kinds of issues are not on top of Italian teachers' minds.

When asked about the digital teaching strategies adopted during the lockdown, online videoconferencing (basically a digital version of frontal instruction) together with 'homework assignments' were the first ones for almost the totality of teachers. 'Online research and laboratory activities' (that is something more sophisticated than mere online lecturing) are much rarer, being used only by 18.3% of pre-school teachers, 31.3% of primary teachers, 44.1% of first-degree secondary school teachers and 40.4% of second-degree secondary school teachers.

Teachers were also asked if their use of digital technologies had increased with the pandemic and if they were willing to use them in the future. As CENSIS recommends, reporting the findings of a survey with almost 3,000 principals, the positive answer given to both questions urges the need to

> create a platform, an institutional reference point that offers guidelines, examples, practical supports, multimedia products [...] and outline an overall plan for the public system of digital education, which, besides ensuring connectivity and technological infrastructure for all schools, coordinates all the investments in innovation, up to now largely assigned on a mere project-basis. (2020, p. 19)[20]

Like teachers, principals felt unprepared to cope with reorganizing teaching through online solutions, proving the inadequacy of a strategy exclusively based on choices made at the local level, by a single institute, sometimes by a single teacher, as we have seen. Therefore, we have 'a "patchy" situation not only region-wise but also between schools and even between classes' (p. 9).

Another important insight derived from CENSIS research is the underdevelopment of the telematic infrastructure and connectivity. According to principals, during the pandemic, Italian schools experienced the effects of the digital divide. In particular,
- 71.5% report that their teachers and students experienced problems with connectivity;
- 82.1% declare that the different technological equipment, connectivity and familiarity of use both among teachers and students were an obstacle to the full functioning of remote teaching;
- 74.8% think that the DAD widened the learning gap among students, depending on their availability of IT tools and supports and the technological culture of their family;

– 84.2% declare that the school had to provide students with hardware to follow remote teaching from home.

These figures confirm the gaps reported by Istat (2020): in 2018–2019, 33% of families had no PC or tablet, a percentage that rises to 41.6% in the southern regions; 12.3% of children between the ages of six and seventeen did not have a PC or tablet at home and of these more than half reside in the South. Even among those who own it, more than half (57%) must share it with their family (only 6.1% live in families with members having their own PC). Indeed, as CENSIS (2020) concludes,

> we are a population of smartphone owners. Much less common among Italian families are personal computers and tablets, devices more suitable for remote learning. Not to mention that even in the houses where a PC is present, it is usually shared among the various members of the family, to study or work. (p. 11)

In other words, the digital divide is still an issue in our country. Among the reasons for not attending remote classes, teachers indicate the digital divide to be the most important, followed by socio-economic disadvantages (INDIRE, 2020a; Ranieri, 2021). Whether you conceive it as a mere question of use vs non-use, access vs non-access, or, more correctly, as the result of a much more complex interplay of factors, the bottom line is the same: students who are already well-resourced are more likely to benefit the most from digital education. Policymakers' long-standing attempts to fix this problem (including those done during the pandemic) by improving technology access and infrastructures in public schools and supporting individuals' digital skills development prove problematic for two fundamental reasons: first because they tend to focus on individuals, bracketing out how inequalities are also the result of broader social structures and conditions of living; second, because they celebrate technology as intrinsically 'good', again bracketing out its complex entrenchment in contemporary neo-liberal discourses about the 'disruptive' power of digital technology, especially when it is provided or even 'donated' by ICT companies. While not denying the need to work on improving access, infrastructures and skills, nor the philanthropic generosity of big tech companies, we also need to theorize better the link between inequalities, technology, private capital and public education (or, if you wish, education as public good), and try to 'design technologies that facilitate more equitable futures for all' (Selwyn et al., 2020, p. 2). We need further research to study the long-term effects and consequences of the increasing platformization and commodification of the school systems across the globe. Of course, the pandemic has not caused this process, but it has undoubtedly reinforced it in the daily experience of educators, students, parents and policymakers in our country as well as around the world.

5   Conclusion

The world pandemic has suddenly accelerated the datafication and platformization of education, bringing all industrialized countries to a generalized adoption of remote teaching to counteract schools and universities' mass closures. In a way, the datafication of education during the pandemic needs to be seen as an epiphenomenal manifestation of two aspirations nurturing each other: on the one hand, the ambition by public institutions to measure education through objective numbers and govern schools through increasingly pervasive technologies of data mining; on the other hand, the aspiration by big tech companies to make education the new capitalist frontier for their data harvesting. Indeed, 'as millions of students sign up to new platforms in order to be able to access education during the pandemic, long-running concerns over data privacy and the use of data for student profiling and control need to be brought back into focus' (Williamson et al., 2020, p. 113).

As in other fields, education datafication implies reducing educational processes into quantifiable bits of information that are eventually inserted into massive digital databases for measurement and calculation. The application of ever more sophisticated data mining techniques and analysis produces a range of specific products such as learning analytics, adaptive learning software, educational bots, etc. The process (and need) to collect large datasets of information in education is not new and certainly pre-exists to digital technologies. However, what is new is not only the more significant amount of data that can be processed but, more importantly, the fact that – thanks to educational platforms – the gap between educational action and data collection is overcome. Data are collected at the very instant in which teaching and learning occur. All single actions teachers and students make (clicking on a content or a link, watching a video tutorial, interacting with others online in a gamified educational challenge, playing a role in a simulation, etc.) produce a bit of information that is then engulfed by a sophisticated infrastructure of data mining and algorithmic processing that is ultimately unknown and unintelligible to them.

Critical attention needs to be given to the actual 'disruptive' efficacy and motivations of corporate interventions in education. Not only do they seem to 'have promised much but delivered less' (Selwyn, 2016, p. 123), but they are also entrenched in paradoxes: they are private but appear to serve the public good; seem neutral, even philanthropic, but are firmly based in a particular set of ideological values and motivations (including the pursuit of profit, raising brand awareness among 'skilled' workers, customers' lock-in); seem to operate locally but their scope and impact are global; appear to replace inefficient top-down, 'big government' policies with bottom-up self-empowering actions while developing a highly centralized structure that remains opaque to their end-users (principals, teachers, students, parents, policymakers).

What education will look like in the post-Covid world depends on the capacity (and willingness) of people to disentangle these paradoxes and contradictions. UNESCO's International Commission on the Futures of Education (2020) has recently proposed 'nine ideas for public action' to address these issues. In particular, Action no. 6 is worth citing as a suggestion for future research and policy commitment:

> The Commission calls for global collaboration among governments, philanthropy, and non-profit organizations to develop and distribute open educational resources and open platforms, recognizing that much of what is currently provided by private companies should become a public undertaking where advancing the interests and capabilities of learners is the sole purpose.

However, two very distinct situations are often confused. It is one thing to employ digital tools in teachers' pedagogical work with students. In digital societies, it is unthinkable to exclude from school the possibilities of access to knowledge and communication that are increasingly seen as a necessary component of daily life – that we correctly speak of 'digital divides' shows how important internet access and device connectivity have become. Here, our efforts should focus on open licensing and open access policies that facilitate no-cost use, reuse, repurposing and adaption. Open educational resources must be prioritized; public education cannot be dependent on digital platforms provided by private companies.

It is a very different thing to design teaching and learning out of ready-made materials and content as this reduces and distorts the work of teachers and students. Public education cannot be defined and controlled by content and methods built outside of the pedagogical space and outside of the human relationships between teachers and students. The forced scramble for materials and platforms that we have seen during the pandemic poses a great risk to the teaching profession and its autonomy and could have serious consequences for the futures of education. We must ensure that any digital transition is not just an effort pushed by technology companies but that teachers, students, governments, civil society representatives and privacy advocates are also represented and shape these transformations (UNESCO, 2020, pp. 16–17).

Notes

1. raiplay.it/video/2017/01/Presa-diretta---Caos-scuola-792dcab5-f1cf-4dc4-a2bb-bae167aae9d7.html
2. https://www.altalex.com/documents/news/2017/05/17/diritto-di-accesso-algoritmo
3. en.unesco.org/covid19/educationresponse
4. https://www.statista.com/chart/21584/gafam-revenue-growth/
5. https://www.holoniq.com/edtech/10-charts-that-explain-the-global-education-technology-market/
6. cercalatuascuola.istruzione.it/cercalatuascuola/
7. istruzione.it/coronavirus/didattica-a-distanza.html
8. When the lockdown started, the French Ministry of Education created the portal apps.education.fr/, including a videoconferencing service and a series of other free and open-source software. French schools could also count on the existing institutional e-learning platform – Ma classe à la maison (cned.fr/maclassealamaison) – hosted on public servers complying with the EU GPDR requirements. Also hosted on public servers is the inter-ministerial videoconferencing platform offered to all public administration departments (numerique.gouv.fr/outils-agents/webconference-etat/).
9. WeSchool, founded in 2016 by Marco De Rossi, currently has 2 million registered students. It has recently announced a capital increase of €6.4M thanks to venture capital (ilsole24ore.com/art/weschool-64-milioni-euro-la-startup-didattica-digitale-ADftcai).
10. solidarietadigitale.agid.gov.it/iniziative/didattica-digitale/
11. lascuolacontinua.it/
12. opendidattica.org/wordpress/
13. https://fare.polito.it/
14. garr.it/it/news-e-eventi/1656-videoconferenza-risorse-garr-per-l-emergenza-covid-19
15. GARR (Gruppo per l'Armonizzazione delle Reti della Ricerca) is the national computer network for universities and research promoted in the late 1980s by the Ministry of Education. It currently includes public research institutes such as CNR, ENEA, INAF, INFN, INGV and the CRUI (Conference of Rectors of Italian Universities).
16. In a detailed analysis of the copyright and data protection terms of corporate platforms used during the pandemic, Ducato et al. (2020) shed light 'on the critical aspects of and potential "creepy" functions hidden in the jungle of terms of service and privacy policies of online services used for ERT (Emergency Remote Teaching)'.
17. *Lock-in* occurs when consumers are confronted with the economic, psychological and social costs of switching from one product and familiarizing themselves with another. Lock-in combines with the *network effect* by which the value of a good depends on the number of customers already using that good.
18. See, for example, Colombo et al., 2020; Santagati & Barabanti, 2020; Ranieri, 2021; Ranieri et al., 2020; Lucisano, 2020. Additional research is presented in a monographic issue of *Lifelong Lifewide Learning* (edaforum.it/ojs/index.php/LLL/issue/view/38) and *Scuola democratica* (rivisteweb.it/issn/1129-731X/earlyaccess).
19. The survey questionnaire is available at: indagine.indire.it/index.php/724785

20 Following the French example, the Italian Ministry of Education has recently announced that it is working on a single institutional digital platform (miur.gov.it/-/scuola-ministero-al-lavoro-su-piattaforma-digitale-unica-azzolina-acceleriamo-innovazione-costruiamo-la-scuola-del-futuro-on).

References

Beer, D. (2019). *The data gaze*. Sage.

Boyd, D., & Crawford, K. (2012). Critical question for Big Data: Provocations for a cultural, technological, and scholarly phenomenon. *Information, Communication & Society, 15*(5), 662–679.

CENSIS. (2020). *Italia sotto sforzo. Diario della transizione. La scuola e i suoi esclusi*. https://www.CENSIS.it/sites/default/files/downloads/Diario%20della%20Transizione.pdf

Colombo, M., Poliandri, D., & Rinaldi, E. E. (2020). Gli impatti dell'emergenza COVID-19 sul sistema scolastico-formativo in Italia. *Scuola democratica*. Advance online publication. doi:10.12828/97098

De Angelis, A. (2020, April 5). Piattaforme digitali, è giusto che Google spadroneggi? Open source ignorate. *Tecnica della scuola*. https://www.tecnicadellascuola.it/piattaforme-digitali-e-giusto-che-google-spadroneggi

De Nardis, L. (2019). The social media challenge to internet governance. In M. Graham & W. H. Dutton (Eds.), *Society and the internet: How networks of information and communication are changing our lives* (pp. 389–402). Oxford University Press.

Ducato, R., Priora, P., Angiolini, C., Giannopoulou, A., Jütte, B. J., Noto La Diega, G., Pascault, L., & Schneider, G. (2020, May 27). Emergency remote teaching: A study of copyright and data protection terms of popular online services (part 1). *Kluwer Copyright Blog*. http://copyrightblog.kluweriplaw.com/2020/05/27/emergency-remote-teaching-a-study-of-copyright-and-data-protection-terms-of-popular-online-services-part-i/

Elias, J. (2020, April 1). California governor says, 'We need more Googles' as company offers free Wi-Fi and Chromebooks to students. *CNBC*. https://www.cnbc.com/2020/04/01/coronavirus-google-offers-wi-fi-chromebooks-to-california-students.html

INDIRE. (2020a). *Indagine tra i docenti italiani. Pratiche didattiche durante il lockdown. Report preliminare (20 luglio 2020)*. https://www.indire.it/wp-content/uploads/2020/07/Pratiche-didattiche-durante-il-lockdown-Report-2.pdf

INDIRE. (2020b). *Indagine tra i docenti italiani. Pratiche didattiche durante il lockdown. Report integrativo (novembre 2020)*. https://www.indire.it/wp-content/uploads/2020/12/Report-integrativo-Novembre-2020_con-grafici-1.pdf

Istat. (2020). *Spazi in casa e disponibilità di computer per bambini e ragazzi.* https://www.istat.it/it/files//2020/04/Spazi-casa-disponibilita-computer-ragazzi.pdf

Jenkins, H., with Clinton, K., Purushotma, R., Robison, A. J., & Weigel, M. (2009). *Confronting the challenges of participatory culture: Media education for the 21st century.* MIT Press. https://direct.mit.edu/books/book/3204/Confronting-the-Challenges-of-Participatory

Kitchin, R. (2014). *The data revolution: Big Data, open data, data infrastructures and their consequences.* Sage.

Klein, N. (2020, May 8). Screen new deal. *The Intercept.* https://theintercept.com/2020/05/08/andrew-cuomo-eric-schmidt-coronavirus-tech-shock-doctrine/

Laney, D. (2001, August 25). 3D management: Controlling data volume, velocity and variety. *AIIM+ Blog.* https://community.aiim.org/blogs/doug-laney/2012/08/25/deja-vvvu-gartners-original-volume-velocity-variety-definition-of-big-data

Lucisano, P. (2020). Fare ricerca con gli insegnanti. I primi risultati dell'indagine nazionale SIRD 'Per un confronto sulle modalità di didattica a distanza adottate nelle scuole italiane nel periodo di emergenza COVID-19'. *Lifelong Lifewide Learning,* 17(36), 3–25 https://doi.org/10.19241/lll.v16i36.551

Magalhaes, J. C., & Couldry, N. (2020, April 27). Tech giants are using this crisis to colonize the welfare system. *Jacobin.* https://www.jacobinmag.com/2020/04/tech-giants-coronavirus-pandemic-welfare-surveillance

McGoey, L. (2015). *No such thing as a free gift: The Gates Foundation and the price of philanthropy.* Verso.

Morozov, E. (2013). *To save everything, click here: The folly of technological solutionism.* PublicAffairs.

OECD. (2016). *Innovating education and educating for innovation: The power of digital technologies and skills.* OECD Publishing. https://doi.org/10.1787/9789264265097-en

O'Neil, C. (2016). *Weapons of math destruction: How Big Data increases inequality and threatens democracy.* Crown Publishers.

Pasquale, F. (2015). *The black box society: The secret algorithms that control money and information.* Harvard University Press.

Perrotta, C., Gulson, K. N., Williamson, B., & Witzenberger, K. (2021). Automation, APIs and the distributed labour of platform pedagogies in Google Classroom. *Critical Studies in Education,* 62(1), 97–113. https://doi.org/10.1080/17508487.2020.1855597

Pievatolo, M. C. (2020, June 8). Teledidattica: proprietaria e privata o libera e pubblica? *ROARS (Return on Academic Research and School).* https://www.roars.it/online/teledidattica-proprietaria-e-privata-o-libera-e-pubblica/

Prinsloo, P. (2019). A social cartography of analytics in education as performative politics. *British Journal of Educational Technology, 50*(6), 2810–2823. doi:10.1111/bjet.12872

Ranieri, M. (2021). Country report on the impact of COVID-19 lockdown on schooling in primary and secondary education. In S. Carretero Gomez et al., *What did we learn from schooling practices during the COVID-19 lockdown?* Publications Office of the European Union. https://publications.jrc.ec.europa.eu/repository/handle/JRC123654

Ranieri, M., Gaggioli, C., & Kaschny Borges, M. (2020). La didattica alla prova del Covid-19 in Italia: uno studio sulla Scuola Primaria. *Praxis Educativa, 15*, 1–20. https://doi.org/10.5212/PraxEduc.v.15.16307.079

Santagati, M., & Barabanti, P. (2020). (Dis)connessi? Alunni, genitori e insegnanti di fronte all'emergenza Covid-19. *Media Education, 11*(2), 109–125. https://doi.org/10.36253/me-9646

Selwyn, N. (2016). *Is technology good for education?* Polity.

Selwyn, N. (2019). *Should robots replace teachers? AI and the future of education.* Polity.

Selwyn, N., Hillman, T., Eynon, R., Ferreira, G., Knox, J., Macgilchrist, F., & Sancho-Gil, G. (2020). What's next for ed-tech? Critical hopes and concerns for the 2020s. *Learning, Media and Technology, 45*(1), 1–6. doi:10.1080/17439884.2020.1694945

UNESCO. (2020). *Education in a post-COVID world: Nine ideas for public action.* https://en.unesco.org/sites/default/files/education_in_a_post-covid_world-nine_ideas_for_public_action.pdf

Van Dijck, J. (2014). Datafication, dataism and dataveillance: Big Data between scientific paradigm and ideology. *Surveillance & Society, 12*(2), 197–208.

Van Dijck, J., Poell, T., & De Waal, M. (2018). *The platform society: Public values in a connective world.* Oxford University Press.

Williamson, B. (2017). *Big Data in education: The digital future of learning, policy and practice.* Sage.

Williamson, B., Eynon, R., & Potter, J. (2020). Pandemic politics, pedagogies and practices: Digital technologies and distance education during the coronavirus emergency. *Learning, Media and Technology, 45*(2), 107–114. doi:10.1080/17439884.2020.1761641

Zuboff, S. (2019). *The age of surveillance capitalism: The fight for a human future at the new frontier of power.* PublicAffairs.

A Post-Commentary from the UK

Educational Challenges after the Covid-19 Pandemic

Spyros Themelis

1   Introduction

Covid-19 and attendant lockdowns are often considered in the burgeoning literature as the cataclysmic events that swept over hitherto well-functioning educational systems around the world. The widespread assumption is that, up until March 2020, when most countries suspended their face-to-face educational activities, education was functioning smoothly. As I show in the remainder of this chapter, nothing could be further from the truth. Before I present relevant evidence, let me dispel from the outset a myth that surrounds the pandemic and government responses to it. This myth has to do with the totally unanticipated and unpredictability of Covid-19. According to Joshua Lederberg (1988), the 1958 Nobel laureate for bacterial genetics, a viral pandemic was very likely to happen: 'The single biggest threat to man's [sic] continued dominance on the planet is the virus.' Others issued similar warnings. For example, Garrett's *The Coming Plague* (1994) or Henig's *The Dancing Matrix* (1993) are two prescient analyses of the possibility and imminent nature of a viral threat facing humanity. Instead, then of asking why we were caught unprepared, it might be more appropriate to ask why such warnings were not heeded. To quote a World Health Organization (WHO) scientist credited with the eradication of smallpox: 'Outbreaks are inevitable. Pandemics are optional' (Brilliant, quoted in Matthewman, 2015, p. 27). Žižek (2020, p. 4) eloquently translated this conundrum into a political question: 'We will have to raise the key question: What is wrong with our system that we were caught unprepared by the catastrophe despite scientists warning us about it for years?' The framework I am proposing interrupts the dominant narrative that places the onus for the devastating consequences of the pandemic on the virus itself. Instead, it searches for answers in the organized responses that were put forward to mitigate its effects and the historical antecedents of these answers. My vantage point is education. Specifically, it is UK education and government responses to the pandemic.

2   The Organization of a Disaster: Underfunding Education

A look at some educational trends just before Covid-19 struck shows that governments in a host of countries were engaging in a major shift in the balance of public versus private financing of education which resulted in the strengthening of the latter and the shrinking of the former. Specifically, in the ten years prior to the pandemic, most OECD countries engineered an increase in the role of the private sector in funding of their education system and an analogous decrease in public funding. The UK saw a substantial increase in the share of private expenditure on education across all stages (i.e. from primary to tertiary), from 23% in 2012 to 35% in 2018, and a corresponding decrease in public expenditure: from 77% to 65%, respectively. In tertiary education alone, the biggest driver of this shift from public to private financing, the share of private expenditure increased by 30%. This trend continued well into early 2020 when Covid-19 struck. In other words, during the pre-pandemic decade the UK underwent an important shift in terms of its funding structure across all three education sectors and mainly in tertiary education. Although the UK was not the only country to be actively involved in expenditure restructuring, it was by far the leader in this trend, outperforming all other OECD countries. In order to make the UK figures presented here comparable, let me discuss another OECD country, which is the focus of this volume: Italy. Italy registered one of the highest increases in private spending (3%) during the same period of time and far greater than the OECD average, which stood at 1%. What is more, Italy has one of the lowest rates in terms of total expenditure on educational institutions, 3.8% of its GDP compared to 5.7% for the UK and 4.5% for all OECD countries (OECD, 2021). This shows that the Italian education system had been drained of public funding prior to the pandemic. What followed is well documented in this volume and is easy to understand. For example, it is evident in Ramella and Rostan's account that it was thanks to the staff members' 'stock of social capital' that the challenge of distance teaching was turned into a learning opportunity. This is echoed by Capogna et al., who note that the 'organizational resilience' on behalf of Italian schools is to be ascribed to the rooting of the previous social capital acted on at different levels individual and collective action inside and outside the school. Likewise, Mesa emphasizes 'the persistent influence of the cultural capital' of the family of origin as well as that of familial economic capital in mitigating or deepening the effects of distance learning. In a similar vein, Barberis et al. show how the weak institutional infrastructure in relation to supporting innovation, such as that associated with delivering education, and more generally, did not support teachers' efforts. As they put it, 'there were limits to the extent to which schools and teachers were prepared for the emergency'. They showed that they reacted quite responsively – but in a vacuum. This vacuum was not accidental, but it was crafted during the pre-Covid-19 years.

What I am highlighting here, is that far from an anomaly, underfunded education systems is an established pattern. Italy is a trend follower, not a trailblazer. Lack of organized response to the pandemic cannot not be explained away by the novelty nor the gravity of the pandemic because situations like this were neither completely novel nor totally unanticipated. In this chapter, I develop a sociological explanation of the responses the UK government put forward to stem Covid-19. I highlight a continuity in these responses and a historical approach to policy priorities that strategically underfunded specific sectors in favour of others. Education and health were the two sectors that have been consistently underfunded and, therefore, less likely to withstand the impact of such a significant threat that the pandemic has been. By contrast, policing and defence have been the beneficiaries of generous sums of public money which increased even during the pandemic.

3 Disaster Explained: It's the Economy, Stupid!

In relation to the initial response the UK prepared to deal with the pandemic, two attitudes were evident: (1) a lack of preparedness for it, and (2) a total lack of willingness to act on it and take the scientists seriously until it was too late. With regard to education, the responses of the UK government can be divided into three phases: (1) denial, (2) reaction and (3) damage limitation. As Timmins (2021) points out,

> the most unforgivable aspect of what happened is not just the failure to make contingency plans in the summer of 2020 but the refusal to do so – when it was already obvious that fresh school closures might well be needed, and that exams might have to be cancelled again. Lessons were not learnt from the first lockdown, with the result that, for both school closures and exams, the story from July 2020 to January 2021 was a case of 'pause, rewind, repeat'. (Timmins, 2021, p. 4)

Any contingency plans that were put forward were based on the outdated flu response plan which was developed in 2011. As a result, during the denial phase, that is to say during the early weeks of the first lockdown (it stared on March 23rd 2020), 'fewer than 2% of all pupils attended on average, peaking at 2% in late May, just before schools partially reopened in June [2020]. Just 5% of vulnerable pupils were in school on average over this period, reaching a peak of 8% by the end of May' (Timmins, 2021, p. 7). However, the government had no means of ensuring that all students who were kept out of school were receiving some form of education. What intensified this lack of a thorough and appropriate plan was the limited and slow response of the UK government in mitigating the effects of the pandemic and avoiding its disastrous spread. This resulted in a lot of confusion, not least among parents, especially those who were key workers and were required to continue working in their normal working environment.

Another issue that exposed the UK government's inability to respond coherently and effectively to the pandemic was its lack of willingness to work closely with the local authorities responsible for managing schools. The latter had been significantly reduced in number over the years and their importance diminished. This development was initiated by the Thatcher government and the Education Reform Act it introduced in 1988. With remarkable efficiency, all ensuing governments worked to further diminish the role and influence of these authorities, which paved the way for new types of schools, namely the academies. Academies run as not-for-profit trusts and they lie outside the control of local authorities. As of 2020, almost three-quarters of secondary schools and one-third of primary schools were outside the control of local authorities. In England, local authorities are associated with the redistribution politics that Labour governments pursued after the Second World War to support the educational needs of the nation and especially of the working class. As such, they are still associated with 'old-style politics' and have been attacked on ideological grounds by both the New Labour and Conservative parties. This factor has contributed to the slow unmaking of the public character of the British education system and had devastating effects during the pandemic. For example, due to the complexity of the new management system and the lack of school aid by local authorities, schools had to wait a long time to receive support, while others never did so. By contrast to the situation in England, Scotland and Wales used local authorities to provide money and resources to schools which were much needed during the pandemic.

Another example of a policy targeted at the most vulnerable is the provision of free school meals (FSMs), which dates back to the 1906 Education Act. This policy became compulsory with the 1944 Education Act and in 1946 the provision of free milk for all school students was also enshrined in legislation. However, free milk provision was terminated in 1980 by the Thatcher administration. FSMs were maintained but the service was privatized. That is to say, it encouraged private companies to compete to provide such meals, which resulted in a decrease in the nutritional quality of school meals. To this day, FSMs are used as a proxy for deprivation and the food security of a lot of disadvantaged families depends on them. During the pandemic, FSMs were replaced by vouchers, which resulted in thousands of kids from low-income families struggling to access food, especially during school holidays, where there were no vouchers provided. As already noted, the government followed a response pattern that was characterized first by denial that the problem existed at all and it accordingly refused to explore any alternatives. Denial here is ideologically driven as any intervention to the free market economy that FSM providers constitute is a heresy to free market capitalism principles. It was not before the celebrity footballer Marcus Rashford publicly intervened by leading a campaign to get food to the most vulnerable school children that the government reacted (in November 2020). However, the issue of food insecurity did not go away and Rashford had to intervene again in order to persuade the government to direct fresh resources in order to avoid food poverty among school kids during the summer of 2021. This second U-turn was even more spectacular than the first one, because this time the government 'put money into an existing local-authority-run programme. Perhaps this was one of the few lessons learnt during the pandemic when it came to schools' (Timmins, 2021, p. 10). For a government that was very busy making policy during the pandemic, its handling of food insecurity is staggering. Specifically, by the end of May 2020, schools received 148 new guidance documents or updates to existing materials. Yet, it allowed thousands of school students and their families to go hungry. This modus operandi raises questions not only about the British government's competence, but also about its priorities. In other words, while the multiple U-turns undoubtedly expose a government ill-prepared to respond to the pandemic effectively, they also reveal a zeal to adhere to the script of free market capitalism and unfettered operation of the markets at any cost.

Although the creation and support of markets (or, more precisely, quasi-markets) in education (Ball, 1993, 2003) is an important issue, it falls outside the scope of this chapter. Instead, I will shed light on the repercussions of another failed government response, this time in relation to the provision of laptops for remote learning. According to Timmins (2021), the education department placed an order with a private provider a month after schools were in lockdown. As most laptops were sourced overseas, 'the first 50,000 of an initial 200,000 order arrived on 11 May, but many schools did not receive supplies until June' (p. 16). What is more, 'complaints about shortages of laptops and routers ran on in England into January [2021]' (p. 17). This reactive approach cost hundreds of school hours for thousands of students, especially for those from disadvantaged backgrounds.

The issues I am discussing here are not isolated incidents or accidents in an otherwise coordinated effort to stem the effects of the pandemic on education. Rather, I argue that it is by design that there were so many serious problems.

Put differently, the calamity of the UK education system and the centrality of the markets within it are not different aspects of reality. Rather, they are part of the reality of UK education, 'they are the two sides of the same political coin' (Wacquant, 2009, p. 292). Following Wacquant, I argue that the structural features 'that have facilitated the organized atrophy' of the UK education system have 'fostered the uncontrolled hypertrophy' of the markets inside it (Wacquant, 2009). In charting the fate of the disadvantaged students in the UK education system, we can also understand how market capitalism has failed them.

4 A Pandemic of Educational Disadvantage?

The total impact of the pandemic on educational inequalities in the UK is currently unknown. However, we can be certain that it is likely to open up an even bigger gap between disadvantaged students and their more affluent counterparts and 'an even greater chasm between those attending outstanding schools, and who have access to parental resources, and those who are not so lucky' (Eyles et al., 2020, p. 6). According to projections published just before the pandemic, it would take 560 years for the disadvantage gap to close if change was to continue at that pace (Hutchinson et al., 2019). However, change was not moving in the right direction. For the first time in over a decade that gap stopped closing and this was before the pandemic started (Hutchinson et al., 2019). Evidence shows that students from disadvantaged backgrounds were less likely to attend school in the period just before lockdown (Sharp et al., 2020). What is more, '[p]upil engagement and disadvantaged pupil engagement were both lower in the most deprived schools. Teachers in the most deprived schools were in contact with fewer pupils' (Sharp et al., 2020, p. 4). More alarmingly, the disadvantage gap has increased for the first time since 2007 among primary school students (Hutchinson et al., 2019). During the pandemic, families from disadvantaged backgrounds faced even bigger challenges in providing their offspring with adequate instruments to support home schooling or providing sufficient space for study at home (Auriemma & Iannaccone, 2020; Reimer et al., 2020).

Undoubtedly, the combination of an already unequal education system and an ill-managed pandemic is set to affect the life chances of a vast number of students. The ones who will bear the brunt the most are the ones from disadvantaged backgrounds. According to a report by the Royal Society,

> 13 cohorts of students have been affected by the lockdown, so from the mid-2030s for the 50 years following that, around a quarter of the entire workforce will have lower skills, with a consequently lower growth rate.

> The present value of such a fall in the growth rate is measured in billions not millions. (DELVE Initiative, 2020)

Apart from loss in educational opportunities, the risk from skills loss owing to school closures is also linked to higher propensity of poverty. For example, 'those with a low level of educational attainment are almost five times as likely to be in poverty now as those with a high level of education' (Serafino & Tonkin, 2014).

The negative effects of Covid-19 have been unevenly distributed not only in terms of social class, but also in relation to intersectional inequities of gender and ethnicity, compounding the longstanding, pre-existing unequal distribution of social 'bads' (Dorling, 2021). Apart from an education system that has been traditionally failing disadvantaged students while increasing the degree of penetration of the markets in it, the UK was not helped in mitigating the effects of the pandemic owing to other structural factors, such as its labour market structure and gender balance which pre-existed the pandemic. Indisputably the latter did not only change the pace of work, but it also changed the meaning and value of it. Old working patterns suddenly became outdated and new patterns emerged. For example, a recent report into homeworking found that '[t]here has been a steep rise in the number of employees working flexibly during lockdown with almost all (86%) employees in our survey having worked from home and 70% of employees working flexitime (flexible starting and ending times of work)' (Chung et al., 2020, p. 6). What is of importance from an educational point of view is that

> 76% of all mothers and 73% of fathers surveyed agreed or strongly agreed that they would like to work flexibly to spend more time with children. A further 64% of fathers and 59% of mothers also said that they would like to reduce their working hours to spend more time with family. (Chung et al., 2020, p. 6)

As a response to parents having spent more time at home during the multiple lockdowns, employees with parental responsibilities seem to have shifted their priorities in favour of family and away from work. However, if this is going to translate into a shift in the balance of the household division of labour and an attendant shift in practices relating to childcare, will have to stand the test of time. In the meantime, evidence suggests that there is a clear gendered inequality in health outcomes and the pandemic has affected women more negatively than men in many other domains (for a similar point, see Mesa, this volume) (Guatimosim, 2020; Minello, 2020). This is probably explained by the fact that women have been more exposed to the pandemic owing to their higher prevalence in education, healthcare and social care jobs and roles in the formal and informal systems. According to the WHO, women make up 70% of this type of workforce (Boniol et al., 2019) while it is estimated that they perform 75% of all unpaid labour (ILO, 2018, p. XXIX). In relation to education, women shouldered the rapid increase in childcare responsibilities and household labour (Yildirim & Eslen-Ziya, 2020). While living spaces were transformed into learning, work and childcare spaces (Clark et al., 2020), domestic roles and responsibilities became less defined, compounding to women's workload and reversely affecting their well-being (Yildirim & Eslen-Ziya, 2020).

In addition, there is also an ethnic differentiation of Covid-19 implications which has by now been well-documented. As I reported elsewhere, the ethnic penalty is multifaceted and permeates all facets of activity:

> Black people are twice as likely to die of Covid-19 than White people; Pakistani and Bangladeshi men are 1.8 times more likely and women of the same heritage 1.6 times at greater risk than their White counterparts. Furthermore, BAME [black, Asian and minority ethnic] people are more likely to find employment in sectors that increase their risk of exposure to Covid-19 infection. The ubiquity of racism is also evident in relation to risk of mortality according to religion, with Jewish and Muslim people at much higher risk of dying of Covid-19. (Themelis, 2022)

5 Conclusions: Lessons for the Future

In conclusion, the evidence presented so far allows us to draw the following conclusions. First, the cost of the pandemic on student achievement and the disadvantage gap is very high and growing. Second, the effects of the pandemic on education are likely to stay with us for decades to come and the cost of remedying them is enormous. Third, it is not only students from disadvantaged backgrounds who will disproportionately pay the price of the pandemic and the way it has been handled by the UK government, but other groups with high exposure to risk, such as women and ethnic minorities.

However, it is important to note that the pandemic has also allowed for some positive gains. The sudden adoption of technology by schools and educational institutions as a medium of instruction has led to a much-needed upskilling, which has been accommodated by the vast majority of the teaching workforce and their students (for a similar point, see Bertozzi & Saruis; Santagati & Barabanti; Di Maggio, this volume). This is a testament to teachers' and students' agility and commitment. It also highlights the importance of the role of the parents in supporting their children's learning and overcoming the health challenges associated with a period of intense psychological stress, such as the pandemic and attendant lockdowns and other restrictions. However, parental support is contingent on family resources and parental educational and socio-economic capital, which has been affecting families from disadvantaged backgrounds disproportionately, given that a high proportion of them had to face job losses and/or income falls.

As Harvey (1989, p. 239) reminds us,

> during phases of maximal change, the spatial and temporal bases for reproduction of the social order are subject to the severest disruption. [...] It is exactly at such moments that major shifts in systems of representation, cultural forms, and philosophical sentiment occur.

However, deep changes also occurred in the organization, management and intensity of interpersonal, professional and social interactions, as well as in the physical and mental health, subjectivity and self-efficacy of social agents who strive to adapt to the drastic change in circumstances around them. In a nutshell, deep changes occur in the ensemble of social relations. These changes are lived through, negotiated, accommodated and resisted, discussed, made sense of and explored by participants in schools and other educational institutions. I discussed such changes through the prism of the UK education system and its chequered history. I showed that the handling of the pandemic by the UK government is consistent with some other major shifts in British (especially English) education over the last few decades and I advanced a sociological explanation of this approach which postulates that the UK had undergone some deep changes in the decades prior to the pandemic. Specifically, the rebalancing of the British education system from a state to a private mode of funding had already occurred a long time before Covid-19 struck. Several policy changes that had been introduced since the early 1980s augmented and entrenched the penetration of the private sector in the educational affairs of the country. This development accounts for a big part of the inequalities in the UK education system and more broadly. The UK has been a leader in this trend in Europe, though it is by no means the only country engaging in such a politics. The politics of neoliberalism has allowed the commodification of education and change in the meaning, role and prospects of education to an unprecedented extent (Ball, 1993; Ball & Gewirtz, 1997). These changes formed a careful, well-crafted and meticulous underlabouring that facilitated the penetration of technology that occurred during the pandemic and made online education and e-learning possible so quickly. The rapid accommodation of such novel modes of teaching and learning by seemingly traditional educational institutions in the UK but also in other countries, such as Italy, underscores the high degree of technological penetration that has been ongoing in the years before the pandemic and has been largely unnoticed. Education during the pandemic experienced a rapid and extended reorganization through its platformization and digitization. Undoubtedly, educational technology has the potential to become another fetishized commodity (Ball, 2003), which risks not only turning schools into 'experimental laboratories' that can allow techno-businesses to take advantage of education but also to foster the rise in the ideology of 'dataism' that Cappello eloquently criticises in this volume. At the same time, the hidden danger is that of the erasure of the social that Ball (2003) forewarned us about and the attendant erosion of the social character of education that the pandemic necessitated and the technology facilitated.

The dangers I am highlighting here are not new. Polanyi (1968) pointed out that the market economy can only function in a market society, that is to say, 'society must be shaped in such a manner as to allow the system to function according to its own laws' (p. 57). Similarly, education can only function in a de-personalized and platformized manner if society is receptive to and accommodating of such changes. I argue that education was ready to enter the virtual tunnel of technology-mediated education because society was ready for it. The novelty that the pandemic introduced is that of the collapse of time and space as well as the removal of the social from education as an institution and a space for (inter-)personal and social development. In other words, the lockdown time-space configuration has been transformed into 'my space, at any time' mode of work. While the capitalist of the pre-pandemic years forced the educational worker into routinized and often alienating forms of labour that required ever increased flexibility and heightened forms of compliance, the pandemic world of educational work comes with embedded forms of output and productivity control and ever-increasing demands to adapt psychologically, mentally, socially and personally. What is more, there is a danger that education could be turned into a form of routinized and automated knowledge delivery and that the struggle will be over the measurement of knowledge as a commodity akin to any other in the marketplace. Apart from stemming and even reversing the increasing penetration of capital into mainstream education, pressing questions to follow up in the post-pandemic world are the following:

– Are students becoming the consumers of pre-packaged forms of knowledge, that is to say, of knowledge contained in knowledge packages and platforms built by private corporations?
– Are teachers becoming merely the delivery instruments of such forms of knowledge?

– Is there a danger that education might become deprived from social innovation, critique and creativity?
 – Is the pandemic forcing the hand of neoliberal governments to take measures that might prove in the future detrimental to society through an uncontrollable elevation of the role of the technological giants (big tech) and an attendant increase in educational inequalities?

The post-war consensus that saw the expansion of public education and the welfare state and has enabled millions of people to escape disadvantage and poverty, seems to be coming to an end. There are warning signs that education is increasingly becoming an affair that governments are leaving to parents, individuals and civil society to deal with. By contrast, central governments prefer to channel money to private companies to sort out some of the major issues facing education, regardless of the effects this approach might have on disadvantage, inequalities and social cohesion. Technology emerged as the main answer during lockdown education to counter the lack of school access by millions of students and the invidious prospect of loss in school time. In post-lockdown education, though, technology cannot be the answer to the underfunding of public education that preceded the pandemic and accounts for a big part of the failed responses to the challenges the pandemic posed, as we saw in relation to the UK. No one can claim that there is a single or an easy solution to the multiple issues facing post-lockdown education. However, re-entering the vicious cycle of denial, reaction and damage limitation as has been the case in the UK since the pandemic started, is not an option. Ultimately, Vegas and Winthrop's (2020) plea 'that strong and inclusive public education systems are essential to the short- and long-term recovery of society and that there is an opportunity to leapfrog toward powered-up schools' is a timely one. The question is whether we are all up to the task and especially if our governments are willing to be on our side. The challenge, as Merico and Scardigno in this volume rightly point out, is not only of considering 'this (new) emergency as an extraordinary opportunity to outline a new, richer, more plural, heterogeneous and polycentric time for education', but to envision public education systems emerging from the pandemic stronger than ever before (Vegas & Winthrop, 2020).

References

Auriemma, V., & Iannaccone, C. (2020). COVID-19 pandemic: Socio-economic consequences of social distancing measures in Italy. *Frontiers in Sociology, 5*, 1–8.

Ball, S. J. (1993). Education markets, choice and social class: The market as a class strategy in the UK and the USA. *British Journal of Sociology of Education, 14*(1), 3–19. doi:10.1080/0142569930140101

Ball, S. J. (2003). *Class strategies and the education market: The middle classes and social advantage*. RoutledgeFalmer.

Ball, S. J., & Gewirtz, S. (1997). Girls in the education market: Choice, competition and complexity. *Gender and Education, 9*(2), 207–222.

Boniol, M., McIsaac, M., Xu, L., Wuliji, T., Diallo, K., & Campbell, J. (2019, March). *Gender equity in the health workforce: Analysis of 104 countries*. Health Workforce Working Paper 1. World Health Organization. https://apps.who.int/iris/bitstream/handle/10665/311314/WHO-HIS-HWF-Gender-WP1-2019.1-eng.pdf

Clark, S., McGrane, A., Boyle, N., Joksimovic, N., Burke, L., Rock, N., et al. (2020). 'You're a teacher you're a mother, you're a worker': Gender inequality during Covid-19 in Ireland. *Gend. Work Organ, 28*(S1), 1–11.

Chung, H., Seo, H., Forbes, S., & Birkett, H. (2020). *Working from home during the Covid-19 lockdown: Changing preferences and the future of work*. University of Kent. https://www.birmingham.ac.uk/Documents/college-social-sciences/business/research/wirc/epp-working-from-home-COVID-19-lockdown.pdf

DELVE Initiative. (2020, July 24). *Balancing the risks of pupils returning to schools*. DELVE Report No. 4. https://rs-delve.github.io/reports/2020/07/24/balancing-the-risk-of-pupils-returning-to-schools.html

Dorling, D. (2021, March 14). If Boris Johnson is serious about levelling up, he would plan for a 2026 census now. *The Guardian*. https://www.theguardian.com/commentisfree/2021/mar/14/gvfgf

Eyles, A., Gibbons, S., & Montebruno, P. (2020, May). *Covid-19 school shutdowns: What will they do to our children's education?* CEP Covid-19 analysis, Paper no. 001. Centre for Economic Performance, London School of Economics and Political Science. https://cep.lse.ac.uk/pubs/download/cepcovid-19-001.pdf

Garrett, L. (1994). *The coming plague: Newly emerging diseases in a world out of balance*. Farrar, Straus and Giroux.

Guatimosim, C. (2020). Reflections on motherhood and the impact of COVID 19 pandemic on women's scientific careers. *Journal of Neurochemistry, 155*, 469–470. https://doi.org/10.1111/jnc.15158

Harvey, D. (1989). *The condition of postmodernity*. Blackwell.

Henig, R. M. (1993). *The dancing matrix*. Vintage Books.

Hutchinson, J., Bonetti, S., Crenna-Jennings, W., & Avinash, A. (2019). *Education in England: Annual report 2019*. Education Policy Institute. https://epi.org.uk/publications-and-research/annual-report-2019/

ILO. (2018). *Care work and care jobs for the future of decent work*. International Labour Organization. https://www.ilo.org/wcmsp5/groups/public/---dgreports/---dcomm/---publ/documents/publication/wcms_633135.pdf

Lederberg, J. (1988). Medical science, infectious disease, and the unity of humankind. *JAMA, 260*(5), 684–685. doi:10.1001/jama.1988.03410050104039

Matthewman, S., & Huppatz, K. (2020). A sociology of Covid-19. *Journal of Sociology, 56*(4), 675–683. doi:10.1177/1440783320939416

Minello, A. (2020). The pandemic and the female academic. *Nature, 28*(4).

OECD. (2021). *Education at a glance 2021: OECD indicators*. OECD Publishing. https://doi.org/10.1787/b35a14e5-en

Polanyi, K. (1968). Our obsolete market mentality. In G. Dalton (Ed.), *Primitive, archaic and modern economies: Essays of Karl Polanyi* (pp. 59–77). Beacon Press.

Reimer, D., Smith, E., Andersen, I. G., & Sortkær, B. (2020). What happens when schools shut down? Investigating inequality in students' reading behavior during Covid-19 in Denmark. *Research in Social Stratification and Mobility, 71*, 100568.

Serafino, P., & Tonkin, R. (2014). *Intergenerational transmission of disadvantage in the UK & EU*. Office for National Statistics. https://webarchive.nationalarchives.gov.uk/ukgwa/20160105214416/http://www.ons.gov.uk/ons/rel/household-income/intergenerational-transmission-of-poverty-in-the-uk---eu/2014/blank.html

Sharp, C., Sims, D., & Rutt, S. (2020). *Schools' responses to Covid-19: Returning pupils to schools*. National Foundation for Educational Research. https://www.nfer.ac.uk/media/4060/schools_responses_to_COVID_19_early_report_final.pdf

Themelis, S. (2022). Colonialisms and class. In A. Maisuria (Ed.), *Encyclopaedia of Marxism and education* (pp. 81–94). Brill.

Timmins, N. (2021). *Schools and coronavirus: The government's handling of education during the pandemic*. Institute for Government. https://www.instituteforgovernment.org.uk/sites/default/files/publications/schools-and-coronavirus.pdf

Vegas, E., & Winthrop, R. (2020). *Beyond reopening schools: How education can emerge stronger than before COVID-19*. Brookings Institute. https://www.brookings.edu/research/beyond-reopening-schools-how-education-can-emerge-stronger-than-before-covid-19/

Wacquant, L. (2009). *Punishing the poor: The neoliberal government of social insecurity*. Duke University Press.

Yildirim, T. M., & Eslen-Ziya, H. (2020). The differential impact of COVID-19 on the work conditions of women and men academics during the lockdown. *Gender, Work & Organization, 28*(S1), 691–697. doi:10.1111/gwao.12529

Žižek, S. (2020). *Pandemic! Covid-19 shakes the world*. OR Books.

Index

accessibility   175, 179, 180, 184

childcare   244, 245

digital divide   20, 56, 105, 152, 155, 192, 197, 230, 231, 233
digital skills   10, 11, 22, 81, 152–154, 157, 170, 171, 175, 181, 231
disadvantage   1, 14, 17, 23, 36, 60, 63, 64, 68, 77, 80, 81, 83, 86, 96, 99, 140, 141, 170, 183, 242, 243–24, 248
distance learning   5, 7, 11, 18–20, 23, 25, 32, 57, 65, 69, 77, 81, 86–89, 91–96, 98, 104, 114, 123, 130, 151–164, 166–171, 192, 193, 205, 209, 210, 212, 239
Durkheim, É.   105–107

educational crisis   118, 119
educational policy   61, 222

faculty   67, 122–130, 132–135, 138, 144–146, 148, 210
family-work conciliation   92

Giddens, A.   12, 106, 111, 116, 117
governance   2, 6, 8, 23, 24, 32, 34, 35, 52, 126, 130, 131, 145, 153, 221, 222, 225

higher education   2, 5, 6, 123, 139, 150, 154, 158, 162, 224

inclusion   6, 151, 197, 198

learning loss   56, 72

online education   20, 46, 81, 175, 179, 180, 182, 184, 188, 246
organisational learning   61

parental involvement   17, 18, 22, 23, 77–82, 84, 85, 93, 97, 98

peer education   51, 151, 168, 187
platforms   5, 14, 19–21, 39, 86, 91, 93, 99, 107–112, 116–118, 122, 124, 127, 135, 142, 144, 146, 154, 186, 198, 200–202, 208, 209, 212, 220–230, 232–235, 247
primary education   16, 213
public fund   33, 34, 223, 239

quality of education   11, 111, 147, 154

resilience   15, 19, 21, 27, 132, 145, 169, 178, 193–195, 202, 203, 209, 239

school autonomy   6
school-family relationship   77, 78, 80, 81, 83–85, 88, 90, 91, 94, 96–98, 198, 207
secondary education   2, 7, 9, 67, 158, 159, 161, 165, 167, 183, 187
Simmel, G.   106, 107
social distancing   12, 17, 27, 64, 69, 84, 104, 106, 107, 110
social inequality/ies   22, 213

teacher training   79, 228
teaching methods   19, 23, 36, 86, 105, 112, 123, 128, 132, 133, 135, 136, 139, 141, 143–146, 148, 168, 175, 176, 179, 186, 187, 189, 197, 210, 229
teaching profession   20, 175–177, 184, 186, 189, 233
territorial inequality/ies   16, 153, 170
trauma   2, 3, 12, 13, 22, 169, 177, 213

university governance   6
university students   18, 99, 104, 110, 112, 115, 123

vulnerability/vulnerable students   25, 180

Weick, K. E.   194, 199